United States Immigration Law

Jeffrey A. Helewitz, JD, LLM, MBA

Second Edition

UPDATED AFTER 9/11/01

Pearson Publications Company
Dallas, Texas

Website: pearsonpub-legal.com

ISBN: 0929563468

Upper Saddle River, N.J. 07458

United States Immigration Law is designed as a textbook for classroom use. The information contained herein is intended only for education and informational purposes.

10 9 8 7 6 5

United States Immigration Law

Jeffrey A. Helewitz, JD, LLM, MBA

Second Edition

UPDATED AFTER 9/11/02

Pearson Publications Company
Dallas, Texas

Website: pearsonpub-legal.com

ISBN: 0-929563-71-9

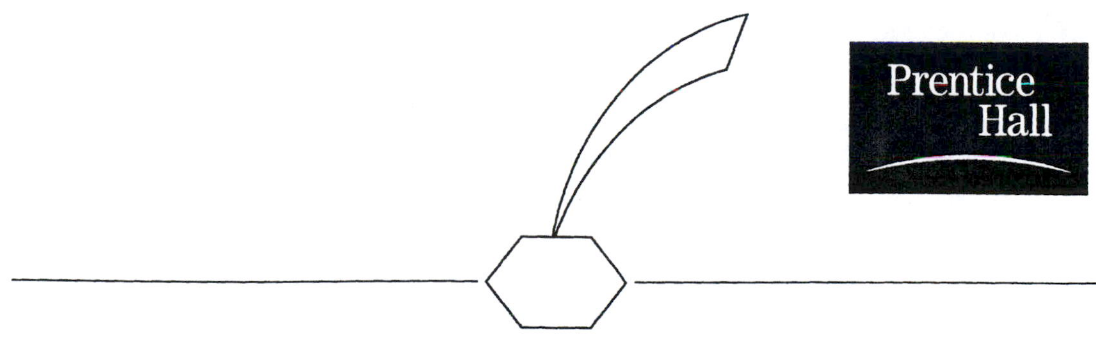

United States Immigration Law is designed as a

textbook for classroom use. The information contained
herein is intended only for education and informational purposes.

DEDICATION

In loving memory of Samuel and Victoria, my favorite immigrants.

ACKNOWLEDGMENTS

This book would not have been possible without the kind and generous assistance of my friend Ingrid Addison, one of my former law students and a former intern at the Immigration and Naturalization Service. Her insightful comments and criticisms proved to be invaluable in the preparation of this text.

Jeffrey A. Helewitz

TABLE OF CONTENTS

FOREWORD

The basis of current U.S. immigration law is the Immigration and Nationality Act of 1952 (INA), as amended by the Immigration Act of 1990, and the accompanying regulations appearing in the Code of Federal Regulations (C.F.R.). Throughout this text, where appropriate, reference is made to the section of the statute, INA, or the regulation, C.F.R., in which the laws being discussed may be found.

Chapter One

HISTORY AND ADMINISTRATION OF U. S. IMMIGRATION LAW

CHAPTER PREVIEW

The recorded history of North America is the story of people leaving their native soil and resettling on the American continent. Some anthropologists today argue that even the "native Americans" are not indigenous to the continent; they, too, are the offspring of earlier immigrants who settled in America before the Europeans. The history of the United States is the history of immigration.

At first, all emigration to North America was open. People were able to come to America and establish roots without restriction. It was only after the European immigrants had established themselves for several generations in what was to become the United States that American immigration policy became restrictive. This restrictive policy limited the number and type of persons those already settled here were willing to welcome. Certain groups, based on the prejudices and fears of the settled populace, were deemed to be "undesirable," and as the American colonies became the United States, and the United States became a continental country, U.S. immigration policy became increasingly exclusive. U.S. immigration law has changed from being an open door to one that is concerned with excluding and expelling persons who are considered "unworthy."

This chapter will focus on the history of U.S. immigration laws, starting from the earliest colonial period and continuing until the most recent immigration enactment in 2000. Each successive immigration law will be analyzed to explain the burgeoning restraints each law placed on immigration. The chapter will conclude with a brief discussion of the various federal agencies that regulate and control immigration to the United States.

Early U.S. Immigration Laws

An **immigrant** is defined as a person who leaves one country to settle permanently in another country. During the colonial period in America's history, immigration was totally free, meaning that whoever wanted to come to North America was free to do so. Of course, not all persons who arrived on North American shores came of their own free will. Many of the early "immigrants" were given no choice in the matter, and arrived in America either as slaves or convicts.

> **Example:** A pauper in London steals some money from a merchant in order to purchase food. The pauper is tried and convicted, and the sentence imposed is transportation to a colonial penal colony.
>
> **Example:** Slave traders arrive in Africa and purchase slaves from African chieftains. These people are then shipped to the American colonies to provide free labor to settle and tame the uncultivated wilderness.

Another category of immigrant settled in America not because of a desire to relocate but in order to flee persecution. Many early European immigrants were more concerned with avoiding death at home than with finding life in the New World.

> **Example**: During the Spanish Inquisition a group of Spanish Jews boarded a ship for the Netherlands. The ship lost its course and wound up in New Amsterdam. The Jewish passengers decided to remain in the New World, hoping to find refuge from European persecution.

Lastly, one of the largest groups to emigrate to America during the colonial period were people seeking opportunities for wealth and advancement that no longer existed for the majority of people in their home countries.

> **Example:** A young man, the tenth child of poor parents, came to America hoping to acquire a small parcel of land so he could afford to marry and raise a family.

This ability to enter the country freely existed as long as America was sparsely populated with European settlers. The primary goal of the early immigrants was to acquire and cultivate the land and to be able to assert dominion over the native Americans to maintain the land so acquired. However, after a period of time, as uncultivated land became more limited, these early settlers decided to restrict entry to the country.

The first law enacted to exclude certain categories of persons from entering America was passed in 1689 by some of the colonies. These colonies excluded entry to "paupers" and criminals. The descendants of the first European immigrants who came to America to escape poverty and persecution for themselves had become so successful that they were now able to become the persecutors.

> **Example**: In 1690 the young son of a poor farmer wanted to come to America to seek his fortune and better his life. Unfortunately, he was classified as a "pauper," having insufficient means to support himself, and was denied entry.

Early Immigration Restrictions

For the first century after the United States became a country, there was very little regulation with respect to immigration. For the most part, the free immigration attitude that existed during the colonial period continued. In 1798 Congress granted the president the authority to expel noncitizens, but the authority remained generally unexercised. In 1802 the first Naturalization Act was passed, which imposed a five-year residency requirement for immigrants before they were entitled to become U.S. citizens. At the time of independence, all Europeans living in the colonies were automatically deemed "citizens," but it was not until the turn of the century that Congress established citizenship guidelines for persons who entered America after 1776.

> **Example:** A young French family came to the United States in 1792 to escape the excesses of the aftermath of the French Revolution. When the Naturalization Act was passed in 1802, the family was qualified to become U.S. citizens because they had resided in the United States for ten years.

Shortly thereafter, Congress passed a law forbidding the importation of slaves that effectively ended that category of "immigrant." The result of this legislation was to create a native industry in breeding people for the slave trade, not a particularly attractive aspect of American immigration policy.

Until the latter part of the nineteenth century, it was still uncertain whether regulation of immigration rested with the federal or state governments. Citizenship was a national concept, and therefore the federal government had early asserted its authority in such matters, but each state was still making independent decisions on admitting foreigners to its borders.

In 1875 the matter was finally decided in *Henderson v. City of New York,* 92 U.S. 259. In that decision the Supreme Court held that state regulations concerning immigration were unconstitutional. In response to that decision, Congress enacted the first national restrictive act limiting the categories of persons who were able to enter the United States. **The Immigration Act of 1875** barred entry to known prostitutes and convicts and further restricted entry for persons who sought admission for "lewd and immoral purposes." These restrictions extended the concept of "undesirable" from the early colonial restrictions discussed above.

Example: In order to escape the squalor of nineteenth century London, and to better their lives, three friends who supported themselves as prostitutes boarded a ship headed for Boston in 1880. When the ship landed, the women were refused entry because they were prostitutes and therefore considered undesirable additions to the population of Boston.

In this same period Congress also outlawed what was known as **coolie labor contracts**. As the colonization of the continent expanded westward, the western territories had been importing cheap indentured labor from China. After a while the European populace of the western territories was worried about the growing size of the Asian population in the area and the consequent loss of jobs for Europeans. The Chinese workers were willing to take jobs at much lower wages than Europeans. The federal response was the banning of contracts employing Chinese labor, thereby causing enactment of the first truly racially discriminatory immigration law in U.S. history.

The first federal act that specifically targeted a group for exclusion based on race and national origin was enacted in 1882 as the **Chinese Exclusion Act**. This statute barred all Chinese immigration (the act remained in effect until 1943), and expanded the categories of persons who were barred from entry to

1. convicts
2. prostitutes
3. lunatics
4. idiots

From this point on, the history of U.S. immigration policy can be viewed as the history of increasing discrimination against foreign-born persons who did not meet certain standards.

Example: A young man boarded a ship in Shanghai bound for North America. When the ship docked in San Francisco, the man attempted to enter the U.S. but was denied entry because he was Chinese. The man was an educated skilled laborer, but he was considered "undesirable" because of his race and national origin.

Example: A German family wanted to send their mentally disabled daughter to Philadelphia to live in a mental institution where they believed she would receive appropriate care. The girl would not be permitted to enter the U.S. because she was considered "undesirable."

The 1882 Act also imposed a **head tax** on each immigrant entering the country in an attempt to discourage poor people who did not actually qualify as "paupers" from immigrating.

The categories of undesirable immigrants were extended by amendment in 1891 to include the following:

5. the diseased
6. paupers
7. polygamists

Now that health (the diseased) became a factor limiting entry, the 1891 Act required that all immigrants undergo a medical examination prior to entry into the country. If the person failed the examination, he or she was sent back to his or her homeland.

Example: A family from Italy arrived in New York, where they were subjected to a medical examination at Ellis Island. The mother was found to be suffering from tuberculosis and was not permitted to enter the country. The family had to decide whether to return home with their mother or to enter New York without her.

In order to administer the law, the 1891 Act established the **Bureau of Immigration.** This bureau has now become the **Immigration and Naturalization Service (INS)**. This federal agency was given the authority to see that the restrictions imposed by the immigration laws were executed.

The 1891 Act also imposed sanctions against persons who were not even in the United States by forbidding activity in foreign countries that encouraged foreign natives to emigrate to America. Exactly how these sanctions were to be imposed is unclear, but its purpose was to limit the growing number of persons who wanted to come to the "golden land."

Example: In order to rid the country of its Jewish population, a Russian group advertised in Russian Jewish communities the benefits of life in the United States. Although these activities took place only in Russia, the Russian group was considered to have violated U.S. law.

Until the end of World War I, the United States government continued to expand the categories of persons who were to be excluded from entry. In 1903, Congress extended the categories to include:

8. epileptics
9. beggars

10. the insane
11. anarchists;

and in 1907 three more categories were added:

12. the feebleminded
13. the tubercular
14. persons with a mental or physical defect.

Also, in 1907, Japanese immigrants were excepted in a special treaty with Japan.

Toward the end of World War I, Congress enacted several pieces of legislation concerned with geographic restrictions (the first was the Chinese Exclusion Act previously discussed). In 1917 Congress precluded immigration of Asians who came from what was called the **Asiatic Barred Zone**. The restriction was primarily racially motivated, because it did not include countries such as Russia and Turkey, whose populations were considered to be racially European. (An attempt to exclude immigration of all blacks was defeated from inclusion in the 1917 Act because of strong lobbying efforts by the NAACP.)

> **Example**: Two people attempt to emigrate to the United States from Asia. The first is an Asian living in Vladivostok; the second is a Korean from Seoul. The first person could enter the country, but the second is excluded because Korea is in the Asiatic Barred Zone.

The 1917 Act also increased the head tax and imposed an ability to read English as a requirement for entry.

The Quota System

After World War I, because of the dramatic increase in immigrants since 1890 and the increasingly larger percentage of the population who were first- or second-generation Americans from non-northern European countries, the United States imposed the first of its quotas in order to limit immigration from non-European nations. The 1921 **Quota Law** limited immigration to 3% of the number of foreign-born persons of that nationality who were residing in the United States in 1910. In other words, if the 1910 census indicated that 1000 persons living in the United States originally emigrated from Argentina, only 30 Argentineans would be permitted to enter the country (3% of 1000). However, there was a non-quota exception if the prospective immigrant lived in the Western Hemisphere for one year prior to immigration. This exception was later revised to a five-year Western Hemisphere residency requirement.

> **Example:** A family from Argentina wanted to emigrate to the United States, but the 30-person quota was already filled. The family was able to enter Spain, a Western Hemisphere country, where they lived for one year so that they could then enter the U.S. under the quota exception.

Because the 1921 law did not limit immigration (especially from the "less desirable" countries) as much as had been expected, Congress enacted a new Quota Law in 1924. This law reduced the quota percentage to 2% of the foreign-born population resident in the U.S. according to the 1890 census. The effect of this law was to reduce dramatically the number of non-Western Hemisphere immigrants who could enter the country because, prior to 1890, immigration from non-Western Hemisphere countries had been limited. The non-quota exception was also limited to Western Hemisphere nationals. Spouses of U.S. citizens were also added to the non-quota exception category.

> **Example:** In the prior example, if the Argentinean family had not emigrated to the United States by 1924, they would now be excluded because they were not nationals of the Western Hemisphere.

In 1929, a new quota formula took effect to limit immigration from non-Western Hemisphere countries even further. The new quota was based on what was known as the **National Origin Formula,** which used the ethnic background of the entire U.S. population to determine immigration limits. A total quota of 150,000 immigrants per year was established, and now, because of the ethnic makeup of the U.S. population at that time, 85% of that total was allocated to people from Northern and Western Europe. These laws remained in effect until after World War II.

The Preference System

The basis of modern U.S. immigration policy is the **Immigration and Nationality Act of 1952 (INA)** (8 U.S.C. §1401). This act kept the nationality quotas of the earlier statutes, but established four preference categories. An **immigration preference** permits those persons within preferred categories to enter the United States ahead of other immigrants. The categories included in the INA were:

1. persons with special job skills and experience
2. family relations of U.S. citizens
3. family relations of foreigners permanently resident in the U.S.
4. spouses of U.S. citizens and permanent residents.

> **Example:** An American soldier is stationed in Japan after World War II. While overseas he marries a Japanese woman. The Japanese spouse is permitted to emigrate to the United States as a preferred-category immigrant.
>
> **Example:** A Brazilian scientist wishes to emigrate to the United States. Because the scientist has special skills and experience in an area the U.S. wishes to encourage, she is permitted to enter the country on an immigration preference.

In 1965 the INA was amended to create a seven-preference category system and to abolish the national origin formula for determining immigration limits. The seven categories created in 1965 were:

1. Unmarried Children of U.S. Citizens

> **Example:** An American citizen has a child with a Romanian citizen while living in Bucharest. The child is given a preference to enter the U.S.

2. The Spouse and Unmarried Children of a Resident Alien

> **Example:** A man from Morocco who is a permanent resident in the United States goes back to Morocco for a visit and marries a woman from his native village. The Moroccan wife is given a preference to enter the United States.

This preference category gave rise to many sham marriages, marriages entered into solely to permit the foreigner to enter the United States under a preference. In 1986, the **Immigration Marriage Fraud Act** was passed, which imposed criminal sanctions on persons who entered into these sham marriages solely to circumvent the immigration law. (See Chapter Three.)

3. Persons with Exceptional Ability

> **Example:** An opera singer from Uruguay wishes to emigrate to the United States. This singer has an international reputation, and because of the singer's exceptional talent he is granted an immigration preference.

4. Professionals

> **Example:** A professor of Islamic history from Qatar is offered a teaching position at Yale. The professor would qualify for a preference as a professional.

5. Other Relatives of U.S. Citizens and Permanent Residents

> **Example:** The foreign sister of a naturalized U.S. citizen may seek an immigration preference for entry as the relative of a U.S. citizen.

6. Needed Workers

> **Example:** The U.S. government has determined that there is a shortage of qualified nurses in the United States, and therefore a preference is given to foreign nurses to enter the U.S.

In 1989, Congress enacted the **Immigration Nursing Relief Act of 1989** in order to encourage immigration of foreign qualified nurses because of a shortage of nurses in the U.S. at that time.

7. Refugees

> **Example:** While on a cultural tour in the United States, a Russian ballet dancer seeks refuge from persecution in his homeland. The dancer would be given a preference, provided he could establish a well-founded fear of persecution in Russia. (See Chapter Eight for a discussion of "Refugees.")

The INA also established a per-country limit on immigration. In 1978, the worldwide quota was increased to 290,000 immigrants per year.

In 1980, the **Refugee Act** was passed, exclusively covering refugees (this will be discussed in Chapter Eight), and in 1989, Congress eliminated the permanent exclusion of persons who had been previously deported from the United States and those who had been convicted of a single marijuana offense.

CURRENT LAW

The most recent comprehensive enactment regulating immigration was the **Immigration Act of 1990,** which amended the INA of 1952. The Immigration Act made major changes in six areas covered by the INA:

1. The Immigration Act increased the overall numerical limitation for immigration to a current annual limit of 675,000 (because of other special provisions in this act, this total numerical limit is actually 800,000).

2. The Immigration Act limited the number of family-sponsored immigrants to a yearly maximum of 465,000.

3. The Immigration Act created five new employment classifications to replace the former categories of skilled and professional workers. The newly created labor categories are:

   a) Priority workers: those persons who are needed to fill labor shortages in the United States. In order to qualify under this classification, such shortage must be first determined by the Department of Labor (28.6% of the employment preference category are allotted to this classification).

Example: The Department of Labor has determined that there is a shortage of computer programmers in the United States. A foreign computer programmer who wants to emigrate to the United States may be given a preference under this category because of the Department of Labor's determination.

   b) Professionals with advanced degrees or exceptional ability in science, art, or business (28.6%)

Example: An Indian professor of ancient Sanskrit wants to come to the United States to teach at an American university. Because of his advanced degree and specialized skills, he would qualify for a preference under this category.

   c) Persons who hold bachelor's degrees, or skilled or unskilled workers (28.6%)

Example: A skilled stonemason from Botswana wants to emigrate to the United States. Because of his specialized skill, he may qualify to enter the country under this labor preference category, even if he is not considered to have exceptional ability.

d) Religious workers and employees of the U.S. working in Hong Kong (Hong Kong has been given special status under U.S. immigration law since 1986, but that ended on January 2, 2002.)

Example: A convent wants to transfer a nun from its house in Ecuador to the Mother House in Minnesota. The nun would qualify as a religious worker.

e) Persons who are considered to be **employment creators**: persons who are able to invest at least $1 million in a business in the United States and who guarantee to employ at least ten U.S. citizens. If the business is to be located in an area of high unemployment, the foreign investor need only invest $500,000.

Example: A native of Saudi Arabia is willing to invest over $1 million in a U.S. business that will employ 15 U.S. citizens. This foreigner would be permitted to enter the U.S. as an employment creator.

In order for a person to enter the U.S. under one of these categories, the Department of Labor must certify that there is a need for such labor.

4. The 1990 Immigration Act created **diversity visas** for natives of countries that are ethnically underrepresented in the general U.S. population. Under this diversity category, nationals of the affected countries can mail applications, which are handled in a random lottery.

Example: The Irish second cousin of a U.S. citizen whose family originally came from Cork cannot obtain a visa as the relative of a citizen because the family tie is too remote. However, under the Immigration Act this cousin could apply for the lottery to obtain a visa as a diversity immigrant, provided Ireland was underrepresented in the general U.S. population.

5. The Immigration Act added four categories of nonimmigrant visas. A **nonimmigrant** is a person who wishes to enter the United Stated for a terminable period of time. The new categories are:

a) persons with extraordinary ability in arts, science, education, business or athletics,
b) athletes and performers,
c) temporary participants in cultural exchange programs, and
d) certain religious occupations.

The nonimmigrant categories will be discussed further in Chapter Four.

6. Finally, the 1990 Act specified the grounds for deporting or excluding aliens. **Deportation** refers to removing aliens who are already in the United States; **exclusion** refers to denying entry to persons who are not yet in the United States. In 1996, these two terms were merged under the single word **removal**. The grounds for *exclusion* under the 1990 Act are:

a) having a communicable disease

b) having been convicted of a crime within the previous 15 years (5 years for minors), although waivers may be granted
c) aliens who are deemed to be a security risk to the United States, such as avowed terrorists
d) communists
e) having misrepresented information in a visa application.

The grounds for *deportation* in the 1990 Act are:

a) marriage fraud: entering into a marriage simply to take advantage of a benefit under the immigration laws
b) national security risk: this ground is left purely up to the discretion of the secretary of state.

The 1990 Act also made some significant changes with respect to the determination of nationality.

Regulation of Undocumented Aliens

The increasingly restrictive policy of the United States with respect to immigration has resulted in a tremendous rise in the number of persons who enter the country without lawful authorization from the American government. These persons, originally called **illegal aliens**, now referred to as **undocumented aliens**, have been the subject of several congressional enactments specifically designed to address the legal problems presented by these persons' presence in the United States. One such act, the Immigration Marriage Fraud Act, has already been discussed.

The first major legislation aimed at stemming the flow of persons entering the country without legal documentation was the **Immigration Reform and Control Act of 1986 (IRCA)**. This statute imposed sanctions on U.S. citizens who directly or indirectly participated in the alien's undocumented entry into the United States, and also granted amnesty to persons who had already entered the country and who were deemed "qualified" to remain in the United States.

Under IRCA, Congress sanctioned all employers who hired illegal aliens after November 6, 1986, and specifically preempted all state criminal statutes covering the employment of illegal aliens.

Example: Acme, Inc., a California corporation involved in agricultural production, hired 300 illegal aliens to harvest its crops in September and October of 1986. Because the aliens had been hired prior to November 6, 1986, IRCA sanctions were not imposed on Acme.

IRCA further granted amnesty to all aliens who illegally entered the United States prior to January 1, 1982, provided that such persons applied for amnesty.

Example: A family from Southeast Asia entered the United States illegally via Canada in 1980. Under IRCA they could qualify for amnesty, permitting them to remain in the country, provided that they applied for amnesty from the government and could provide proof of their date of entry and continued stay in the U.S.

Because of a shortage of agricultural workers, IRCA granted temporary and permanent resident status to qualified agricultural workers. In order to be considered "qualified," the worker must have met the following four requirements:

1. The person must generally meet the requirements established by the IRCA for admissibility to the United States;
2. The person cannot have been convicted of either one felony or three misdemeanors;
3. The person cannot have participated in persecuting people in the person's homeland; and
4. If male, the person must have registered for U.S. Selective Service (the draft).

All information given to the government by the alien to meet the requirements of IRCA was expressly declared to be confidential, and IRCA imposed penalties for breach of any such confidentiality.

One part of IRCA did cover legal entry to the United States. In what came to be known as the NP-5 and OP-1 programs, IRCA created methods of increasing legal immigration. The NP-5 program created a first come, first served, mail registration for visas for persons in 36 countries whose visas were reduced by the quota system enacted in 1965. Under the NP-5 program over 330,000 visas were issued to persons from the affected countries.

The OP-1 program was a lottery based on a one-time registration program that affected nationals of 162 countries that had used less than 29% of their maximum quota in fiscal year 1988.

Also, under a special IRCA provision, quotas for colonial nationals (most specifically Hong Kong) were increased from 600 to 5,000 annual visas. This was an attempt to encourage immigration from the Eastern Hemisphere and to provide a haven for Hong Kong nationals who did not wish to remain in the colony after the transfer of power to the People's Republic of China.

In 1996, the federal government responded to the increasingly large number of undocumented aliens residing in and entering the United States by enacting the **Illegal Immigration Reform and Immigrant Responsibility Act of 1996** (Pub. L. 104-208). This Act only affects noncitizens and nonpermanent resident aliens who are residing in, or attempting to enter, the country without proper documentation. This statute also increased the penalties for persons removed from the United States. The specific provisions of this act will be discussed in later chapters where problems of deportation and exclusion ("removal") of aliens are discussed.

In December of 2000, the most recent federal immigration law came into effect. The **Legal Immigration and Family Equity Law Act** that effects Section 245(i) of the INA in a form of amnesty program will be discussed in subsequent chapters.

Federal Regulation of Immigration and Nationality

The ability of the federal government to regulate questions of immigration and nationality has never been successfully challenged. The basis of the federal authority is Article I, §8 clause 4 of the U.S. Constitution, which grants the federal government the ability to determine a person's citizenship.

To administer the various laws discussed above, the federal government, under the authority of the Executive Branch, has created several agencies to oversee their implementation.

The Department of State — The Department of State has responsibility for maintaining U.S. embassies and consulates abroad, to oversee American interests in foreign countries, and to protect the rights of U.S. citizens abroad. The Department of State is also in charge of **immigration officers**, government officials who maintain the U.S. against noncitizen entry.

The Department of Justice — The Department of Justice is given the primary authority with respect to immigration matters as the supervising agency of the **Immigration and Naturalization Service (INS).** The INS is headed by a commissioner appointed by the president. This commissioner is assisted by four associate commissioners and a general counsel who sit in the national office in Washington, DC. The INS maintains four regional offices (Burlington, Vermont; Ft. Snelling, Minnesota; Laguna Nigel, California; and Dallas, Texas), and thirty-four district offices headed by district directors who are responsible for the maintenance of records and information and for the investigation, examination, and removal of aliens. The INS also maintains **border patrols** to guard against illegal entry into the United States.

As part of the administrative process for immigration matters, a specialty court called the **Immigration Court** has been established as part of the INS, and decrees of this court may be appealed to the **Board of Immigration Appeals (BIA)**, which is directly accountable to the attorney general. The BIA has five permanent and two temporary judges.

The Department of Labor (DOL) — The Department of Labor is responsible for certifying the need for workers who wish to enter the United States under the labor visa categories, and the DOL also identifies areas of high unemployment for the employment creator category.

The Department of Health and Human Services — This department is responsible for administering the medical examination to those immigrants whose health status must be certified.

The U.S. Congress — On the legislative side, not only does the Congress enact the statutes that affect all immigration, but it also has the power to pass **private legislation**, bills that affect only one individual or one small group. By means of a **private bill,** a person who might not otherwise qualify to enter or remain in the United States may have his or her matter taken up by a member of Congress, who may press for enactment of a bill permitting that alien to remain in the country. This is a widely used but not widely known resource in immigration law.

Example: An alien has illegally been in the United States for several years but does not qualify for amnesty under any statute so that she can remain in the country. The alien is a brilliant writer, and a member of Congress has read and been impressed by her work. Because of her special skill, the member of Congress enters a bill to permit the alien to remain in the U.S. as an exception to the immigration law, and the bill is passed. The alien is now legally in the U.S. because of private legislation.

A complete discussion of the procedures involved in administering the immigration and nationality laws appears in the following chapters.

ETHICAL CONSIDERATIONS

Despite the fact that the United States is truly a country composed of immigrants, over the last century, American policies with respect to the continued resettlement of foreign nationals to North

America can be viewed as an expression of discrimination based on race, nationality, ethnic background, and Judeo-Christian prejudices. As the federal laws became more and more restrictive, the prejudices of the American rulers could be clearly documented. Specific racial categories have been earmarked for exclusion, such as Chinese and Southeast Asians (the attempt to exclude Africans failed because of the NAACP), and persons from non-European countries generally have been given limited opportunities to immigrate. The standards adopted by the Congress can be seen to reflect the standards of the country as a whole, and it is important to note that it was only after the civil rights movement of the 1960s that the immigration laws became slightly less prejudicial.

Today, the focus of immigration law is not so much to limit entry to the country but to expel persons who have already entered without proper documentation. The rights of citizens versus the rights of the undocumented aliens have become the battleground for current legislation, and since the 1980s illegal immigrants have been the focus of retribution. The question remains, however, whether concerns over the "illegality" of these peoples' entry is based on their racial and/or ethnic background (primarily Asian and Latin American).

CHAPTER REVIEW

The history of the United States is the history of immigration and world population migration. Starting from an unrestricted policy of immigration, since the late 1800s U.S. policy has become increasingly restrictive with respect to who may be permitted to enter the country.

The earliest restrictions concerned convicts, prostitutes, paupers, and the Chinese, but these categories quickly extended to include the mentally and physically disabled, polygamists, those who were viewed as politically subversive, and people with health-related problems. When the quota system was first introduced, its purpose and effect were to exclude immigrants from non-Western Hemisphere countries. Later, after World War II, a preference underscored those considered to be the most desirable immigrants because of education, wealth, and family relationships.

Despite, or because of, these growing restrictions, more and more people entered the United States, many currently residing in the country without legal authorization. In response to the growing number of undocumented aliens, since the 1980s Congress had geared its efforts to expel these persons from the country. America's open door policy has now become a forced exit.

CHAPTER VOCABULARY

Asiatic Barred Zone — 1917 congressional act barring certain Asian immigrants but exempting others.

Board of Immigration Appeals (BIA) — The Department of Justice board created to hear appeals from the immigration court.

Border patrol — Government officials authorized to maintain U.S. borders and to keep out undocumented aliens.

Bureau of Immigration — Forerunner of the INS created to administer the immigration laws.

Chinese Exclusion Act of 1882 — Federal statute designed to limit immigration of Chinese nationals.

Coolie labor contract — Contract used to hire Chinese immigrants at low wages.

Deportation — The process of removing aliens from the United States (now termed “removal”).

Diversity visa — Classification of preference given to persons who come from countries underrepresented in the U.S. population.

Employment creator — Alien given preference if he or she guarantees to invest at least $1 million in a U.S. business and employ at least ten U.S. citizens.

Exclusion — Process of denying an alien the right to enter the U.S. (now termed “removal”).

Head tax — Fee that immigrants formerly paid when entering the United States.

Illegal Immigration Reform and Immigrant Responsibility Act of 1996 — Most recent federal statute concerning undocumented aliens.

Immigrant — Person from one country who wishes to resettle permanently in another country.

Immigration Act of 1875 — The first national act restricting the categories of persons permitted to enter the U.S.

Immigration Act of 1990 — Current federal legislation governing immigration.

Immigration Court — Specialty court established to hear immigration matters.

Immigration Marriage Fraud Act — Enacted in 1986 to prevent sham marriages designed to circumvent immigration law.

Immigration and Nationality Act of 1952 (INA) — The federal statute that forms the basis of current immigration law.

Immigration and Naturalization Service (INS) — Federal agency under the Department of Justice authorized to implement the immigration laws.

Immigration Nursing Relief Act of 1989 — Enacted in 1989 to alleviate shortage of nurses in the U.S.

Immigration officer — Government official under the Department of State whose function is to maintain U.S. borders and make the initial determination on an application for naturalization.

Immigration preference — Under the INA, four categories of persons receive preference over other immigrants.

Immigration Reform and Control Act of 1986 (IRCA) — Federal law designed to deal with the question of undocumented aliens residing in the United States.

Legal Immigration and Family Equity Law Act — Federal law permitting certain undocumented aliens to adjust their status to lawful status.

National Origin Formula — One of the early methods of limiting immigration of persons from non-Western Hemisphere countries.

Nationality Act of 1802 — First federal statute dealing with questions of nationality.

Nonimmigrant — Alien who wishes to enter the country for a terminable period of time rather than permanently.

Quota — Method of limiting the number of aliens who may enter the country each year.

Refugee Act of 1980 — Federal statute covering the entry of refugees into the country.

Removal — The process of denying entry to aliens and removing undocumented aliens from the country.

Undocumented aliens — Formerly "illegal aliens." Persons who enter the U.S. without lawful authorization.

EDITED JUDICIAL DECISIONS

Two judicial decisions are included to highlight the material discussed in the chapter. *Henderson v. The City of New York* is the Supreme Court case that established federal supremacy in immigration matters. *Jean v. Nelson, Commissioner, Immigration and Naturalization Service* discusses the problems encountered by undocumented aliens.

HENDERSON v. THE CITY OF NEW YORK
92 U.S. 259 (1875)

OPINION:

In the case of the *City of New York v. Miln*, reported in 11 Pet. 103, the question of the constitutionality of a statute of the State concerning passengers in vessels coming to the port of New York was considered by this court. It was an act passed Feb. 11, 1824, consisting of several sections.

The first section, the only one passed upon by the court, required the master of every ship or vessel arriving in the port of New York from any country out of the United States, or from any other State of the United States, to make report in writing, and on oath, within twenty-four hours after his arrival, to the mayor of the city, of the name, place of birth, last legal settlement, age, and occupation of every person brought as a passenger from any country out of the United States, or from any of the United States into the port of New York, or into any of the United States, and of all persons landed from the ship, or put on board, or suffered to go on board, any other vessel during the voyage, with intent of proceeding to the city of New York. A penalty was prescribed of seventy-five dollars for each passenger not so reported, and for every person whose name, place of birth, last legal settlement, age, and occupation should be falsely reported.

The other sections required him to give bond, on the demand of the mayor, to save harmless the city from all expense of support and maintenance of such passenger, or to return any passenger, deemed liable to become a charge, to his last place of settlement; and required each passenger, not a citizen of the United States, to make report of himself to the mayor, stating his age, occupation, the name of the vessel in which he arrived, the place where he landed, and name of the commander of the vessel. We gather from the report of the case that the defendant, Miln, was sued for the penalties claimed for refusing to make the report required in the first section. A division of opinion was certified by the judges of the Circuit Court on the question, whether the act assumes to regulate commerce between the port of New York and foreign ports, and is unconstitutional and void.

This court, expressly limiting its decision to the first section of the act, held that it fell within the police powers of the States, and was not in conflict with the Federal Constitution.

From this decision Mr. Justice Story dissented, and in his opinion stated that Chief Justice Marshall, who had died between the first and the second argument of the case, fully concurred with him in the view that the statute of New York was void, because it was a regulation of commerce forbidden to the States.

In the Passenger Cases, reported in 7 How. 283, the branch of the statute not passed upon in the preceding case came under consideration in this court. It was not the same statute, but was a law relating to the marine hospital on Staten Island. It authorized the health commissioner to demand, and, if not paid, to sue for and recover, from the master of every vessel arriving in the port of New York from a foreign port, one dollar and fifty cents for each cabin passenger, and one dollar for each steerage passenger, mate, sailor, or mariner, and from the master of each coasting vessel twenty-five cents for each person on board. These moneys were to be appropriated to the use of the hospital.

The defendant, Smith, who was sued for the sum of $295 for refusing to pay for 295 steerage passengers on board the British ship "Henry Bliss," of which he was master, demurred to the declaration on the ground that the act was contrary to the Constitution of the United States, and void. From a judgment against him, affirmed in the Court of Errors of the State of New York, he sued on a writ of error, on which the question was brought to this court.

It was here held, at the January term, 1849, that the statute was "repugnant to the constitution and laws of the United States, and therefore void." 7 How. 572.

Immediately after this decision, the State of New York modified her statute on that subject, with a view, no doubt, to avoid the constitutional objection; and amendments and alterations have continued to be made up to the present time.

As the law now stands, the master or owner of every vessel landing passengers from a foreign port is bound to make a report similar to the one recited in the statute held to be valid in the case of *New York v. Miln*; and on this report the mayor is to endorse a demand upon the master or owner that he give a bond for every passenger landed in the city, in the penal sum of $300, conditioned to indemnify the commissioners of emigration, and every county, city, and town in the State, against any expense for the relief or support of the person named in the bond for four years thereafter; but the owner or consignee may commute for such bond, and be released from giving it, by paying, within twenty-four hours after the landing of the passengers, the sum of one dollar and fifty cents for each one of them. If neither the bond be given nor the sum paid within the twenty-four hours, a penalty of $500 for each pauper is incurred, which is made a lien on the vessel, collectible by attachment at the suit of the Commissioner of Emigration.

Conceding the authority of the Passenger Cases, which will be more fully considered hereafter, it is argued that the change in the statute now relied upon requiring primarily a bond for each passenger landed, as an indemnity against his becoming a future charge to the state or county, leaving it optional with the ship-owner to avoid this by paying a fixed sum for each passenger, takes it out of the principle of the case *of Smith v. Turner* – the Passenger Case from New York. It is said that the statute in that case was a direct tax on the passenger, since the act authorized the shipmaster to collect it of him, and that on that ground alone was it held void; while in the present case the requirement of the bond is but a suitable regulation under the power of the State to protect its cities and towns from the expense of supporting persons who are paupers or diseased, or helpless women and children, coming from foreign countries.

In whatever language a statute may be framed, its purpose must be determined by its natural and reasonable effect; and if it is apparent that the object of this statute, as judged by that criterion, is to compel the owners of vessels to pay a sum of money for every passenger brought by them from a foreign shore, and landed at the port of New York, it is as much a tax on passengers if collected from them, or a tax on the vessel or owners for the exercise of the right of landing their passengers in that city, as was the statute held void in the Passenger Cases.

To require a heavy and almost impossible condition to the exercise of this right, with the alternative of payment of a small sum of money, is, in effect, to demand payment of that sum. To suppose that a vessel, which once a month lands from three hundred to one thousand passengers, or from three thousand to twelve thousand per annum, will give that many bonds of $300 with good sureties, with a covenant for four years, against accident, disease, or poverty of the passenger named in such bond, is absurd, when this can be avoided by the payment of one dollar and fifty cents collected of the passenger before he embarks on the vessel.

Such bonds would amount in many instances, for every voyage, to more than the value of the vessel. The liability on the bond would be, through a long lapse of time, contingent on circumstances which the bondsman could neither foresee nor control. The cost of preparing the bond and approving sureties, with the trouble incident to it in each case, is greater than the sum required to be paid as commutation. It is inevitable, under such a law, that the money would be paid for each passenger, or the statute resisted or evaded. It is a law in its purpose and effect imposing a tax on the owner of the vessel for the privilege of landing in New York passengers transported from foreign countries.

It is said that the purpose of the act is to protect the State against the consequences of the flood of pauperism immigrating from Europe, and first landing in that city.

But it is a strange mode of doing this to tax every passenger alike who comes from abroad.

The man who brings with him important additions to the wealth of the country, and the man who is perfectly free from disease, and brings to aid the industry of the country a stout heart and a strong arm, are as much the subject of the tax as the diseased pauper who may become the object of the charity of the city the day after he lands from the vessel.

No just rule can make the citizen of France landing from an English vessel on our shore liable for the support of an English or Irish pauper who lands at the same time from the same vessel.

So far as the authority of the cases of *New York v. Miln* and Passenger Cases can be received as conclusive, they decide that the requirement of a catalogue of passengers, with statements of their last residence, and other matters of that character, is a proper exercise of State authority and that the requirement of the bond, or the alternative payment of money for each passenger, is void, because forbidden by the constitution and laws of the United States. But the Passenger Cases (so called because a similar statute of the State of Massachusetts was the subject of consideration at the same term with that of New York) were decided by a bare majority of the court. Justices McLean, Wayne, Catron, McKinley, and Grier held both statutes void; while Chief Justice Taney, and Justices Daniel, Nelson, and Woodbury, held them valid. Each member of the court delivered a separate opinion, giving the reasons for his judgment, except Judge Nelson, none of them professing to be the authoritative opinion of the court. Nor is there to be found, in the reasons given by the judges who constituted the majority, such harmony of views as would give that weight to the decision which it lacks by reason of the divided judgments of the members of the court. Under these circumstances, with three cases before us arising under statutes of three different States on the same subject, which have been discussed as though open in this court to all considerations bearing upon the question, we approach it with the hope of attaining a unanimity not found in the opinions of our predecessors.

As already indicated, the provisions of the Constitution of the United States, on which the principal reliance is placed to make void the statute of New York, is that which gives to Congress the power "to regulate commerce with foreign nations." As was said in *United States v. Holliday*, 3 Wall. 417, "commerce with foreign nations means commerce between citizens of the United States and citizens or subjects of foreign governments." It means trade, and it means intercourse. It means commercial intercourse between nations, and parts of nations, in all its branches. It includes navigation, as the principal means by which foreign intercourse is effected. To regulate this trade and intercourse is to prescribe the rules by which it shall be conducted. "The mind," says the great Chief Justice, "can scarcely conceive a system for regulating commerce between nations which shall exclude all laws concerning navigation, which shall be silent on the admission of the vessels of one nation into the ports of another;" and he might have added, with equal force, which prescribed no terms for the admission of their cargo or their passengers. *Gibbons v. Ogden*, 9 Wheat. 190.

Since the delivery of the opinion in that case, which has become the accepted canon of construction of this clause of the Constitution, as far as it extends, the transportation of passengers from European ports to those of the United States has attained a magnitude and importance far beyond its proportion at that time to other branches of commerce. It has become a part of our commerce with foreign nations, of vast interest to this country, as well as to the immigrants who come among us to find a welcome and a home within our borders. In addition to the wealth which some of them bring, they bring still more largely the labor which we need to till our soil, build our railroads, and develop the latent resources of the country in its minerals, its manufactures, and its agriculture. Is the regulation of this great system a regulation of commerce? Can it be doubted that a law which prescribes the terms on which vessels shall engage in it is a law regulating this branch of commerce?

The transportation of a passenger from Liverpool to the city of New York is one voyage. It is not completed until the passenger is disembarked at the pier in the latter city. A law or a rule emanating from any lawful authority, which prescribes terms or conditions on which alone the vessel can discharge its passengers, is a regulation of commerce; and, in case of vessels and passengers coming from foreign ports, is a regulation of commerce with foreign nations.

The accuracy of these definitions is scarcely denied by the advocates of the State statutes. But assuming, that, in the formation of our government, certain powers necessary to the administration of their internal affairs are reserved to the States, and that among these powers are those for the preservation of good order, of the health and comfort of the citizens, and their protection against pauperism and against contagious and infectious diseases, and other matters of legislation of like character, they insist that the power here exercised falls within this class, and belongs rightfully to the States.

This power, frequently referred to in the decisions of this court, has been, in general terms, somewhat loosely called the police power. It is not necessary for the course of this discussion to attempt to define it more accurately than it has been defined already. It is not necessary, because whatever may be the nature and extent of that power, where not otherwise restricted, no definition of it, and no urgency for its use, can authorize a State to exercise it in regard to a subject-matter which has been confided exclusively to the discretion of Congress by the Constitution.

Nothing is gained in the argument by calling it the police power. Very many statutes, when the authority on which their enactment's rest is examined, may be referred to different sources of power, and supported equally well under any of them. A statute may at the same time be an exercise of the taxing power and of the power of eminent domain. A statute punishing counterfeiting may be for the protection of the private citizen against fraud, and a measure for the protection of the currency and for the safety of the government which issues it. It must occur very often that the shading which marks the line between one class of legislation and another is very nice, and not easily distinguishable.

But, however difficult this may be, it is clear, from the nature of our complex form of government, that, whenever the statute of a State invades the domain of legislation which belongs exclusively to the Congress of the United States, it is void, no matter under what class of powers it may fall, or how closely allied to powers conceded to belong to the States.

"It has been contended," says Marshall C.J., "that if a law passed by a State, in the exercise of its acknowledged sovereignty, comes into conflict with a law passed by Congress in pursuance of the Constitution, they affect the subject and each other like equal opposing powers. But the framers of our Constitution foresaw this state of things, and provided for it by declaring the supremacy, not only of itself, but of the laws made in pursuance thereof. The nullity of any act inconsistent with the Constitution is produced by the declaration that the Constitution is supreme." Where the Federal government has acted, he says, "In every such case the act of Congress or the treaty is supreme; and the laws of the State, though enacted in the exercise of powers not controverted, must yield to it." 9 Wheat. 210.

It is said, however, that, under the decisions of this court, there is a kind of neutral ground, especially in that covered by the regulation of commerce, which may be occupied by the State, and its legislation be valid so long as it interferes with no act of Congress, or treaty of the United States. Such a proposition is supported by the opinions of several of the judges in the Passenger Cases; by the decisions of this court in *Cooly v. The Board of Wardens*, 12 How. 299; and by the cases of *Crandall v. Nevada*, 6 Wall. 35, and *Gilman v. Philadelphia*, 3 Wall. 713. But this doctrine has always been controverted in this court, and has seldom, if ever, been stated without dissent. These decisions, however, all agree, that under the commerce clause of the Constitution, or within its compass, there are powers, which, from their nature, are exclusive in Congress; and, in the case of *Cooly v. The Board of Wardens*, it was said, that "whatever subjects of this power are in their nature national, or admit of one uniform system or plan of regulation, may justly be said to be of such a nature as to require exclusive legislation by Congress." A regulation which imposes onerous, perhaps impossible, conditions on those engaged in active commerce with foreign nations, must of necessity be national in its character. It is more than this; for it may properly be called international. It belongs to that class of laws which concern the exterior relation of this whole nation with other nations and governments. If our government should make the restrictions of these burdens on commerce the subject of a treaty, there could be no doubt that such a treaty would fall within the power conferred on the President and the Senate by the Constitution. It is in fact, in an eminent degree, a subject which concerns our international relations, in regard to which foreign nations ought to be considered and their rights respected, whether the rule be established by treaty or by legislation.

It is equally clear that the matter of these statutes may be, and ought to be, the subject of a uniform system or plan. The laws which govern the right to land passengers in the United States from other countries ought to be the same in New York, Boston, New Orleans, and San Francisco. A striking evidence of the truth of this proposition is to be found in the similarity, we might almost say in the identity, of the statutes of New York, of Louisiana, and California, now before us for consideration in these three cases.

It is apparent, therefore, that, if there be a class of laws which may be valid when passed by the States until the same ground is occupied by a treaty or an act of Congress, this statute is not of that class.

The argument has been pressed with some earnestness, that inasmuch as this statute does not come into operation until twenty-four hours after the passenger has landed, and has mingled with, or has the right to mingle with, the mass of the population, he is withdrawn from the influence of any laws which Congress might pass on the subject, and remitted to the laws of the State as its own citizens are. It might be a sufficient answer to say that this is a mere evasion of the protection which the foreigner has a right to expect from the Federal government when he lands here a stranger, owing allegiance to another government, and looking to it for such protection as grows out of his relation to that government.

But the branch of the statute which we are considering is directed to and operates directly on the ship owner. It holds him responsible for what he has done before the twenty-four hours commence. He is to give the bond or pay the money because he has landed the passenger, and he is given twenty-four hours' time to do this before the penalty attaches. When he is sued for this penalty, it is not because the man has been here twenty-four hours, but because he brought him here, and failed to give the bond or pay one dollar and fifty cents.

The effective operation of this law commences at the other end of the voyage. The master requires of the passenger, before he is admitted on board, as a part of the passage-money, the sum which he knows he must pay for the privilege of landing him in New York. It is, as we have already said, in effect, a tax on the passenger, which he pays for the right to make the voyage, — a voyage only completed when he lands on the American shore. The case does not even require us to consider at what period after his arrival the passenger himself passes from the sole protection of the constitution, laws, and treaties of the United States, and becomes subject to such laws as the State may rightfully pass, as was the case in regard to importation's of merchandise in *Brown v. Maryland*, 12 Wheat. 417, and in the License Cases, 5 How. 504.

It is too clear for argument that this demand of the owner of the vessel for a bond or money on account of every passenger landed by him from a foreign shore is, if valid, an obligation which he incurs by bringing the passenger here, and which is perfect the moment he leaves the vessel.

We are of the opinion that this whole subject has been confided to Congress by the Constitution; that Congress can more appropriately and with more acceptance exercise it than any other body known to our law, state or national; that by providing a system of laws in these matters, applicable to all ports and to all vessels, a serious question, which has long been a matter of contest and complaint, may be effectually and satisfactorily settled.

Whether, in the absence of such action, the States can, or how far they can, by appropriate legislation, protect themselves against actual paupers, vagrants, criminals, and diseased persons, arriving in their territory from foreign countries, we do not decide. The portions of the New York statute which concern persons who, on inspection, are found to belong to these classes, are not properly before us, because the relief sought is to the part of the statute applicable to all passengers alike, and is the only relief which can be given on this bill.

The decree of the Circuit Court of New York, in the case of *Henderson et al. v. Mayor of the City of New York et al.*, is reversed, and the case remanded, with direction to enter a decree for an injunction in accordance with this opinion.

The statute of Louisiana, which is involved in the case of *Commissioners of Immigration v. North German Lloyd*, is so very similar to, if not an exact copy of, that of New York, as to need no separate consideration. In this case the relief sought was against exacting the bonds or paying the commutation-money as to all passengers, which relief the Circuit Court granted by an appropriate injunction; and the decree in that case is accordingly affirmed.

JEAN v. NELSON, COMMISSIONER, IMMIGRATION AND NATURALIZATION SERVICE

472 U.S. 846 (1985)

Petitioners, the named representatives of a class of undocumented and unadmitted aliens from Haiti, sued respondent Commissioner of the Immigration and Naturalization Service (INS). They alleged, *inter alia*, that they had been denied parole by INS officials on the basis of race and national origin. See 711 F.2d 1455 (CA11 1983) (panel opinion) (Jean I). The en banc Eleventh Circuit concluded that any such discrimination concerning parole would not violate the Fifth Amendment to the United States Constitution because of the Government's plenary authority to control the Nation's borders. That court remanded the case to the District Court for consideration of petitioners' claim that their treatment violated INS regulations, which did not authorize consideration of race or national origin in determining whether or not an excludable alien should be paroled. 727 F.2d 957 (1984) (Jean II). We granted certiorari. 469 U.S. 1071. We conclude that the Court of Appeals should not have reached and decided the parole question on constitutional grounds, but we affirm its judgment remanding the case to the District Court.

Petitioners arrived in this country sometime after May 1981, and represent a part of the recent influx of undocumented excludable aliens who have attempted to migrate from the Caribbean basin to South Florida. Section 235(b) of the Immigration and Nationality Act, 66 Stat. 199, 8 U. S. C. §1225(b), provides that "[every] alien . . . who may not appear to the examining immigration officer at the port of arrival to be clearly and beyond a doubt entitled to land shall be detained for further inquiry to be conducted by a special inquiry officer." Section 212(d)(5)(A) of the Act, 66 Stat. 188, as amended, 8 U. S. C. §1182(d)(5)(A), authorizes the Attorney General "in his discretion" to parole into the United States any such alien applying for admission "under such conditions as he may prescribe for emergent reasons or for reasons deemed strictly in the public interest." The statute further provides that such parole shall not be regarded as an admission of the alien, and that the alien shall be returned to custody when in the opinion of the Attorney General the purposes of the parole have been served.

For almost 30 years before 1981, the INS had followed a policy of general parole for undocumented aliens arriving on our shores seeking admission to this country. In the late 1970's and early 1980's, however, large numbers of undocumented aliens arrived in South Florida, mostly from Haiti and Cuba. Concerned about this influx of undocumented aliens, the Attorney General in the first half of 1981 ordered the INS to detain without parole any immigrants who could not present a prima facie case for admission. The aliens were to remain in detention pending a decision on their admission or exclusion. This new policy of detention rather than parole was not based on a new statute or regulation. By July 31, 1981, it was fully in operation in south Florida.

Petitioners, incarcerated and denied parole, filed suit in June 1981, seeking a writ of habeas corpus under 28 U. S. C. §2241 and declaratory and injunctive relief. The amended complaint set forth two claims pertinent here. First, petitioners alleged that the INS's change in policy was unlawfully effected without observance of the notice-and-comment rulemaking procedures of the Administrative Procedure Act (APA), 5 U. S. C. §553. Petitioners also alleged that the restrictive parole policy, as executed by INS officers in the field, violated the equal protection guarantee of the Fifth Amendment because it discriminated against petitioners on the basis of race and national origin. Specifically, petitioners alleged that they were impermissibly denied parole because they were black and Haitian.

The issue we must resolve is aptly stated by petitioners:

"This case does not implicate the authority of Congress, the President, or the Attorney General. Rather, it challenges the power of low-level politically unresponsive government officials to act in a manner which is contrary to federal statutes . . . and the directions of the President and the Attorney General, both of whom provided for a policy of non-discriminatory enforcement." Brief for Petitioners 37.

Petitioners urge that low-level INS officials have invidiously discriminated against them, and notwithstanding the new neutral regulations and the statutes, these low-level agents will renew a campaign of discrimination against the class members on parole and those members who are currently detained. Petitioners contend that the only adequate remedy is "declaratory and injunctive relief" ordered by this Court, based upon the Fifth Amendment. The limited statutory remedy ordered by the court in Jean II, petitioners contend, is insufficient. For their part respondents are also eager to have us reach the Fifth Amendment issue. Respondents wish us to hold that the equal protection component of the Fifth Amendment has no bearing on an unadmitted alien's request for parole.

"Prior to reaching any constitutional questions, federal courts must consider nonconstitutional grounds for decision." *Gulf Oil Co. v. Bernard*, 452 U.S. 89, 99 (1981); *Mobile v. Bolden*, 446 U.S. 55, 60 (1980); *Kolender v. Lawson*, 461 U.S. 352, 361, n. 10 (1983), citing *Ashwander v. TVA*, 297 U.S. 288, 347 (1936) (Brandeis, J., concurring). This is a "fundamental rule of judicial restraint." *Three Affiliated Tribes of Berthold Reservation v. Wold Engineering*, 467 U.S. 138 (1984). Of course, the fact that courts should not decide constitutional issues unnecessarily does not permit a court to press statutory construction "to the point of disingenuous evasion" to avoid a constitutional question. *United States v. Locke*, 471 U.S. 84, 96 (1985). As the Court stressed in *Spector Motor Co. v. McLaughlin*, 323 U.S. 101, 105 (1944), "[if] there is one doctrine more deeply rooted than any other in the process of constitutional adjudication, it is that we ought not to pass on questions of constitutionality . . . unless such adjudication is unavoidable." See also *United States v. Gerlach Livestock Co.*, 339 U.S. 725, 737 (1950); *Larson v. Valente*, 456 U.S. 228, 257 (1982) (STEVENS, J., concurring).

Had the court in Jean II followed this rule, it would have addressed the issue involving the immigration statutes and INS regulations first, instead of after its discussion of the Constitution. Because the current statutes and regulations provide petitioners with nondiscriminatory parole consideration – which is all they seek to obtain by virtue of their constitutional argument – there was no need to address the constitutional issue.

Congress has delegated its authority over incoming undocumented aliens to the Attorney General through the Immigration and Nationality Act, 8 U. S. C. §1101 *et seq*. The Act provides that any alien "who [upon arrival in the United States] may not appear to [an INS] examining officer . . . to be clearly and beyond a doubt entitled to land" is to be detained for examination by a special inquiry officer or immigration judge of the INS. 8 U. S. C. §§1225(b), 1226(a); see 8 C.F.R. §236.1 (1985). The alien may request parole pending the decision on his admission. Under 8 U. S. C. §1182(d)(5)(A),

"[the] Attorney General may . . . parole into the United States temporarily under such conditions as he may prescribe for emergent reasons or for reasons deemed strictly in the public interest any alien applying for admission to the United States."

The Attorney General has delegated his parole authority to his INS District Directors under new regulations promulgated after the District Court's order in this case. See 8 C.F.R. §212.5 (1985). Title 8 C.F.R. §212.5 provides a lengthy list of neutral criteria which bear on the grant or denial of parole. Respondents concede that the INS's parole discretion under the statute and these regulations, while exceedingly broad does not extend to considerations of race or national origin. Respondents' position can best be seen in this colloquy from oral argument:

"Question: You are arguing that constitutionally you would not be inhibited from discriminating against these people on whatever ground seems appropriate. But as I understand your regulations, you are also maintaining that the regulations do not constitute any kind of discrimination against these people, and . . . your agents in the field are inhibited by your own regulations from doing what you say the Constitution would permit you to do."

"Solicitor General: That's correct." Tr. of Oral Arg. 28-29.

See also Brief for Respondents 18-19; 8 U. S. C. §1182(d)(5)(A); 8 C.F.R. §212.5 (1985); cf. Statement of the President, United States Immigration and Refugee Policy (July 31, 1981), 17 Weekly Comp. of Pres. Doc. 829 (1981). As our dissenting colleagues point out, post, at 862-863, the INS has adopted nationality-based criteria in a number of regulations. These criteria are noticeably absent from the parole regulations, a fact consistent with the position of both respondents and petitioners that INS parole decisions must be neutral as to race or national origin. neutral on their face must be applied in a neutral manner, we think that interpretation arrives with some authority in this Court.

Accordingly, we affirm the en banc court's judgment insofar as it remanded to the District Court for a determination whether the INS officials are observing this limit upon their broad statutory discretion to deny parole to class members in detention. On remand the District Court must consider:

1. whether INS officials exercised their discretion under §1182(d)(5)(A) to make individualized determinations of parole, and
2. whether INS officials exercised this broad discretion under the statutes and regulations without regard to race or national origin.

Petitioners protest, however, that such a nonconstitutional remedy will permit lower-level INS officials to commence parole revocation and discriminatory parole denial against class members who are currently released on parole. But these officials, while like all others bound by the provisions of the Constitution, are just as surely bound by the provisions of the statute and of the regulations. Respondents concede that the latter do not authorize discrimination on the basis of race and national origin. These class members are therefore protected by the terms of the Court of Appeals' remand from the very conduct which they fear. The fact that the protection results from the terms of a regulation or statute, rather than from a constitutional holding, is a necessary consequence of the obligation of all federal courts to avoid constitutional adjudication except where necessary. The judgment of the Court of Appeals remanding the case to the District Court for consideration of petitioner's claims based on the statute and regulations is

Affirmed.

EXERCISES

1. Do you believe that the U.S. should place any restrictions on immigration? Why or why not? Is your answer influenced by the events of September 11, 2001?
2. A large number of aliens are residing in the country without legal authorization. What do you think would be an appropriate action to take with respect to these people? What, if anything, should be done to reduce or eliminate the problem of illegal entry into the United States?

3. From where did your ancestors emigrate? Would they be permitted to enter the country now based on current law?
4. Do you believe that aliens should be permitted to enter the U.S. to fill a labor void, or should funds be used to train U.S. citizens to fill these job vacancies? Explain.
5. The text briefly discusses private legislation. What is your opinion of such specialized enactments? Do they serve a legitimate purpose? Do you believe that such private bills are constitutional? Why or why not?

Chapter Two

CITIZENSHIP AND NATIONALITY

CHAPTER PREVIEW

Immigration refers to the migration of people from their place of citizenship or nationality to a geographic location to which they owe no automatic allegiance. Consequently, the threshold question with respect to immigration is the determination of a person's citizenship or nationality. One cannot immigrate to one's own homeland.

Citizenship is defined as belonging to a political community that submits to the dominion of a government. **Nationality** is typically used as a political subdivision of citizenship. For example, prior to the breakup of the Soviet bloc in Europe, a person may have been a citizen of Yugoslavia but a Serbian national; Serbia was a political subdivision of Yugoslavia, but the central Yugoslavian government controlled Serbia. A person who does not owe allegiance to a country because of citizenship or nationality is considered to be an **alien** with respect to that country.

Example: At the turn of the century the United States controlled many geographic possessions, i.e., Puerto Rico, Guam, etc. The Supreme Court determined that persons who lived in these areas were U.S. nationals but not U.S. citizens. They were afforded many privileges as U.S. nationals but were not given all the rights of U.S. citizens. These cases are known as the **insular cases**.

Being a citizen of a country entitles a person to certain rights. With respect to immigration, a person has the right to reside in the country of his or her citizenship. A citizen cannot be expelled from his or her homeland, nor can a citizen be barred from entry or reentry to the country of his or her citizenship.

Example: An American citizen is convicted of armed robbery and rape. After serving his time in prison, he is free to live anywhere in the United States. A citizen cannot be expelled from the country of his citizenship no matter what crimes he may commit.

Example: An immigrant to the United States is convicted of armed robbery and rape after being in the country only seven months. After serving his prison term, the immigrant can be removed from the United States; he has no automatic right of residence because he is not a citizen.

Example: An American citizen goes to Mexico on vacation for two weeks. When she returns to the United States she must be admitted because she is a citizen.

Example: A Mexican citizen wishes to enter the United States. The Mexican citizen is stopped at the U.S. border because she has no valid entry documents. Because she is not a U.S. citizen, she has no automatic right of entry.

Citizenship also imposes several obligations on the citizen, such as the obligation to perform military service and to serve on a jury. With respect to immigration law, a person's citizenship or nationality must first be ascertained to determine whether or not the immigration laws apply to him or her.

This chapter will examine how citizenship is determined, how one may change one's citizenship, and under what circumstances citizenship may be lost. Remember, a person cannot emigrate to the country where the person is a citizen.

OBTAINING CITIZENSHIP BY BIRTH

There are two methods whereby a person becomes a citizen. The first method is involuntarily determined by the person's birth. The second method of acquiring citizenship results from a voluntary act by the person, known as **naturalization**.

Under American law a person acquires citizenship by birth by one of two methods. The first method is by the geographical location of the person's birth. This method of obtaining citizenship is known as ***jus soli***, place of birth.

> **Example:** A person is born in Kansas City, Kansas. This person is automatically an American citizen by the doctrine of *jus soli*.

The second method of obtaining citizenship by birth is through the blood of one's parents. A child is automatically considered to be a citizen of the country of citizenship of his or her parents. This concept is known as ***jus sanguinis***, by blood.

> **Example:** An American couple is vacationing in Paris, France, when the woman gives birth. The child is automatically considered an American citizen because of the citizenship of the parents.

Take note that historically, under American law, the concept of *jus soli* and *jus sanguinis* did not apply to Native Americans or slaves. It should also be noted that although some countries recognize the concept of **dual citizenship**, a person owing allegiance to two countries simultaneously, the United States historically did not recognize this status. If an American citizen holds dual citizenship under the laws of another country, he or she must renounce the foreign citizenship if he or she wishes to remain in the United States after attaining the age of 18.

The specific requirements for obtaining U.S. citizenship by birth were detailed in the 1952 Act discussed in the previous chapter. This statute specifies three methods of U.S. citizenship by birth:

1. **Birth Within the United States (*jus soli*)** (INA §301(a)). The Act distinguishes between persons who are born to individuals subject to United Sates jurisdiction and those who are born to individuals not subject to U.S. jurisdiction, even if the person is born within the U.S. Persons born to diplomats or other aliens who are in the United States as a public official detailed to the United States are not considered to be U.S. citizens. Persons born in the United States who are the children of U.S. citizens or nationals, or children of persons who are in the United States pursuant to a private interest, are deemed citizens of the United States. Persons born to individuals who are in the United States without legal authorization may not be deemed U.S. citizens.

Example: A child is born to the wife of the captain of a foreign government hospital ship docked in U.S. waters for refueling. This child is not a U.S. citizen because the parents are government officials.

Example: A child is born to the wife of the captain of a foreign pleasure craft while it is docked in U.S. waters for refueling. This child is a U.S. citizen because the parents were in the U.S. on a private vessel.

Children born to **enemy aliens**, (so designated by the secretary of state), while in the United States are not U.S. citizens.

2. **Birth in United States Territories (*jus soli*).** The United States owned several territories as of the date of the 1952 Act, and citizenship for persons born in those locales was dependent upon the territory in question.
   a) Hawaii. Persons born in Hawaii on or after July 7, 1898, were U.S. citizens; persons born in Hawaii prior to that date became U.S. citizens on April 30, 1900 (30 Stat. §750). Since August 21, 1959, Hawaii has been a state.
   b) Alaska. Anyone except Native Americans who were born in Alaska after March 30, 1867, were U.S. citizens (15 Stat. §539). Native Americans born or living in Alaska as of June 2, 1924, are considered to be U.S. citizens (43 Stat. §253). Since June 3, 1959, Alaska has been a state.
   c) Puerto Rico. Persons born in Puerto Rico after January 13, 1941, are U.S. citizens (54 Stat. §1137). Persons born between April 11, 1899, and January 12, 1941, became U.S. citizens as of January 13, 1941, provided they were residing in a territory controlled by the United States.
   d) Canal Zone. A person born in the Canal Zone is a U.S. citizen if one of his or her parents is a U.S. citizen (INA §303(a)).
   e) Virgin Islands. Persons born in the Virgin Islands after January 17, 1912, are U.S. citizens. Additionally, any Danish citizen living in the Virgin Islands on that date who did not retain his or her Danish citizenship became a U.S. citizen (the U.S. Virgin Islands were formerly owned by Denmark) (INA §306(a)(1)).
   f) Guam. All persons born in Guam on or after April 11, 1899, are U.S. citizens, and all persons living in Guam prior to that date were declared U.S. citizens on August 1, 1950, if they resided on Guam or any other U.S. territory (INA §307).
   g) The Philippines. The Philippines became independent of the United States in 1946, and consequently all persons born there after that date are not U.S. citizens. Prior to independence, Filipinos were considered U.S. nationals but not U.S. citizens (INA §308).

3. **Born Outside the United States and its Territories (*jus sanguinis*).** Determining U.S. citizenship for persons born outside the United States is fairly complicated and depends on three factors: the citizenship of the parent; residence of the parent within the United States; and the date of birth.

For persons born outside the United States before May 24, 1934, the person was considered a U.S. citizen if the *parents* were citizens and the *father* had resided in the United States prior to the birth of the child (1 Stat. §103).

Example: A child was born in Hong Kong on May 23, 1934, of U.S. citizens. The mother had lived in the United States until her marriage at age 24; the father had never lived in the U.S. even though he was a U.S. citizen. This child is not considered to be a U.S. citizen.

Persons born outside the United States between May 24, 1934 and January 12, 1941 were considered U.S. citizens if the person's father *or mother* was a U.S. citizen and the citizen parent had resided in the United States prior to the birth (48 Stat. §797).

Example: In the preceding example, if the child had been born on May 24, 1935, instead of May 23, the child would be considered a U.S. citizen.

Persons born outside the United States between January 13, 1941 and December 23, 1952 were considered U.S. citizens if both parents were U.S. citizens, or one parent was a U.S. citizen and the other a U.S. national, and the citizen parent had resided in the United States or its possessions (54 Stat. §1138). If only one parent was a U.S. citizen and the other was an alien, the child was only deemed to be a U.S. citizen if the citizen parent lived in the United States for ten years, at least five of which occurred after attaining the age of 16. Furthermore, the child would lose his or her U.S. citizenship if the child did not reside in the United States for a period totaling five years between the ages of 13 and 21.

Example: A child was born to a U.S. father and an alien mother in the mother's homeland. The child first came to the United States at the age of 18. This child would not be a U.S. citizen because the child could not reside in the United States for the requisite five years between the ages of 13 and 21.

For persons born outside the United States after December 23, 1952, if both parents are U.S. citizens, the child is a U.S. citizen. If only one parent is a U.S. citizen and the other is a U.S. national, the citizen parent must have been physically present in the United States for one year prior to the child's birth for the child to be considered a U.S. citizen (INA §301(d)). If one parent is a U.S. citizen and the other is an alien, the citizen parent must have been present in the United States for a period of ten years, at least five of which occurred after the parent attained the age of 14 (INA §301 (g)). This requirement was amended in 1986 to a physical presence of five years, two of which occur after attaining the age of 14.

The provisions of the 1952 Act were amended in 1966 to include periods of overseas service on behalf of the United Sates government as counting toward the residency requirement, if the parent was either the one in service or was the dependent of the one in service.

Example: The citizen parent of a child born in Germany had been an "Army brat," having lived overseas with her parents who were in military service for the United States government all over the world. Because the citizen parent was the dependent of persons serving in the U.S. military overseas, her U.S. residence included the periods during which she was so dependent, and the child is a U.S. citizen.

OBTAINING CITIZENSHIP BY NATURALIZATION

The second method of acquiring citizenship is by naturalization. **Naturalization** is the process whereby the citizen of one country voluntarily decides to become the citizen of another country. In the United States, the INS determines whether or not an alien meets the requirements to become a United States citizen. Remember, acquiring citizenship by naturalization is a voluntary action on the part of the person desiring the new citizenship; it is not automatically determined

Requirements. In order to become a naturalized U.S. citizen, one must meet four statutory requirements:

1. **Residence** (INA §316). The alien seeking to become a U.S. citizen must be resident in the United States for a period of five years. During this five-year period prior to applying for naturalization, the person must have been physically present in the United States for at least 2½ years and must have resided in the district in which he or she petitions for naturalization for at least three months prior to submitting the petition. The residence cannot be founded on an illegal entry into the United States.

> **Example:** A petitioner for naturalization has lived in the United States for six years. The petitioner entered the United States on a valid visa, and has lived at his present address for two years. This person would meet the residency requirement to petition for naturalization.
>
> **Example:** A person seeking naturalization as a U.S. citizen has been physically present in the United States for over 15 years, but entered the country without proper documentation. This person does not meet the residency requirement to petition for naturalization.

The residency requirement mandates a continuous residency, but the continuity is not broken by absences of up to six months. Absences from the country for a period of more than six months but less than one year create rebuttable presumptions of a break in continuity. An absence for more than one year conclusively destroys continuity, and the alien must complete a new period of continued residence.

> **Example:** An alien permanently resides in the United States and goes back to her homeland for a three-month visit one summer. This vacation does not destroy her continued residence in the U.S.
>
> **Example:** An alien permanently residing in the United States has to go back to his homeland to care for his ailing father. The alien is away from the United States for eight months. There is a presumption that his residence is broken, but the alien may overcome the presumption by documenting the medical need for the absence.
>
> **Example:** An alien permanently residing in the United States returns to his homeland for 15 months to take care of a family business. In this instance the continuous residence in the United States is broken, and the alien must start a new residency period.

There is an exception to the requirement of physical presence in the United States for persons who leave the country for a year or more. The exception applies if the person is in the service of the U.S. government, a U.S. institution of research, a U.S. corporation engaged in foreign trade, a public international organization to which the United States is a member, or a religious organization. Also, the alien must already have been in the United States for one year prior to their departure. To obtain this exemption, the alien must file Form N-470.

> **Example:** After living in the United States for two years, an alien is sent by her employer, a U.S. corporation, to the company's office in Santiago, Chile, for a two-year period. The alien may obtain an exemption for the residency requirement by filing Form N-470 and proving that her absence is for the purpose of developing foreign trade to benefit the U.S. corporation.

An alien may also be considered to have **constructive residence** in the United States if he or she served on a U.S. public vessel or a vessel whose home port is the United States (this does not include service as part of the military). This service is considered to count toward the residency requirement.

> **Example:** An alien is employed as a cook on a U.S. pleasure ship. While serving on board, the alien is deemed to be in continuous residence in the United States.

Also, a person who is involuntarily absent from the United States may have the period of involuntary absence excused from the residency requirement. Examples of involuntary absence would be kidnapping while overseas or being detained overseas during periods of armed conflict.

2. **Age** (INA §334). In order to be able to petition to become a naturalized U.S. citizen, the petitioner must be at least 18 years of age. A petition may be filed on behalf of a minor by the minor's natural or adoptive parent.

> **Example:** A family emigrates to the United States after the birth of their child. After five years, the parents petition for U.S. citizenship on behalf of themselves and their minor child.

3. **Literacy** (INA §312). To be granted U.S. citizenship an alien must be able to demonstrate an understanding of the English language. There is an exception to this language requirement for persons over the age of 55 who have been resident in the United States for 15 years.

In addition to the English language requirement, the petitioner must pass an examination demonstrating a knowledge of American history. An interpreter may be used for any person who has been exempted from the language requirement. Also, a person who has a demonstrated physical disability that would interfere with taking the examination may also be exempted.

> **Example:** A man emigrated from Israel with his adult children 18 years ago. The man is 62 years old and knows no English. If he applies for U.S. citizenship, he will be exempted from the English language requirement, and a Hebrew interpreter will be provided for him to take the examination to test his knowledge of American history.

4. **Moral Character** (INA §316(a)). A person seeking U.S. citizenship by naturalization must demonstrate good moral character. A person is considered to lack good moral character if, at any time in the five years prior to filing the petition, the petitioner was
   a) a habitual drunkard

b) a polygamist
c) receiving the principal source of his or her income from gambling
d) convicted of two or more gambling offenses
e) found to have given false testimony to obtain a benefit under the immigration laws
f) convicted and jailed for 180 days or more, regardless of when the offense was committed
g) at any time convicted of murder.

The preceding list is not exclusive, and a person may be considered to lack good moral character even if the person does not fall into one of these categories. Under the statute, the attorney general is not limited to the preceding five-year period when determining the petitioner's character, but may also consider any act committed by the applicant that relates to moral character.

Relaxed Requirements. The INA permits relaxed requirements for certain categories of individuals:

1. Children: a child may seek naturalization by petition filed by the parent, and the child does not have to meet the literacy or moral character requirements. (INA §323(a)).
2. Spouses: the spouse of a U.S. citizen may apply for naturalization after only three years of residence in the United States. (INA §319).
3. Military Service: a lawful resident who honorably serves in the U.S. military may apply for naturalization after having served in the U.S. military for periods totaling three years. (INA §328).

THE NATURALIZATION PROCESS

The application procedure for an alien seeking to become a naturalized U.S. citizen is a multistep process:

1. THE APPLICATION (INA §334(a)). The alien first files Form N-400 with the Immigration and Naturalization Service. The application must include three identical photographs, the applicant's alien registration number, biographical information, and proof of the applicant's legal entry into the United States. Fingerprints, formerly required, are no longer necessary. (See Appendices 2-1, 2-2, and 2-3.)

2. THE EXAMINATION (INA §335(b)). Every applicant must be personally examined before a **naturalization officer**. The applicant, unless exempted, must take and pass a test to determine the applicant's knowledge of the English language and American history. At the examination, the applicant may present witnesses to testify as to the applicant's qualifications for citizenship. The applicant may be represented by an attorney or other authorized person, who may view the proceeding but who may not participate. The examination may be videotaped or recorded, and such tape is admissible in any future proceeding. After the examination, the alien is apprised of the officer's decision. The applicant may request a hearing before an immigration officer if the petition is denied. (See Appendix 2-4.)

3. A HEARING ON THE DENIAL OF AN APPLICATION (INA §336(a)). If the application is denied, the alien has the right to a hearing before an immigration officer different from the one who initially denied the application. The hearing must be held within 180 days after the request for a hearing is filed, and the hearing may be taped. If

the immigration officer does not render a decision within 120 days after the hearing, the applicant may seek redress in the federal district court where the issue is decided *de novo*.

4. THE OATH (INA §337). If the applicant has been approved for citizenship, citizenship will be granted in court after the applicant takes an oath of allegiance to the United States. If the court cannot administer the oath within 45 days, the applicant may have the oath administered by the INS.

5. CERTIFICATE OF NATURALIZATION (INA §338). After the oath of allegiance is administered, the new citizen will be issued a certificate of naturalization, which is proof of citizenship. This certificate contains the number of the petition and the certificate, the date of naturalization, the name, signature, place of residence, personal description and signed photograph of the naturalized citizen, and a statement by the INS that the person described in the certificate has met all the requirements to be a citizen of the United States.

LOSS OF NATIONALITY

Pursuant to the provisions of the Immigration and Nationality Act, a person may lose his or her citizenship in one of the following ways:

1. By expatriation pursuant to Section 349(a) of the INA.
2. By denaturalization pursuant to Section 340(a) of the INA.

Expatriation. Expatriation is the voluntary abandonment of one's citizenship by becoming a citizen or subject of another country. There are generally six methods whereby a citizen becomes an expatriate:

a) Becoming a naturalized citizen of another country (INA §349(a)(1))

Example: A woman from Iran emigrated to the United States in 1990. After living in America for the requisite number of years, she applied for and was granted U.S. citizenship. By becoming a naturalized citizen of the United States, she had expatriated herself from Iran.

b) Swearing an oath of allegiance to a foreign state (INA §349(a)(2))

Example: An American citizen who is Jewish visits Israel after graduating from college. The American decides he wants to stay in Israel and swears an oath of allegiance to Israel. The American has lost his U.S. citizenship by an act of expatriation.

c) Serving in the military of a foreign state (INA §349(a)(3)). If an American citizen voluntarily enters into the military service of a government hostile to the United States with a view to renouncing U.S. citizenship, such military service constitutes an act of expatriation.

Example: An American citizen of Iraqi heritage flies to Baghdad to join Iraqi forces in the attempt to oust all foreigners, especially Americans, from Iraqi soil. This act may constitute an act of expatriation.

d) Employment with a foreign government (INA §349(a)(4)). If an American citizen accepts employment with a foreign government that requires an oath of allegiance as a condition of such employment, the American will be expatriated. Be aware, though, that not all employment by foreign governments constitutes an act of expatriation, and each instance must be individually analyzed.

e) Formal renunciation (INA §349(a)(5) & (6)). Whenever an American formally renounces his or her citizenship, the American has fulfilled an act of expatriation, regardless of the reason for the renunciation.

Example: Barbara Hutton, the Woolworth heiress, was married to a Dane living in London. In order to save on income taxes, she renounced her U.S. citizenship; as the wife of a Danish subject, she was automatically considered to be Danish.

f) Committing an act of treason or subversion (INA §349(a)(7)). Whenever a naturalized American is *convicted* of an act of treason or subversion, pursuant to the INA the American loses his or her citizenship. Note that the provision of the statute has never been tested for its constitutionality.

In order for an American to lose his or her citizenship by an act of expatriation, the person must be at least 18 years of age, and the burden of proof with respect to an act of expatriation is by a preponderance of the evidence.

Denaturalization. The INA specifies five grounds by which a naturalized U.S. citizen may lose such citizenship:

a) By the concealment of a material fact or a willful misrepresentation of information in order to obtain a Certificate of Naturalization (INA §340(a)). A fact is deemed to be "material" if it would have caused a denial of the person's application, or might have led to an investigation of facts that would warrant denial of the application.

Example: An applicant for U.S. citizenship concealed the fact that he had actively participated in the persecution and execution of an ethnic minority in the applicant's homeland. This is considered a material fact that would warrant denying an application for naturalization.

b) Illegal procurement of naturalization (INA §101(f)(6)). This can occur whenever the applicant had been granted naturalization where no facts existed to substantiate one or more of the requirements to become a naturalized citizen.

> **Example:** The applicant lied on his application, but the fact was not considered "material." Because giving false testimony indicates a lack of good moral character, the person could be denaturalized.

c) Abandoning U.S. residence within one year of naturalization (INA §340(d)).

> **Example:** An alien living in the United States became a U.S. citizen, but retired from employment within one year of naturalization and left the United States to return to his original homeland. If it can be shown that the person never intended to return to the United States on a permanent basis, he could be denaturalized.

d) Refusal to appear as a witness before a Congressional Committee investigating the naturalized citizen's alleged subversive activities within ten years of naturalization. This is a very limited ground for denaturalization (INA §340(a)).

e) Becoming a member of a subversive organization within five years of naturalization (INA §340)).

These last two grounds for denaturalization are attempts to prevent subversives from obtaining U.S. citizenship only to work for the overthrow of the American government.

ETHICAL CONSIDERATIONS

Several ethical considerations become apparent when considering the process of becoming a citizen of the United States. What is the responsibility of the United States government with respect to persons born in the United States of persons who are illegally residing in the country after the expiration of a valid visa? If the government removes the parents because they do not have a legal right to reside in the United States, isn't the government forcing the infant U.S. citizen to be removed or orphaned?

When the statute prescribes that a person be of "good moral character" and indicates certain criteria that are left open to interpretation, such as being a habitual drunkard, the statute is opening the door for an abuse of discretion on the part of the government officials authorized to administer the law. Furthermore, if a Moslem adheres to the dictates of Islam by having several wives, does that mean that he lacks "good moral character" because he does not adhere to Judeo-Christian concepts?

Finally, what constitutes a "subversive activity?" In a country that challenged its own native-born citizens for their beliefs during the McCarthy era, it would appear to be a dangerous concept to specify "subversive" without differentiating between political ideas and physical acts such as organizing an insurrection.

CHAPTER REVIEW

It is impossible for a person to emigrate to the United States if the person is already a U.S. citizen. Consequently, the primary question that must be addressed when considering application of the U.S. immigration laws is the citizenship or nationality of the person in question.

Under the INA a person may become a U.S. citizen either by birth or by naturalization. A person is deemed to be a U.S. citizen by birth if

- the person is born within the geographic confines of the United States or
- the person is born abroad if one or both of the person's parents is a U.S. citizen, and
- the citizen parent has actually resided in U.S. territory for a minimum statutory period.

A person may become a U.S. citizen by naturalization, provided the person has legally entered the United States, has lived here for a minimum period of time, is conversant with the English language and American history, is of good moral character, and applies for citizenship by naturalization with the INS.

An American may lose his or her American citizenship either by expatriation, voluntarily renouncing such citizenship, or by denaturalization. Denaturalization may occur whenever a naturalized citizen is found to have failed to meet the requirements for naturalization even though a Certificate of Naturalization had been issued.

CHAPTER VOCABULARY

Alien — A person who is not a citizen of the country in question.

Citizenship — Owing allegiance to a particular geographic and political unit.

Constructive residence — Meeting U.S. residency requirements for naturalization by serving on a U.S. public vessel or a vessel with a U.S. home port.

Denaturalization — The process by which a naturalized citizen loses citizenship.

Dual citizenship — Owing allegiance to two countries at the same time; not recognized by the United States.

Expatriation — A voluntary act by which a citizen renounces his or her citizenship.

Enemy aliens — Citizens and nationals of countries the United States has declared an enemy of the country.

Immigration — The migration of people from their place of citizenship or nationality to a geographic location to which they owe no automatic allegiance.

Immigration officer — Government official under the Department of State whose function is to maintain U.S. borders and make the initial determination on an application for naturalization.

Insular cases — Refers to Supreme Court determination that persons in the U.S. territories were U.S. nationals, but not U.S. citizens.

Jus sanguinis — Citizenship by blood.

Jus soli — Citizenship by place of birth.

Nationality — A political subdivision of citizenship.

Naturalization — The process of becoming a citizen of a country by a voluntary act.

Naturalization officer — A government official authorized to handle the naturalization process.

EDITED JUDICIAL DECISIONS

The following two cases underscore some of the concepts discussed in the main text. *United States of America v. Breyer* analyzes certain problems with respect to naturalization, and *Rogers v. Bellei* discusses the concept of *jus sanguinis.*

UNITED STATES OF AMERICA v. BREYER

841 F. Supp. 679 (E. D. Pa. 1993)

This is a denaturalization action filed by the United States government pursuant to Section 340(a) of the Immigration and Nationality Act of 1952, as amended, 8 U.S.C. §1451(a). The court has jurisdiction under 28 U.S.C. §1345 and 8 U.S.C. §§1421(a) and 1451(a).

On July 7, 1993, the court granted the government's motion for summary judgment with respect to counts I and II of its complaint. United States v Breyer, 829 F. Supp. 773 (E.D.Pa. 1993). The court found that the defendant, Johann Breyer, advocated or assisted in the persecution of people because of race, religion or national origin as an armed guard at the Buchenwald concentration camp and the Auschwitz death camp. Because of the defendant's assistance in persecution, Section 13 of the Displaced Persons Act of 1948 ("DPA"), as amended, made the defendant's entry visa into the United States invalid. The court also found that the defendant's service as a member of the SS Totenkopf of the Waffen-SS constituted participation in a movement hostile to the United States and thus rendered him ineligible to receive an entry visa under Section 13 of the DPA. The court concluded that because the defendant was ineligible for the entry visa he obtained in order to enter the United States, the defendant failed to satisfy all the statutory requirements for naturalization. Therefore, the court held that the defendant's citizenship by naturalization was illegally procured. The government withdrew the other counts of the complaint at trial.

The defendant responded to the government's motion for summary judgment that he was a citizen by birth because his mother was born in the United States. The court examined this affirmative defense separately because it found it to be a distinct issue from that of naturalization. The court found that Section 1993 of the Revised Statute of 1874 as applied to the defendant was unconstitutional since it conferred United States citizenship to foreign-born offspring of United States citizen fathers but not to United States citizen mothers. The court concluded that this statute was unconstitutional because there was no legitimate good faith basis for the gender discrimination and it therefore violated the equal protection component of the Fifth Amendment due process clause. The court expressly reserved the factual issue of the birthplace of the defendant's mother for trial.

The court conducted the bench trial on the remaining issues during four days in September, 1993, and October, 1993. The focus of the trial was the birthplace of the defendant's mother. After carefully reviewing the testimony and the exhibits, and the suggested findings of fact and conclusions of law submitted by the parties, the court sets forth the following findings of fact and conclusions of law.

II. FINDINGS OF FACT (Deleted)

III. CONCLUSIONS OF LAW

The court's conclusions of law are as follows:

(a) Defendant's Mother's Birthplace

43. The defendant must prove that his mother was born in the United States by a preponderance of the evidence. See, *United States v. Ghaloub*, 385 F.2d 567, 570 (2d Cir. 1966); *De Vargas v. Brownell*, 251 F.2d 869 (5th Cir. 1958); *Delmore v. Brownell*, 236 F.2d 598 (3d Cir. 1956).

44. The absence of an official birth record is not decisive as to whether a person is born in the United States because other proof can be adduced to establish this claim. See, *Liacakos v. Kennedy*, 195 F. Supp. 630 (D.D.C. 1961); 4 Gordon & Mailman, Immigration Law and Practice §99.02[1][b].

45. In the absence of a contemporaneous official record of birth, secondary evidence can establish a person's birthplace. See 4 Gordon & Mailman, Immigration Law and Practice

§ 99.02[1][e].

46. From the secondary evidence produced at trial, the defendant has proven by a preponderance of the evidence that his mother, Katharina Susanna Breyer, was born in the United States of America on December 23, 1897.

47. Under the Fourteenth Amendment to the United States Constitution, "all persons born or naturalized in the United States, and subject to the jurisdiction thereof, are citizens of the United States and of the State, wherein they reside."

48. The court finds that since the defendant's mother was born in the United States, she was a United States citizen by birth.

(b) Remedy for Unconstitutionality of Section 1993

49. The court has previously found that Section 1993 of the Revised Statute of 1874, as it applied to the defendant on the date of his birth in 1925, was unconstitutional as a violation of the equal protection component of the Fifth Amendment's due process clause since United States citizen mothers were not included in the benefits conferred by the statute. When the defendant was born, Section 1993 awarded United States citizenship to the foreign-born offspring of United States citizen fathers but not to United States citizen mothers. See, *United States v. Breyer*, 829 F. Supp. 773 (E.D.Pa. 1993).

50. A court can remedy a constitutionally under-inclusive scheme either by declaring the statute a nullity and ordering that the benefits not be extended to the members of the class intended to benefit or by extending the coverage of the statute to include those who are aggrieved by the exclusion. See, *Heckler v. Mathews*, 465 U.S. 728, 738, 104 S. Ct. 1387, 79 L. Ed. 2d 646 (1984); *Welsh v. United States*, 398 U.S. 333, 361, 90 S. Ct. 1792, 26 L. Ed. 2d 308 (1970).

51. The court finds that the proper remedy for Section 1993's constitutional defect is to include United States citizen mothers under the statute so that their foreign-born offspring are awarded citizenship. To hold otherwise and remedy Section 1993 by declaring it a nullity would involve stripping citizenship from foreign-born offspring of male citizens who have enjoyed that citizenship for decades. Such a result is impossible to countenance.

52. The government urges that any remedy fashioned by the court be nonretroactive and only apply to future cases.

53. Retroactivity is "overwhelmingly the norm." *James B. Bean Distilling Co. v. Georgia*, 501 U.S. 529, 111 S. Ct. 2439, 115 L. Ed. 2d 481 (1991). There is a "normal rule of

retroactive application." *Harper v. Virginia Dept. of Taxation,* U.S. , 113 S. Ct. 2510, 125 L. Ed. 2d 74 (1993).

54. In order for the remedy to be nonretroactive, the court must consider these factors: (1) whether its decision establishes a new principle of law, either by overruling clear past precedent on which the litigants may have relied or by deciding an issue of first impression whose resolution was not clearly foreshadowed; (2) after reviewing the prior history of the rule in question, its purpose and its effect, whether the retrospective operation of the rule will retard its operation; (3) whether retroactivity will produce substantial inequitable results. See, *Chevron Oil Co. v. Huson,* 404 U.S. 97. 106-107, 92 S. Ct. 349, 30 L. Ed. 2d 296 (1971).

55. After reviewing the three Chevron factors, the court rejects the government's position of nonretroactivity and finds that the remedy of inclusion of United States mothers should be applied retroactively.

(a) Clearly, the court's decision that Section 1993 is unconstitutional establishes a new principle of law since the decision involved an issue of first impression within the Third Circuit. However, it is equally clear that this resolution of the issue was clearly foreshadowed. Thus, the first Chevron factor favors a nonretroactive application of Section 1993's remedy, but only slightly.

(b) The retroactive application of Section 1993's remedy of including mothers will promote, rather than retard, the principles of equal protection of the law. When the court declared Section 1993 unconstitutional, it examined the history and purpose of the statute and found no legitimate and bona fide reason existed to justify the statute's gender discrimination. By retroactively applying Section 1993's remedy of inclusion to the defendant, the court would be promoting the prohibition against gender discrimination. Thus, the second Chevron factor favors the retroactive application of Section 1993's remedy.

(c) The retroactive application of including mothers under the coverage of Section 1993 will not produce substantially inequitable results since foreign-born offspring of United States fathers born before 1934 will retain their United States citizenship. Thus, the third Chevron factor also favors the retroactive application of Section 1993's remedy.

56. The court concludes that the remedy for the unconstitutionality of Section 1993 is to retroactively include United States mothers under the statute so that their foreign-born offspring that were born before 1934 would be United States citizens.

(c) Defendant's Citizenship by Birth Defense

57. The court declines the government's request to treat the defendant's affirmative defense of citizenship by birth as a permissive counterclaim under Rule 13(b) of the Federal Rules of Civil Procedure because the parties did not present evidence or argument on the issues of whether the defendant's mother was still a United States citizen when the defendant was born and whether the defendant was still a United States citizen when he entered this country.

58. A person seeking a declaration of citizenship may apply pursuant to Section 341(a) of the Immigration and Naturalization Act, 8 U.S.C. §1452(a), for a certificate of citizenship from the United States Attorney General based upon statutory authority.

59. A party must have exhausted his or her administrative remedies before a federal district court can issue a declaration of United States nationality or citizenship pursuant to

8 U.S.C. §1503(a). See *Whitehead v. Haig*, 794 F.2d 115 (3d Cir. 1986); *Linzalone v. Dulles*, 120 F. Supp. 107 (S.D.N.Y. 1954).

60. The defendant has not exhausted his administrative remedies since he is currently appealing to the Administrative Appeals Unit of the Immigration and Nationalization Service ("INS") an adverse decision by the District Director of the Philadelphia INS that denied his application for a certificate of citizenship.

61. The court will abstain from resolving the issue of defendant's citizenship by birth so that he can properly exhaust his administrative remedies.

(d) Defendant's Naturalization Certificate

62. The government previously prevailed on counts I and II of its complaint because the defendant's citizenship was illegally procured by his failure to comply with the statutory requirements for naturalization. See, *United States v. Breyer*, 829 F. Supp. 773 (E.D.Pa. 1993).

63. The defendant's certificate of naturalization must be revoked since his citizenship by that means was illegally procured. 8 U.S.C. §1451(a).

64. Assuming, arguendo, that defendant is ultimately declared a citizen by birth, his certificate of naturalization is an extraneous document and the revocation of this document will have no effect on his standing as a United States citizen.

An appropriate order follows.

ORDER

AND NOW, this 20th day of December, 1993, based on the foregoing findings of fact and conclusions of law, IT IS HEREBY ORDERED that:

1. Defendant procured his Certificate of Naturalization illegally.

2. The November 7, 1957 order of the United States District Court for the Eastern District of Pennsylvania admitting defendant to United States citizenship IS REVOKED AND SET ASIDE.

3. Defendant's Certificate of Naturalization No. 7992538 IS HEREBY CANCELED and defendant shall surrender Certificate of Naturalization to the United States Attorney for the Eastern District of Pennsylvania within sixty (60) days of the date of this order.

4. This order shall not prejudice the defendant's right to pursue his claim of citizenship by birth through the appropriate administrative channels.

ROGERS v. BELLEI

401 U.S. 815 (1971)

Under constitutional challenge here, primarily on Fifth Amendment due process grounds, but also on Fourteenth Amendment grounds, is §301 (b) of the Immigration and Nationality Act of June 27, 1952, 66 Stat. 236, 8 U. S. C. §1401 (b).

Section 301 (a) of the Act, 8 U. S. C. §1401 (a), defines those persons who "shall be nationals and citizens of the United States at birth." Paragraph (7) of §301 (a) includes in that definition a person born abroad "of parents one of whom is an alien, and the other a citizen of the United States" who has met specified conditions of residence in this country. Section 301 (b), however, provides that one who is a citizen at birth under §301 (a)(7) shall lose his citizenship unless, after age 14 and before age 28, he shall come to the United States and be physically present here continuously for at least five years. We quote the statute in the margin.

The plan thus adopted by Congress with respect to a person of this classification was to bestow citizenship at birth but to take it away upon the person's failure to comply with a post-age-14 and pre-age-28 residential requirement. It is this deprival of citizenship, once bestowed, that is under attack here.

I

The facts are stipulated:

1. The appellee, Aldo Mario Bellei (hereinafter the plaintiff), was born in Italy on December 22, 1939. He is now 31 years of age.

2. The plaintiff's father has always been a citizen of Italy and never has acquired United States citizenship. The plaintiff's mother, however, was born in Philadelphia in 1915 and thus was a native-born United States citizen. She has retained that citizenship. Moreover, she has fulfilled the requirement of §301 (a)(7) for physical presence in the United States for 10 years, more than five of which were after she attained the age of 14 years. The mother and father were married in Philadelphia on the mother's 24th birthday, March 14, 1939. Nine days later, on March 23, the newlyweds departed for Italy. They have resided there ever since.

3. By Italian law the plaintiff acquired Italian citizenship upon his birth in Italy. He retains that citizenship. He also acquired United States citizenship at his birth under Rev. Stat. §1993, as amended by the Act of May 24, 1934, §1, 48 Stat. 797, then in effect. That version of the statute, as does the present one, contained a residence condition applicable to a child born abroad with one alien parent.

4. The plaintiff resided in Italy from the time of his birth until recently. He currently resides in England, where he is employed as an electronics engineer with an organization engaged in the NATO defense program.

5. The plaintiff has come to the United States five different times. He was physically present here during the following periods:

April 27 to July 31, 1948

July 10 to October 5, 1951

June to October 1955

December 18, 1962 to February 13, 1963

May 26 to June 13, 1965.

On the first two occasions, when the plaintiff was a boy of eight and 11, he entered the country with his mother on her United States passport. On the next two occasions, when he was 15 and just under 23, he entered on his own United States passport and was admitted as a citizen of this country. His passport was first issued on June 27, 1952. His last application approval, in August 1961, contains the notation "Warned abt. 301 (b)." The plaintiff's United States passport was periodically approved to and including December 22, 1962, his 23d birthday.

6. On his fifth visit to the United States, in 1965, the plaintiff entered with an Italian passport and as an alien visitor. He had just been married and he came with his bride to visit his maternal grandparents.

7. The plaintiff was warned in writing by United States authorities of the impact of §301 (b) when he was in this country in January 1963 and again in November of that year when he was in Italy. Sometime after February 11, 1964, he was orally advised by the American Embassy at Rome that he had lost his United States citizenship pursuant to §301 (b). In November 1966 he was so notified in writing by the American Consul in Rome when the plaintiff requested another American passport.

8. On March 28, 1960, plaintiff registered under the United States Selective Service laws with the American Consul in Rome. At that time he already was 20 years of age. He took in Italy, and passed, a United States Army physical examination. On December 11, 1963, he was asked to report for induction in the District of Columbia. This induction, however, was then deferred because of his NATO defense program employment. At the time of deferment he was warned of the danger of losing his United States citizenship if he did not comply with the residence requirement. After February 14, 1964, Selective Service advised him by letter that, due to the loss of his citizenship, he had no further obligation for United States military service.

Plaintiff thus concededly failed to comply with the conditions imposed by §301 (b) of the Act....

III

The two cases primarily relied upon by the three-judge District Court are, of course, of particular significance here.

Schneider v. Rusk, 377 U.S. 163 (1964). Mrs. Schneider, a German national by birth, acquired United States citizenship derivatively through her mother's naturalization in the United States. She came to this country as a small child with her parents and remained here until she finished college. She then went abroad for graduate work, was engaged to a German national, married in Germany, and stayed in residence there. She declared that she had no intention of returning to the United States. In 1959, a passport was denied by the State Department on the ground that she had lost her United States citizenship under the specific provisions of §352 (a)(1) of the Immigration and Nationality Act, 8 U. S. C. §1484 (a)(1), by continuous residence for three years in a foreign state of which she was formerly a national. The Court, by a five-to-three vote, held the statute violative of Fifth Amendment due process because there was no like restriction against foreign residence by native-born citizens.

... The dissent (Mr. Justice Clark, joined by JUSTICES HARLAN and WHITE) based its position on what it regarded as the long acceptance of expatriating naturalized citizens who voluntarily return to residence in their native lands; possible international complications; past decisions approving the power of Congress to enact statutes of that type; and the Constitution's distinctions between native-born and naturalized citizens.

Afroyim v. Rusk, 387 U.S. 253 (1967). Mr. Afroyim, a Polish national by birth, immigrated to the United States at age 19 and after 14 years here acquired United States citizenship by naturalization. Twenty-four years later he went to Israel and voted in a political election there.

In 1960 a passport was denied him by the State Department on the ground that he had lost his United States citizenship under the specific provisions of §349 (a)(5) of the Act, 8 U. S. C. §1481 (a)(5), by his foreign voting. The Court, by a five-to-four vote, held that the Fourteenth Amendment's definition of citizenship was significant; that Congress has no "general power, express or implied, to take away an American citizen's citizenship without his assent," 387 U.S., at 257; that Congress' power is to provide a uniform rule of naturalization and, when once exercised with respect to the individual, is exhausted, citing Mr. Chief Justice Marshall's well-known but not uncontroversial dictum in *Osborn v. Bank of the United States*, 9 Wheat. 738, 827 (1824); and that the "undeniable purpose" of the Fourteenth Amendment was to make the recently conferred "citizenship of Negroes permanent and secure" and "to put citizenship beyond the power of any governmental unit to destroy," 387 U.S., at 263. *Perez v. Brownell,* 356 U.S. 44 (1958), a five-to-four holding within the decade and precisely to the opposite effect, was overruled.

The dissent (MR. JUSTICE HARLAN, joined by JUSTICES Clark, STEWART, and WHITE) took issue with the Court's claim of support in the legislative history, would elucidate the Marshall dictum, and observed that the adoption of the Fourteenth Amendment did not deprive Congress of the power to expatriate on permissible grounds consistent with "other relevant commands" of the Constitution. 387 U.S., at 292.

It is to be observed that both Mrs. Schneider and Mr. Afroyim had resided in this country for years. Each had acquired United States citizenship here by the naturalization process (in one case derivative and in the other direct) prescribed by the National Legislature. Each, in short, was covered explicitly by the Fourteenth Amendment's very first sentence: "All persons born or naturalized in the United States and subject to the jurisdiction thereof, are citizens of the United States and of the State wherein they reside." This, of course, accounts for the Court's emphasis in Afroyim upon "Fourteenth Amendment citizenship." 387 U.S., at 262.

IV

. . .

The statutory pattern developed and expanded from (a) one, established in 1790 and enduring through the Revised Statutes and until 1934, where citizenship was specifically denied to the child born abroad of a father who never resided in the United States; to (b), in 1907, a governmental protection condition for the child born of an American citizen father and residing abroad, dependent upon a declaration of intent and the oath of allegiance at majority; to (c), in 1934, a condition, for the child born abroad of one United States citizen parent and one alien parent, of five years' continuous residence in the United States before age 18 and the oath of allegiance within six months after majority; to (d), in 1940, a condition, for that child, of five years' residence here, not necessarily continuous, between ages 13 and 21; to (e), in 1952, a condition, for that child, of five years' continuous residence here, with allowance, between ages 14 and 28.

The application of these respective statutes to a person in plaintiff Bellei's position produces the following results:

1. Not until 1934 would that person have had any conceivable claim to United States citizenship. For more than a century and a half no statute was of assistance. Maternal citizenship afforded no benefit. One may observe, too, that if Mr. Bellei had been born in 1933, instead of in 1939, he would have no claim even today. *Montana v. Kennedy*, supra.

2. Despite the recognition of the maternal root by the 1934 amendment, in effect at the time of plaintiff's birth, and despite the continuing liberalization of the succeeding statutes, the plaintiff still would not be entitled to full citizenship because, although his mother met the condition for her residence in the United States, the plaintiff never did fulfill the residential condition imposed for him by any of the statutes.

3. This is so even though the liberalizing 1940 and 1952 statutes, enacted after the plaintiff's birth, were applicable by their terms to one born abroad subsequent to May 24, 1934, the date of the 1934 Act, and were available to the plaintiff.

Thus, in summary, it may be said fairly that, for the most part, each successive statute, as applied to a foreign-born child of one United States citizen parent, moved in a direction of leniency for the child. For plaintiff Bellei the statute changed from complete disqualification to citizenship upon a condition subsequent, with that condition being expanded and made less onerous, and, after his birth, with the succeeding liberalizing provisions made applicable to him in replacement of the stricter statute in effect when he was born. The plaintiff nevertheless failed to satisfy any form of the condition.

. . .

VI

This takes us, then, to the issue of the constitutionality of the exercise of that congressional power when it is used to impose the condition subsequent that confronted plaintiff Bellei. We conclude that its imposition is not unreasonable, arbitrary, or unlawful, and that it withstands the present constitutional challenge.

1. The Congress has an appropriate concern with problems attendant on dual nationality. *Savorgnan v. United States*, 338 U.S. 491, 500 (1950); N. Bar-Yaacov, Dual Nationality xi and 4 (1961). These problems are particularly acute when it is the father who is the child's alien parent and the father chooses to have his family reside in the country of his own nationality. The child is reared, at best, in an atmosphere of divided loyalty. We cannot say that a concern that the child's own primary allegiance is to the country of his birth and of his father's allegiance is either misplaced or arbitrary.

The duality also creates problems for the governments involved. MR. JUSTICE BRENNAN recognized this when, concurring in *Kennedy v. Mendoza-Martinez*, 372 U.S. 144, 187 (1963), a case concerning native-born citizens, he observed: "We have recognized the entanglements which may stem from dual allegiance . . . ." In a famous case MR. JUSTICE DOUGLAS wrote of the problem of dual citizenship. *Kawakita v. United States*, 343 U.S. 717, 723-736 (1952). He noted that "one who has a dual nationality will be subject to claims from both nations, claims which at times may be competing or conflicting," id., at 733; that one with dual nationality cannot turn that status "into a fair-weather citizenship," id., at 736; and that "circumstances may compel one who has a dual nationality to do acts which otherwise would not be compatible with the obligations of American citizenship," ibid. The District Court in this very case conceded:

"It is a legitimate concern of Congress that those who bear American citizenship and receive its benefits have some nexus to the United States." 296 F.Supp., at 1252.

2. There are at least intimations in the decided cases that a dual national constitutionally may be required to make an election. In *Perkins v. Elg*, 307 U.S. 325, 329 (1939), the Court observed that a native-born citizen who had acquired dual nationality during minority through his parents' foreign naturalization abroad did not lose his United States citizenship "provided

that on attaining majority he elects to retain that citizenship and to return to the United States to assume its duties." In *Kawakita v. United States*, 343 U.S., at 734, the Court noted that a dual national "under certain circumstances" can be deprived of his American citizenship through an Act of Congress. In *Mandoli v. Acheson*, 344 U.S. 133, 138 (1952), the Court took pains to observe that there was no statute in existence imposing an election upon that dual nationality litigant.

These cases do not flatly say that a duty to elect may be constitutionally imposed. They surely indicate, however, that this is possible, and in Mandoli the holding was based on the very absence of a statute and not on any theory of unconstitutionality. And all three of these cases concerned persons who were born here, that is, persons who possessed Fourteenth Amendment citizenship; they did not concern a person, such as plaintiff Bellei, whose claim to citizenship is wholly, and only, statutory.

3. The statutory development outlined in Part IV above, by itself and without reference to the underlying legislative history, committee reports, and other studies, reveals a careful consideration by the Congress of the problems attendant upon dual nationality of a person born abroad. This was purposeful and not accidental. It was legislation structured with care and in the light of then apparent problems.

4. The solution to the dual nationality dilemma provided by the Congress by way of required residence surely is not unreasonable. It may not be the best that could be devised, but here, too, we cannot say that it is irrational or arbitrary or unfair. Congress first has imposed a condition precedent in that the citizen parent must have been in the United States or its possessions not less than 10 years, at least five of which are after attaining age 14. It then has imposed, as to the foreign-born child himself, the condition subsequent as to residence here. The Court already had emphasized the importance of residence in this country as the talisman of dedicated attachment, *Weedin v. Chin Bow*, 274 U.S., at 666-667, and said: "It is not too much to say, therefore, that Congress at that time [when Rev. Stat. §1993 was under consideration] attached more importance to actual residence in the United States as indicating a basis for citizenship than it did to descent from those who had been born citizens of the colonies or of the states before the Constitution. As said by Mr. Fish, when Secretary of State, to Minister Washburn, June 28, 1873, in speaking of this very proviso, the heritable blood of citizenship was thus associated unmistakably with residence within the country which was thus recognized as essential to full citizenship. Foreign Relations of the United States, Pt. 1, 1873, p. 259." 274 U.S., at 665-666.

The same policy is reflected in the required period of residence here for aliens seeking naturalization. 8 U. S. C. §1427 (a).

5. We feel that it does not make good constitutional sense, or comport with logic, to say, on the one hand, that Congress may impose a condition precedent, with no constitutional complication, and yet be powerless to impose precisely the same condition subsequent. Any such distinction, of course, must rest, if it has any basis at all, on the asserted "premise that the rights of citizenship of the native born and of the naturalized person are of the same dignity and are coextensive," *Schneider [*835] v. Rusk*, 377 U.S., at 165, and on the announcement that Congress has no "power, express or implied, to take away an American citizen's citizenship without his assent," *Afroyim v. Rusk*, 387 U.S., at 257. But, as pointed out above, these were utterances bottomed upon Fourteenth Amendment citizenship and that Amendment's direct reference to "persons born or naturalized in the United States." We do not accept the notion that those utterances are now to be judicially extended to citizenship not based upon the Fourteenth Amendment and to make citizenship an absolute. That it is not an absolute is demonstrated by the fact that even Fourteenth Amendment citizenship by

naturalization, when unlawfully procured, may be set aside. *Afroyim v. Rusk*, 387 U.S., at 267.

6. A contrary holding would convert what is congressional generosity into something unanticipated and obviously undesired by the Congress. Our National Legislature indulged the foreign-born child with presumptive citizenship, subject to subsequent satisfaction of a reasonable residence requirement, rather than to deny him citizenship outright, as concededly it had the power to do, and relegate the child, if he desired American citizenship, to the more arduous requirements of the usual naturalization process. The plaintiff here would force the Congress to choose between unconditional conferment of United States citizenship at birth and deferment of citizenship until a condition precedent is fulfilled. We are not convinced that the Constitution requires so rigid a choice. If it does, the congressional response seems obvious.

7. Neither are we persuaded that a condition subsequent in this area impresses one with "second-class citizenship." That cliché is too handy and too easy, and, like most clichés, can be misleading. That the condition subsequent may be beneficial is apparent in the light of the conceded fact that citizenship to this plaintiff was fully deniable. The proper emphasis is on what the statute permits him to gain from the possible starting point of noncitizenship, not on what he claims to lose from the possible starting point of full citizenship to which he has no constitutional right in the first place. His citizenship, while it lasts, although conditional, is not "second-class."

8. The plaintiff is not stateless. His Italian citizenship remains. He has lived practically all his life in Italy. He has never lived in this country; although he has visited here five times, the stipulated facts contain no indication that he ever will live here. He asserts no claim of ignorance or of mistake or even of hardship. He was warned several times of the provision of the statute and of his need to take up residence in the United States prior to his 23d birthday.

We hold that §301 (b) has no constitutional infirmity in its application to plaintiff Bellei. The judgment of the District Court is reversed.

EXERCISES

1. A very wealthy woman lives overseas and has been advised to renounce her U.S. citizenship in order to save on income and estate taxes. Several years after expatriation, the country where the woman resides undergoes a revolution and she wishes to return to the Untied States as a citizen. How would you argue on her behalf? How would you argue against her reentry as a U.S. citizen?
2. A man from Saudi Arabia wants to emigrate to the Untied States with his three wives. He and his wives are devout Moslems. The family is denied entry. Justify the government's decision.
3. What factors would you look at to determine the voluntariness of a U.S. citizen's act of expatriation?
4. Go to the library and find three judicial decisions that discuss which factors constitute "illegal procurement of naturalization."
5. What is your opinion of the residency requirement for the U.S. citizen parent of a person born outside the United States? Is this fair to the child whose citizenship is in question? Is it constitutional to penalize a child for the acts of the parent? How can the INA position be justified?

Chapter Three

IMMIGRANT CATEGORIES

CHAPTER PREVIEW

Once it has been determined that a person is an **alien**, a citizen of a country other than the United States, and the alien has decided to enter the country, the alien may be eligible to enter either as an immigrant or as a nonimmigrant. An **immigrant** is an alien who wishes to become a permanent resident in the United States. A **nonimmigrant** is an alien who wishes to enter the United States for a limited period of time. This chapter will discuss the methods available for an alien to be able to enter the United States as an immigrant. Chapter Four covers the nonimmigrant classifications.

Aliens who wish to become immigrants to the United States fall into two categories:

1. aliens subject to numerical limitation (quotas); and
2. aliens who are not subject to numerical limitations.

These categories are delineated in the Immigration Act of 1990, which amended the INA. The United States still maintains an annual quota for immigrants who do not fall into special categories, limiting worldwide entry to 675,000 persons each year. There is no numerical limitation to entry for those aliens who fall into the special category of being an immediate relative of a U.S. citizen. This chapter will focus on the requirements to qualify as an immigrant; subsequent chapters will discuss the procedures to obtaining visas. (A **visa** is an official document issued by the government authorizing entry into the United States for aliens.)

NUMERICAL LIMITATIONS

The United States limits immigration of all persons who are not immediate family members of U.S. citizens to a maximum of 675,000 each year. Within this overall quota limit, this general category is further subdivided into three preference categories: an order of priority to obtain one of the 675,000 annual visas. The three preference categories are

1. family-sponsored aliens
2. aliens who meet certain employment-related criteria
3. diversity aliens.

Family-Sponsored Aliens (INA §203)

Of the 675,000 visas subject to numerical limitations, 226,000 are allocated to this category. Additionally, any unused visas from the employment-related category can be added to this group.

The category of family-sponsored visas subject to numerical limitation is available for the nonimmediate relatives of U.S. citizens and permanent resident aliens. Within this preference category, the class is further subdivided into four groups, with a specific number of visas allotted to each such subdivision. The categories are:

a) Unmarried sons and daughters of U.S. citizens. The term "sons and daughters" is used to distinguish these people as adults rather than children. The children of U.S. citizens may enter the United States without reference to numerical limitations. A total of 23,400 visas are allotted to this group, plus any unused visas from the other family-sponsored categories. This category does not include children younger than 21 years of age.

Example: A former Ethiopian who emigrated to the United States and has become a naturalized U.S. citizen wants to bring over his unmarried 24-year-old son. The son would qualify for entry under the first preference category for family-sponsored visas.

b) Spouses, minor and unmarried children of lawful permanent residents. A **lawful permanent resident** is an alien who has entered the country with an immigrant visa. 114,200 visas are allotted to this category, with a further subdivision of 77% of this total being apportioned to spouses and minor children.

Example: In the previous example, prior to the Ethiopian's becoming a naturalized U.S. citizen, he was living in the country as a permanent resident. While here under that classification, his wife was able to join him by obtaining a visa under this family-sponsored category.

c) Married sons and daughters of U.S. citizens. 23,400 visas, plus unused visas from the first and second categories, are allotted to this group.

Example: The naturalized U.S. citizen from the previous examples wants to bring his married daughter to the United States. The married daughter would fall into this third preference category of family-sponsored visas.

d) Siblings of U.S. citizens (provided that the U.S. citizen is at least 21 years old). The remaining visas, plus any unused visas from the first two categories, are allotted to this group.

Example: While in the United States on business, an Asian couple gives birth to a child who becomes a U.S. citizen by birth. Fifteen years later this child comes to the United States to go to school, and his siblings try to get a visa to enter the country as immigrants. The application for these siblings would be denied because the citizen sibling is younger than 21.

Employment-Related Visas

(INA §101(a)) This category of immigrant preference is allotted 140,000 visas, plus any unused visas from the family-sponsored category. This preference encourages persons with special and needed job skills to immigrate to the United States. This category is subdivided into five preferences:

a) Priority workers. A **priority worker** is defined as any of the following:
   - a person of "extraordinary ability" in science, arts, business, athletics, or entertainment
   - outstanding professors and researchers
   - executives and managers of multinational organizations.

Example: After the breakup of the Soviet Union, an Olympic figure skater decided to emigrate to the United States. Because the figure skater had "extraordinary ability," the skater would be permitted to enter under the employment-related category for priority workers.

b) Professionals who have advanced degrees and persons of exceptional abilities in the arts, sciences or business. 40,000 visas are allocated to this category, plus any unused priority worker visas. Persons who obtain visas under this category must prove that they have a job offer in the United States, unless such requirement has been waived by the attorney general.

Example: An Australian anthropologist has been offered a teaching position at UCLA. This person could enter under the second preference category for employment-related visas.

c) Skilled and other workers in short supply, and professionals who only hold bachelor's degrees. 40,000 visas are available for persons who qualify under this category, plus any unused visas from the first two employment-related categories. There must be a determination by the Department of Labor that there is indeed a short supply of workers in the area, and no more than 10,000 of these visas are permitted to be given to "other," or unskilled, workers.

Example: A skilled stonemason from Italy wants to emigrate to the United States. It has been determined that there is a shortage of skilled stonemasons in the United States, and consequently the mason may be entitled to a visa under this third employment-related preference category.

d) Special immigrants. A **special immigrant** is defined to be a religious worker or the former employee of a U.S. government or international organization. This category, which is limited to 10,000 visas, includes such persons as resident aliens returning from abroad, former U.S. citizens, ministers and religious workers, and employees of U.S. government agencies overseas who have worked for the agency for a minimum of 15 years.

Example: An Indian woman has worked as a secretary in the U.S. embassy in New Delhi for 20 years. She now wants to emigrate to the United States. She qualifies for entry as a special immigrant.

Also included in this category are persons considered to be **commuter aliens**, citizens of Canada or Mexico who enter and leave the United States daily in order to work in the country. These persons are given **green cards**, U.S. government authorization to work in the United States.

Example: A Canadian lives in Windsor, Ontario, and travels to Detroit each weekday to work in an automobile factory. This Canadian is a commuter alien.

e) Employment creator. As discussed in the first chapter, this category consists of aliens who will invest a minimum of $1 million ($500,000 in areas of high unemployment) and guarantee to employ at least ten U.S. citizens. In this category the alien is only given a provisional visa for two years in order to avoid fraud, after which time the alien's application will be reviewed to make sure that the alien has in fact invested the funds. This group is allotted 10,000 visas.

Example: A wealthy Egyptian citizen wants to emigrate to the United States. The Egyptian plans to invest $2 million in a factory in Rhode Island to manufacture costume jewelry, and plans to employ 20 people. The Egyptian may qualify as an employment creator and may be given a provisional two-year visa.

Diversity Visas

This category of visa, which began in 1995, is designed to attract aliens whose country of origin was a "low admission" country within the previous five years. Low admission refers to the percentage of available visas that were used by citizens of that country. The purpose behind this program is to create diversity in immigration and to avoid favoring certain nations. 55,000 visas are allotted to this preference category. Additionally, special visas are available for residents of Hong Kong who may wish to emigrate to the United States, depending upon how conditions are affected by the takeover of the colony by the People's Republic of China. This special provision extends until January 1, 2002.

There are no subsets in this preference group, and the visas are issued on a lottery basis. An alien may only submit one application per year, and must have attained a high school education or its equivalent, or have at least two years of work experience.

Example: An alien who does not qualify under any other preference applies for a diversity visa. Because diversity visas are issued by lottery, the alien fails to obtain a visa. The alien may submit a new application the following year. This method of entry to the United States is very haphazard.

VISAS NOT SUBJECT TO NUMERICAL LIMITATIONS

This category of immigrant is limited to the spouse, child or parent of a U.S. citizen, and is not subject to any yearly numerical limitations. (INA §201(b)) Note that this category only addresses the immediate family of U.S. citizens; for nonimmediate family members or relations of permanent residents, the numerical limitations apply.

Spouse

In order to qualify to enter the United States as the spouse of a U.S. citizen, the person seeking entry must prove that the marriage is valid and subsisting. The marital status must be proved by clear and convincing evidence, and the marriage may not have been consecrated by proxy unless the marriage has been subsequently consummated. Also, marriages that violate U.S. public policy, such as incestuous or polygamous relationships, will fail to qualify the alien as a legitimate spouse.

The purpose for having these requirements is to ensure that the marriage is not a sham relationship entered into solely or exclusively to gain entry into the United States. As a consequence, a two-year provisional residency is imposed on the alien before permanent resident status will be granted. This period is used to prove the legitimacy of the marriage. However, the couple may separate, if legal grounds exist, without jeopardizing the alien's status, provided that the marriage was not entered into fraudulently.

Example: While studying at a university overseas, an American student falls in love with and marries a citizen of the foreign country. The alien spouse may be entitled to enter the United States for a provisional period of two years, after which the marital relationship will be reviewed by the INS, and a permanent resident status may be awarded to the spouse.

Example: While studying at a foreign university, an American student is approached by a citizen of the foreign country and offered $10,000 if the American will marry the alien so that the alien may enter the United States. The American agrees and the ceremony takes place, but the marriage is never consummated and they do not live together. This "spouse" will not be permitted entry to the U.S. because the marriage is a sham.

Example: While studying at a university overseas, an American student falls in love with and marries a citizen of the foreign country. The couple returns to the United States and the spouse is granted provisional entry as the spouse of an American citizen. Once in the U.S., the citizen spouse begins abusing the immigrant spouse, both physically and mentally, and the immigrant spouse leaves the citizen. This separation will not adversely affect the immigrant's status, because the marriage was legitimately entered into, and legal grounds exist for the separation.

If an alien marries a U.S. citizen during removal proceedings (see Chapters Six and Seven), the marriage will not halt the proceedings and, if the alien is removed, he or she may not apply for entry as the spouse of a U.S. citizen for a minimum of two years.

Child

Several different categories of persons may be described as the "child" of a U.S. citizen. First of all, the child must be unmarried and under the age of 21 in order to qualify for a visa. The child must be the legitimate child of the U.S. citizen, either legitimate at birth or legally legitimized before the child attains the age of 18. Legitimization may occur by the marriage of the parents or a legally sufficient act of legitimization pursuant to appropriate law. If the child is illegitimate, parentage must be proved or acknowledged.

Example: An alien emigrates to the United States after the death of his wife, leaving his two infant children in the care of his parents. The immigrant eventually becomes a naturalized U.S. citizen. His children may now enter the United States as the legitimate children of a citizen.

Example: While serving with the U.S. Armed Forces during the Gulf War, an American fathers a child by a Kuwaiti woman. When the soldier discovers that he is a father, he acknowledges the child as his pursuant to the laws of the military, of the soldier's state, and of Kuwait. This child may now enter the U.S. as the acknowledged child of a U.S. citizen.

A stepchild may enter the U.S. as the "child" of a U.S. citizen, provided that the child was younger than 18 when he or she became the stepchild.

Example: An American citizen marries a Brazilian widow who has two children, eight and ten years old. These children would qualify as the stepchildren of a U.S. citizen.

If the child was adopted, the adoption must have occurred before the child attained the age of 16, and the adopted child must have resided with the adoptive U.S. parent for at least two years.

> **Example:** A U.S. citizen is working overseas when she marries an alien widower who has an eight-year-old child whom she adopts. When the citizen and the spouse return to the United States three years later, the adopted child may be granted a visa as the child of a U.S. citizen.

Many Americans who are unable to adopt children domestically seek to adopt children overseas. These children may be admitted to the United States, provided that the child so adopted is either orphaned, abandoned by the parents, or it can be demonstrated that the natural parents are unable to support the child and have relinquished parental rights. The adopted alien child must be adopted by a U.S. citizen and the citizen's spouse jointly, or, if adopted by an unmarried U.S. citizen, the citizen must be at least 25 years old.

> **Example:** A lesbian wants to adopt a child but is precluded from adopting a child under her state's law. She travels to Russia where she adopts an orphaned baby. The woman is 30 years old. This child would be able to enter the country as the child of a U.S. citizen.

Parent

Any person who is considered a parent under the definition of "child" discussed above may be allowed a visa as the immediate relative of a U.S. citizen, provided that the child is younger than 21 years of age and the child is a U.S. citizen. The natural parents of a child who is a U.S. citizen because the child was adopted by a U.S. citizen after determining that the child qualified as an orphan are precluded from entry. Also, it is questionable whether an alien may enter the United States, legally or illegally, give birth inside the country to a child who would automatically be a U.S. citizen by birth, and then claim entry as the parent of a U.S. citizen.

> **Example:** A Korean child was abandoned by his parents and was placed in an orphanage in Seoul. An American couple adopts the child. The natural mother cannot now seek entry as the parent of a U.S. citizen; her abandonment of her infant terminates her relationship to the child.

ETHICAL CONSIDERATIONS

Many ethical considerations may be encountered when dealing with immigrants. Because so many people want to become permanent residents of the United States, both aliens and any Americans who help the aliens enter may be involved in unethical practices in order to obtain an immigrant visa.

Marriage fraud is probably the most common ethical problem associated with immigration, which is why Congress found it necessary to enact the Immigration Marriage Fraud Act to attempt to eliminate the situation. Aliens and Americans who enter into sham marriages so that the alien can gain entry to the United States are committing fraud.

People may also lie with respect to their family relationships, educational backgrounds, and work experience in order to obtain a visa to the United States. The fact that limitations are imposed on the number of persons who may enter the country as immigrants provides a backdrop for people to falsify information on visa applications just so they can become permanent residents.

Also, for a country whose history is based on free immigration, it may be considered an ethical or moral dilemma to decide to limit immigration.

CHAPTER REVIEW

All persons who wish to come to the United States to live on a permanent basis are called immigrants, and the ability of such persons to enter the country is limited. The United States has established two categories for immigrants. The first category, the modern adaptation of the quota system, imposes a ceiling of 675,000 immigrant visas annually for all persons who are not the immediate relatives of U.S. citizens. Within this category of persons subject to numerical limitations for entry, the INA, as amended in 1990, established three broad preference classifications: family-sponsored immigrants of U.S. citizens and permanent residents; employment-related immigrants; and diversity immigrants. A specific number of visas are allotted to each classification, and the classifications (except for diversity immigrants) create priorities that create a system of preferences within the preferences.

The second category of immigrant, those who qualify as the spouse, child or parent of a U.S. citizen, are permitted to enter the United States without any numerical limitation. However, these persons must be able to document the existence of a family.

CHAPTER VOCABULARY

Alien — Any person who owes allegiance to a country other than the United States.

Commuter alien — Citizen of Canada or Mexico who enters and leaves the United States every day to work.

Diversity immigrant — Immigrant classification for persons whose country of origin has had few immigrants in the past few years.

Green card — Document authorizing an alien to work in the U.S.

Immigrant — Citizen of one country who wishes to relocate to another country for an indefinite period of time.

Lawful permanent resident — An alien who has entered the U.S. with an immigrant visa.

Nonimmigrant — Citizen of one country who wishes to enter another country for a limited period of time.

Numerical limitations — Ceiling on the number of visas that can be issued to the persons who are not the immediate family members of U.S. citizens.

Priority worker — Classification of immigrant in the employment-related category who has extraordinary skills and abilities.

Special immigrant — A religious worker or the former employee of a U.S. government or international organization.

Visa — Government document permitting an alien to enter the country.

EDITED JUDICIAL DECISIONS

Azizi v. Thornburgh addresses the question of imposing a two-year residency requirement on spouses of U.S. citizens before being granted immigrant status, and *Hall v. McLaughlin* discusses the requirements to obtain an employment-related visa.

AZIZI v. THORNBURGH

908 F.2d 1130 (2d Cir. 1990)

Plaintiff-appellant Saboet Azizi ("Mrs. Azizi"), a naturalized citizen of the United States, and her husband, plaintiff-appellant Feim Azizi ("Mr. Azizi"), a citizen of Yugoslavia, appeal from a summary judgment entered in the United States District Court for the District of Connecticut (Nevas, J.) on August 4, 1989 rejecting their constitutional challenges to section 5 of the Immigration Marriage Fraud Amendments of 1986 ("IMFA"), 8 U.S.C. §§1154(h), 1255(e) (1988). On appeal, the Azizis maintain that the two-year foreign residency requirement imposed by section 5 on an alien spouse who marries a United States citizen during the pendency of a deportation or exclusion proceeding violates their rights to equal protection and due process. While we are cognizant of the hardships imposed by this legislation upon aliens and their spouses who enter into legitimate marriages during deportation proceedings, we conclude that section 5 is a valid exercise of Congress' plenary power to regulate immigration and naturalization.

BACKGROUND

Mr. Azizi, a citizen of Yugoslavia, illegally entered the United States on or about February 24, 1986. Thereafter, the Immigration and Naturalization Service ("INS") instituted a deportation proceeding against him by issuing an order to show cause and notice of hearing. On June 10, 1986, Mr. Azizi conceded that his entry was unlawful but applied for political asylum. Prior to a determination on his application for political asylum, Mr. Azizi married Saboet Elmazi, a Yugoslavian native and naturalized citizen of the United States. A hearing was held in January 1987, after which the Immigration Judge denied Mr. Azizi's application for asylum but granted him until July the privilege of departing voluntarily. According to the Azizis, the Immigration Judge advised Mrs. Azizi that her husband's departure could be prevented by filing a petition for "immediate relative" status in his behalf. See 8 U.S.C. §1151(b).

Immediately following the deportation hearing, Mrs. Azizi filed an immigrant visa petition seeking to have Mr. Azizi qualified as an immediate relative. Pursuant to section 5 of the IMFA, an alien who marries a United States citizen during the pendency of deportation proceedings must reside outside the United States for two years before a petition predicated on immediate relative status will be considered by the INS. Id. §§1154(h), 1255(e). In violation of section 5, the INS accepted the immigrant visa petition and approved it on June 23, 1987. Mr. Azizi did not file an appeal from the January deportation order, believing he was no longer subject to the order. He did not depart from the United States, and the period for voluntary departure expired.

Mr. Azizi was arrested in November 1987 for failure to comply with the deportation order. He moved immediately to reopen his case before the Immigration Judge, but the motion was denied. On December 9, 1987, the Azizis commenced this action in the district court for the purpose of obtaining relief from the deportation order. On the following day, the INS revoked its approval of Mr. Azizi's visa petition on the ground that it was granted in violation of section 5 of the IMFA. The Azizis amended their complaint to challenge the revocation on constitutional grounds. After pre-trial proceedings were concluded, plaintiffs moved for summary judgment, and defendant cross-moved for the same relief. The district court granted defendant's cross-motion for summary judgment, *Azizi v. Thornburgh*, 719 F. Supp. 86 (D.Conn. 1989), and this appeal ensued.

DISCUSSION

Every year, thousands of aliens seek immigrant visas to enter the United States. The Immigration and Nationality Act ("INA") imposes numerical quotas on the number of aliens permitted to immigrate to this country. 8 U.S.C. §1151(a). Immigrant visas are allocated in accordance with a preference system, which limits eligibility to categories prescribed by the (INA. Id. §1153(a)). However, aliens who fit within the "immediate relative" class are exempt from the numerical quotas. Id. §1151(a), (b). A spouse, child or parent of a United States citizen is considered an immediate relative and may qualify for permanent resident status. Id. §1151(b).

An alien who marries a United States citizen and obtains permanent resident status while no deportation proceeding is pending is permitted to remain in this country on a conditional basis for two years. Id. §1186a(a)(1), (b). If, at the end of the second anniversary of the marriage, the Attorney General determines that the marriage is bona fide, the conditional status is removed. Id. §1186a(c)(1). In contrast, pursuant to section 5 of the IMFA, an alien who marries a United States citizen during the pendency of a deportation proceeding must reside outside the United States for two years after the marriage. Id. §1154(h). Upon expiration of this two-year period, the alien spouse may seek permanent resident status. See id. §§1154(h), 1255(e).

I. Equal Protection

The Azizis contend that section 5 of the IMFA denies them their fourteenth amendment right to equal protection of the laws because it classifies citizens and aliens in a manner that violates the fundamental right to marry. They maintain that, because section 5 infringes on their right to marry, a strict scrutiny analysis must be employed in reviewing the statute. Specifically, the Azizis point to the fact that the two-year foreign residency requirement places an onerous burden on citizen/alien marriages without prior consideration of the validity of those marriages.

While we recognize the fundamental nature of the right to marry, we also must consider that "control over matters of immigration is a sovereign prerogative, largely within the control of the executive and the legislature." *Landon v. Plasencia*, 459 U.S. 21, 34, 74 L. Ed. 2d 21, 103 S. Ct. 321 (1982). Perhaps in no area is the legislative power "more complete." *Oceanic Steam Navigation Co. v. Stranahan*, 214 U.S. 320, 339, 53 L. Ed. 1013, 29 S. Ct. 671 (1909). Because of Congress' plenary authority, our review of legislation involving matters of immigration and naturalization is limited. *Fiallo v. Bell*, 430 U.S. 787, 792, 52 L. Ed. 2d 50, 97 S. Ct. 1473 (1977). Congressional authority in this area extends to the establishment of alien classifications as a basis for determining immigration eligibility. See id. at 794; *Kleindienst v. Mandel*, 408 U.S. 753, 766, 33 L. Ed. 2d 683, 92 S. Ct. 2576 (1972). Such classifications will be upheld against a constitutional challenge if a rational basis exists for their adoption. See *Guan Chow Tok v. INS*, 538 F.2d 36, 38-39 (2d Cir. 1976) (*per curiam*); accord *Anetekhai v. INS*, 876 F.2d 1218, 1224 (5th Cir. 1989).

Recognizing Congress' broad power to classify aliens for immigration purposes, the Azizis maintain that section 5 infringes upon the exercise of their fundamental right to marry. In Fiallo, the Supreme Court upheld the constitutionality of a section of the INA that excluded illegitimate children and their natural fathers from the preferential status granted the "child" or "parent" of a United States citizen. 430 U.S. at 799-800. The Court was not persuaded by the appellants' contention that a strict level of scrutiny must be adopted because the classification impinged on fundamental familial relationship rights of citizens and aliens. Id. at 794. In the same vein, we reject the Azizis' contention that a strict level of scrutiny must be adopted here because section 5 affects their right to marry.

The classes created by section 5 derive from the distinction between citizen/alien marriages that occur before and those that occur after commencement of a deportation or exclusion proceeding. While great deference must be accorded Congress' decision to classify aliens in such a manner, the government must demonstrate some legitimate reason for adoption of the classification. *Francis v. INS*, 532 F.2d 268, 272-73 (2d Cir. 1976).

Section 5 is aimed at preventing an alien from circumventing a potential deportation or exclusion order by entering into a sham marriage after receiving notice of the commencement of a deportation or exclusion proceeding. H.R.Rep. No. 906, 99th Cong., 2d Sess. 6, reprinted in 1986 U.S.Code Cong. & Admin.News 5978, 5978. In enacting this legislation as a preventive measure, Congress recognized that "aliens who are engaged in deportation proceedings are more likely than other aliens to enter into fraudulent marriages in order to avoid being expelled from the country." *Almario v. Attorney General*, 872 F.2d 147, 152 (6th Cir. 1989) (quoting *Smith v. INS*, 684 F. Supp. 1113, 1117 (D.Mass. 1988)); Anetekhai, 876 F.2d at 1222; cf. Guan Chow Tok, 538 F.2d at 38-39. Having identified a potential for fraudulent marriages during the pendency of a deportation proceeding, Congress had a rational basis for prescribing a two-year foreign residency period as a prerequisite to permanent resident status. Accordingly, we find that section 5 of the IMFA does not run afoul of the equal protection clause of the fourteenth amendment.

II. Due Process

The Azizis advance several arguments in support of their contention that section 5 violates their due process rights. They assert that section 5 places an unconstitutional burden on their fundamental right to marry, without affording them the opportunity to substantiate the legitimacy of their marriage. As previously noted, section 5 is a legitimate preventive measure designed to deter fraudulent citizen/alien marriages during the pendency of deportation proceedings. Almario, 872 F.2d at 151-52. Obviously, any statute aimed at eradicating fraudulent marriages could not avoid affecting marital relationships. In light of our limited scope of review, we find the Azizis' contention unavailing.

Next, the Azizis contend that the absence of a hearing deprives Mrs. Azizi of her property interest in an approved visa for Mr. Azizi. It is not disputed that, when Congress grants property rights to illegal aliens, the fifth amendment protects against the deprivation of those rights without due process of law. See *Mathews v. Diaz*, 426 U.S. 67, 77, 48 L. Ed. 2d 478, 96 S. Ct. 1883 (1976); see also *Board of Regents v. Roth*, 408 U.S. 564, 569-70, 33 L. Ed. 2d 548, 92 S. Ct. 2701 (1972). However, the Azizis cannot succeed on their due process challenge, because they do not have an inherent property right in an immigrant visa, and section 5 does not grant them any such property interest. Through the enactment of section 5, Congress conferred immediate relative status only on the class of alien spouses who marry when no deportation or exclusion proceedings are pending. See Anetekhai, 876 F.2d at 1223; Almario, 872 F.2d at 151-52; see also *Cleveland Bd. of Educ. v. Loudermill*, 470 U.S. 532, 541, 84 L. Ed. 2d 494, 105 S. Ct. 1487 (1985); Diaz, 426 U.S. at 80, 83. The power to define the class of alien spouses who qualify for immediate relative status is within the plenary authority vested in Congress over matters of immigration and naturalization. Since the Azizis married after commencement of the deportation proceeding, they cannot demonstrate the right to an immigrant visa and therefore they do not have the requisite property interest necessary to prevail on their procedural due process challenge.

In addition, the Azizis contend that section 5 creates an irrebuttable presumption that all citizen/alien marriages entered into during the pendency of deportation proceedings are fraudulent and, if the marriage fails within the two-year foreign residency period, that the marriage is deemed to be *void ab initio* for immigration purposes. In rejecting this contention, we agree with the reasoning adopted by the other circuits that have addressed this challenge to section 5 and conclude that there is no irrebuttable presumption, because aliens who enter into marriages during the pendency of deportation proceedings "are not absolutely precluded from obtaining the 'immediate relative' status available to other aliens," but are only denied consideration of a petition for immediate relative status for two years. See *Escobar v. INS*, No. 89-5037, slip op. at 5-6 (D.C.Cir. Feb. 2, 1990), withdrawn pending reh'g en banc, No. 89-5037 (D.C.Cir. Apr. 25, 1990); Anetekhai, 876 F.2d at 1223; Almario, 872 F.2d at 152-53. The enactment of section 5 does not represent a congressional determination that all marriages entered into during deportation proceedings are fraudulent. Congress simply implemented a decision to remove any incentive for aliens facing deportation or expulsion to enter into a fraudulent marriage. See Escobar, No. 89-5037, slip op. at 5-6; Anetekhai, 876 F.2d at 1223; Almario, 872 F.2d at 152-53; cf. *Weinberger v. Salfi*, 422 U.S. 749, 777, 45 L. Ed. 2d 522, 95 S. Ct. 2457 (1975) (social security provision denying death benefits to widow or step-child based on duration of relationship upheld in face of challenge that it created irrebuttable presumption that marriage was fraudulent); *Michael H. v. Gerald D.*, 491 U.S. 110, 109 S. Ct. 2333, 2340-41, 105 L. Ed. 2d 91 (1989) (state law presumption that husband of child's mother is child's father does not violate putative father's due process rights).

The Azizis' final due process challenge is grounded on the contention that section 5 does not create a substantive classification but rather an unconstitutional procedure adopted to stem the influx of illegal aliens. By characterizing the IMFA as procedural rather than substantive, they urge us to scrutinize the statute under procedural due process standards. Further, the Azizis reject the position that the deferential Fiallo standard is applicable to the due process challenge, contending that the standard applies only to Congress' power to classify aliens and not to an alien's right to a fair procedure when attempting to prove immediate relative status.

A finding that section 5 is a procedural rather than a substantive legislative enactment would require us to determine "whether the procedures meet the essential standard of fairness under the Due Process Clause." Plasencia, 459 U.S. at 35. The Azizis' attempt to invoke the holding of Plasencia as support for their position is misplaced. In Plasencia, an exclusion hearing was mandated by statute. The Supreme Court's discussion focused on a permanent resident alien's due process challenge to the adequacy of the exclusion hearing. Id. at 32-37. Reliance on Plasencia is inapposite because section 5 does not grant a statutory entitlement to a hearing.

We are not persuaded by attempts to characterize the statute as procedural. Through the enactment of the IMFA, Congress attempted to achieve a reduction in the incidence of "marriage fraud." H.R.Rep. No. 99-906, 99th Cong., 2d Sess. 6, reprinted in 1986 Code Cong. & Admin.News at 5978. Congress determined that "although in theory participating in a fraudulent marriage makes an individual liable to both criminal and administrative sanctions, in practice it is very difficult to revoke or rescind an alien's status, deport him, or even locate him or his spouse." Id. Section 5 addresses this perceived abuse by creating two distinct classes of alien spouses, those who marry prior to and those who marry after the commencement of deportation proceedings.

According to the Azizis, a manifest problem with section 5 is that resourceful individuals may circumvent the two-year foreign residency period in a number of ways. While loopholes may exist in the statutory scheme, the statute is not irrational simply because it is an imperfect solution to the problems Congress intended to eradicate. See Salfi, 422 U.S. at 780.

Prior to the enactment of the IMFA, aliens qualifying for immediate relative status included all alien spouses. Motivated by the perceived need to deter marriage fraud, section 5 amended the INA to refine the qualifications of those claiming immediate relative status. The definition of "spouse" for purposes of immigration is now limited to those who have married prior to the commencement of a deportation hearing and precludes, for a period of two years, consideration of any alien who marries during the pendency of a proceeding.

8 U.S.C. §§1154(h), 1255(e). The position advanced by the Azizis is merely an invitation to expand the substantive categories created by the IMFA. We reject this entreaty. See Anetekhai, 876 F.2d at 1223; Escobar, No. 89-5037, slip op. at 1 (Wald, Ch.J., dissenting); see also Almario, 872 F.2d at 151-52. Contra Escobar, No. 89-5037, slip op. at 6. Accordingly, we hold that section 5 is an exercise of Congress' broad power to enact substantive legislation, classifying the groups of aliens who qualify for immediate relative status.

III. Estoppel

The Azizis contend that the government should be estopped from denying immediate relative status to Mr. Azizi, because the Immigration Judge allegedly told them that Mr. Azizi could apply for immediate relative status, and the INS approved the immigrant visa petition. The government avers that we lack jurisdiction to hear this claim because Mr. Azizi failed to exhaust available administrative remedies. We find it unnecessary to pass on the government's contention, because the Azizis's estoppel claim fails as a matter of law. "The government can be estopped where the traditional elements of estoppel and 'affirmative misconduct' are present." *Scime v. Bowen*, 822 F.2d 7, 9 n. 2 (2d Cir. 1987) (quoting *Corniel-Rodriguez v. INS*, 532 F.2d 301, 302 (2d Cir. 1976)); see *INS v. Miranda*, 459 U.S. 14, 19, 74 L. Ed. 2d 12, 103 S. Ct. 281 (1982) (per curiam). We agree with the district court that the Azizis have alleged only negligent conduct on the part of the INS. In the absence of affirmative misconduct, estoppel may not be invoked against the government.

CONCLUSION

The district court properly granted summary judgment dismissing appellants' equal protection and due process challenges. As well, it correctly concluded that the government may not be estopped in the absence of an allegation of affirmative misconduct. Accordingly, we affirm.

HALL v. MCLAUGHLIN
864 F.2d 868 (D.C. Cir. 1989)

Appellant Eric Hall, a Pakistani national, is a founder and corporate president of appellant Hall Enterprises, Inc. Hall Enterprises in 1982 applied to the Secretary of Labor (the "Secretary") for "labor certification," which entails a determination that the employment of an alien – in this case, the continued employment of Eric Hall as corporate president – would not displace qualified available domestic workers and would not adversely affect the market for domestic labor. Had the Secretary granted labor certification, Eric Hall would have become eligible for an immigrant visa, i.e., a visa authorizing permanent residence in the United States. Without labor certification, his continued presence in the United States is subject to successive extensions of the nonimmigrant visa he now holds.

The Secretary denied labor certification on the premise that Eric Hall and Hall Enterprises are effectively one and the same, so that no genuine employment relationship exists. The lack of a genuine employment relationship, the Secretary held, brings Eric Hall under a regulation prohibiting the grant of labor certification to any alien who works for himself. Appellants' challenge to the Secretary's decision was dismissed by the district court. Appellants seek reversal of the district court's order, claiming that the Secretary acted arbitrarily and capriciously in finding the absence of a genuine employment relationship. Because we find that the Secretary's application of her regulations was rational and consistent with prior labor certification decisions, we affirm the district court.

I. BACKGROUND

A. Statute and Regulations

Section 212 of the Immigration and Nationality Act, 8 U.S.C. §1182 (the "Act"), provides that several enumerated classes of aliens are to be denied visas and excluded from the United States. Among these are aliens seeking to enter the country for the purpose of performing skilled or unskilled labor, unless the Secretary grants labor certification to a particular alien based on criteria set out in the statute. Id. §212(a) (14), 8 U.S.C. §1182 (a) (14). Specifically, the Act provides that labor certification is not to be granted unless the Secretary certifies that —

(A) there are not sufficient workers who are able, willing, qualified (or equally qualified in the case of aliens who are members of the teaching profession or who have exceptional ability in the sciences or the arts), and available at the time of application for a visa and admission to the United States and at the place where the alien is to perform such skilled or unskilled labor, and (B) the employment of such aliens will not adversely affect the wages and working conditions of the workers in the United States similarly employed. Id. If labor certification is denied, the alien is subject to exclusion from the United States unless he can obtain a visa on some other grounds. Id. If labor certification is granted, the alien not only is removed from the class of excludable aliens but also becomes eligible for an immigrant visa. 8 U.S.C. §1153(a) (6). By law, a certain number of immigrant visas are allotted annually to each country of origin. 8 U.S.C. §1152(a). An alien to whom labor certification is granted becomes a "sixth-preference" alien, or, for a narrow category of professionals and exceptionally talented persons, a "third-preference" alien. 8 U.S.C. §1153(a) (3), (a) (6). The "sixth preference," which Eric Hall seeks, means five other categories of aliens are further ahead in line for the allocation of immigrant visas to aliens originating from a given country. 8 U.S.C. §1153(a). The Secretary has promulgated regulations to govern the labor certification process in general and specifically to implement the worker availability standard. 20 C.F.R. Part 656 (1988). Under the regulations, an application indicating a genuine employer-employee relationship receives entirely different treatment from that accorded an application arising from circumstances deemed to constitute self-employment.

An application for certification is to be filed by an employer seeking to employ a particular alien. 20 C.F.R. §656.21(a). The application must contain, among other things, a job description setting minimum qualifications; the qualifications must meet certain requirements and must not be unduly restrictive. Id. §656.21(b) (2). In a case not involving self-employment, processing of the application begins with a determination by the Secretary, on the basis of general labor market data, as to the availability of qualified domestic workers for the job. If the data indicate that none are available, certification must be granted. See *Production Tool Corp. v. Employment and Training Admin.*, 688 F.2d 1161, 1170 (7th Cir. 1982); *Acupuncture Center of Washington v. Dunlop*, 177 U.S. App. D.C. 367, 543 F.2d 852, 858-60 (D.C. Cir.), cert. denied, 429 U.S. 818, 50 L. Ed. 2d 78, 97 S. Ct. 62 (1976); 20

C.F.R. 656.24(b) (2) (ii)-(iv). If it is determined that qualified workers are likely to be available locally, the employer must engage in recruitment efforts, in cooperation with the local job service office, to determine whether any of those workers are willing to take the job opportunity. 20 C.F.R. §656.21(f), 656.21(g), 656.24(b) (2) (i). If qualified United States workers do apply for the job, the applicant alien is denied labor certification; if not, the alien merits certification.

Where a genuine employer-employee relationship is not present, a different set of rules applies and labor certification is denied outright in all cases. 20 C.F.R. §§656.20 (c) (8), 656.50. This per se rule barring certification for self-employed persons is applied not only to solo practitioners, but also to aliens who have an ownership stake in a corporation under circumstances deemed to amount to self-employment. The Secretary's rationale for the rule is that the best way to determine whether labor certification would harm United States workers is to require the employer to undertake a genuine effort to recruit a domestic worker. See Br. for Appellee 11-16. Self-employment, in the Secretary's view, offers no opportunity for genuine recruitment. The Secretary posits that under certain circumstances (the exact nature of which we discuss, infra Part II), a corporation that applies for certification on behalf of an alien who is its part-owner cannot be expected to make a serious effort to replace the alien with a United States worker. The present case concerns the application of the self-employment regulations to an alien who is not self-employed in the solo sense but is part-owner of the business enterprise that applied for certification on his behalf.

B. Facts and Prior Proceedings

Eric Hall, a Pakistani national, currently resides in the United States under an E-2 visa, which is a form of nonimmigrant visa that permits an alien to come to the United States to develop and direct the operations of a business enterprise in which he has invested a substantial amount of capital. 8 U.S.C. §1101(a) (15) (E) (ii). Continued residence in the United States under an E-2 visa requires that the alien periodically obtain an extension of his visa from the Immigration and Naturalization Service. 8 C.F.R. §214.2(e) (1988). Although extensions are routinely granted and E-2 status is therefore considered nearly as desirable as permanent resident status, Eric Hall now seeks an immigrant visa which would confer permanent resident status.

Eric Hall and his wife Marjorie established Hall Enterprises in August 1982, incorporating it under the laws of Maryland. Initially, each of the Halls owned 50 percent of the stock. The company is engaged in the business of importing and exporting Pakistani furniture, giftware and military spare parts. On December 12, 1982, Eric Hall sold 490 of his 500 shares of Hall Enterprises stock to Joseph J. Bernot, retaining an option to repurchase under certain conditions. Two weeks later, on December 29, 1982, Hall Enterprises applied for labor certification for Eric Hall, who was already serving as corporate president.

A Labor Department certifying officer denied certification on March 13, 1985. The certifying officer found that there was no job opportunity clearly open to United States workers as the regulations require; no employer-employee relationship truly existed, in that the alien controlled the corporation that had declined to supplant him with a United States worker. The certifying officer based these findings on the presence of family members (including Eric Hall) in the corporate structure, the Hall family's ownership of 51 percent of the stock, the transfer of most of Eric Hall's stock just two weeks prior to the application for certification, and the premise that Eric Hall's position as president made it unlikely that he would be replaced by a qualified United States worker. Appellants' Appendix ("A.A.") 64-66....

C. Issues Under Review

Appellants challenge the Secretary's determination that the relationship between Eric Hall and Hall Enterprises did not constitute genuine "employment," within the meaning of 20 C.F.R. §656.50. They allege that the Secretary acted arbitrarily and capriciously in finding that Eric Hall did not work "for an employer other than [him]self." We undertake our review of the Secretary's action using the "arbitrary or capricious" test embodied in the Administrative Procedure Act §10(e) (2) (A), 5 U.S.C. §706(2) (A). See *Acupuncture Center of Washington v. Dunlop,* 543 F.2d at 859; *Pesikoff v. Secretary of Labor*, 163 U.S. App. D.C. 197, 501 F.2d 757, 761 (D.C. Cir.), cert. denied, 419 U.S. 1038, 42 L. Ed. 2d 315, 95 S. Ct. 525 (1974).

At the administrative level, the appellants did not challenge the regulations' insistence upon an "employment" relationship. See Administrative Record ("A.R.") 9-17 (Hall Enterprises' brief before the ALJ). Thus we need not decide the question of whether the blanket denial of labor certification to all self-employed aliens rests on a permissible interpretation of the Immigration and Nationality Act. We address only the Secretary's application of her self-employment rule to Eric Hall and Hall Enterprises.

II. FIDELITY TO ADMINISTRATIVE PRECEDENT

The appellants' main argument is that the Secretary's application of the self-employment rule was inconsistent with prior labor certification decisions. Before the ALJ, they cited Richard's Custom Autos, 5 ILCR 1-218 (1983), and Cohen-Verdi, Inc., 3 ILCR 1-887 (1982), for the proposition that an alien's partial ownership of the employer corporation does not indicate the absence of an "employment" relationship so long as the corporation is not "a sham or scheme for obtaining the alien's labor certification." Richard's Custom Autos, 5 ILCR at 1-220. In the present case, as appellants correctly point out, the ALJ found that Hall Enterprises was not a sham developed solely to obtain certification. A.A. 70. We do not, however, believe that the Secretary's prior decisions mandate a finding of "employment" in every case where the corporation is not a sham.

A. Requirement of Consistency in Agency Actions

Reasoned decision making requires treating like cases alike; an agency may not casually ignore its own past decisions. Divergence from agency precedent demands an explanation. Judge Leventhal, in *Greater Boston Television Corp. v. FCC*, 143 U.S. App. D.C. 383, 444 F.2d 841 (D.C. Cir.1970), cert. denied, 403 U.S. 923, 29 L. Ed. 2d 701, 91 S. Ct. 2233 (1971), provided the classic direction for a reviewing court:

[A]n agency changing its course must supply a reasoned analysis indicating that prior policies and standards are being deliberately changed, not casually ignored, and if an agency glosses over or swerves from prior precedents without discussion it may cross the line from the tolerably terse to the intolerably mute.(citations omitted).

But, of course, an agency runs the risk of intolerable muteness only when it "glosses over or swerves from" its precedents. Where the reviewing court can ascertain that the agency has not in fact diverged from past decisions, the need for a comprehensive and explicit statement of its current rationale is less pressing. Thus, in other equally perceptive words of Judge Leventhal – if satisfied that the agency has taken a hard look at the issues with the use of reasons and standards, the court will uphold its findings, though of less than ideal clarity, if the agency's path may reasonably be discerned, though of course the court must not be left to guess as to the agency's findings or reasons.

Greater Boston Television, 444 F.2d at 851 (citations omitted); see *Union Mechling Corp. v. United States*, 185 U.S. App. D.C. 57, 566 F.2d 722, 725 (D.C. Cir. 1977). See also *Apex Oil Co. v. Federal Energy Admin.*, 443 F. Supp. 647, 651 (D.D.C. 1977) (Greater Boston test asks whether the agency's "change in the application of the established criteria was significant enough to require an explanation," and, if so, whether such an explanation was provided).

Thus, where a particular agency action does not appear to be inconsistent with prior decisions, the agency's explanation need not be elaborate....

B. Consistency of Application of Self-Employment Rule

So viewed, the decision of the Secretary in the present case – "though of less than ideal clarity" – must be upheld. We conclude that the Secretary did not "swerve" from her prior decisions. Consequently, her explanation need only be sufficient to permit the court to discern the path she has taken. The Secretary has met this burden.

The appellants say that the present case is controlled by a line of prior decisions beginning with Cohen-Verdi, Inc., 3 ILCR 1-887 (1982) and culminating in Richard's Custom Autos, 5 ILCR 1-218 (1983). These cases set out a two-part inquiry for determining whether a genuine "employment" relationship exists between the applying employer and the alien employee.

In Cohen-Verdi, Inc., the Secretary denied labor certification on two grounds, one of which was the employer's failure to show that, in light of the alien applicant's part-ownership, the corporation was not "a sham and a scheme for obtaining the Alien's labor certification." Cohen-Verdi, Inc., 3 ILCR at 1-889.

Certification was also denied in Marriott Farms, Inc., 4 ILCR 1-362 (1982), on the ground that a genuine employment relationship had not been established. This ruling was predicated on the ALJ's finding that – the alien has been the princi[pal] initiator of Marriott Farms, Inc. As such,the corporation has come to rely heavily upon the alien's skills and contacts so that, were it not for the alien, the corporation would probably cease to exist....

The seminal ruling in Richard's Custom Autos blended these two tests, which for the sake of brevity we will label the "sham" and "inseparability" tests. In Richard's Custom Autos, the ALJ ordered the grant of labor certification. 5 ILCR at 1-220. Significantly, she relied on the criteria in both Cohen-Verdi and Marriott Farms for discerning the existence of a genuine employment relationship. She considered the facts in light of both tests and made the following two findings:

[The employer] is an ongoing business that is not likely to cease to exist without the alien. The employer has also established that its corporate shell is not a sham or scheme for obtaining the alien's labor certification.

5 ILCR at 1-220 (emphasis added). Having concluded that both tests pointed to the presence of a self-employment relationship, the ALJ granted certification.

Under the line of cases culminating in Richard's Custom Autos, the alien must prevail on both tests in order to merit certification. The ALJ's use of the word "also" in the quoted passage makes this clear. The two prior cases are consistent with this analysis, since in both Cohen-Verdi, Inc. and Marriott Farms, Inc. the alien flunked one of the two tests and certification was denied. (In neither case was there a need to apply both tests, since failing either one precluded the alien from obtaining certification.)

Appellants here assert that the nonsham nature of Hall Enterprises entitles them to labor certification. Yet, as we have seen, both Marriott Farms, Inc. and Richard's Custom Autos impose an inseparability test. Only Cohen-Verdi, Inc. fails to mention the inseparability factor. The question therefore is whether the Secretary has impermissibly swerved from Cohen-Verdi, Inc. without indicating her rationale for the departure. We think not. To the extent that Marriott Farms, Inc. and Richard's Custom Autos do modify Cohen-Verdi, Inc. by adding an inseparability component to the sham test, the Secretary has adequately explained her rationale for doing so. Just as a sham corporation could not be expected to make an independent determination of its need for the alien alter ego, neither could a bona fide corporation whose continued existence depends on the alien founder be expected to make a similar choice. The two situations are the functional equivalents of one another in that a genuine test of the labor market is unlikely in both instances. The citation of both Cohen-Verdi, Inc. and Marriott Farms, Inc. in Richard's Custom Autos, and the latter's use of both tests conjunctively, belie any contention that the Secretary "casually ignored" her own precedents.

Thus neither Cohen-Verdi, Inc. nor any other case brought to our attention has held that where the applicant corporation is not a sham, an employment relationship is conclusively established. Cohen-Verdi, Inc. stated that where a corporation is a sham, certification is to be denied. Marriott Farms, Inc. held that inseparability (also) defeats certification, and Richard's Custom Autos showed how the sham and inseparability tests work in tandem. The ALJ in this case employed both tests to decide if a true employment relationship was present.

Logic of course dictates that the two factors should be considered independently. The "sham" question determines only whether the corporation was fraudulently established for the sole purpose of obtaining certification for the alien. The "inseparability" question considers whether the corporation, even if legitimately established, relies so heavily on the pervasive presence and personal attributes of the alien that it would be unlikely to continue in operation without him. This latter question is appropriate because a company that depends so heavily on the alien that it would probably shut down without him is unlikely to make any real choice between him and a "qualified" United States worker.

[Discussion of Dissenting Arguments omitted]

III. EVIDENTIARY SUPPORT FOR THE ALJ's DECISION (omitted)

CONCLUSION

Tenets of reasoned decision making require an agency to justify any significant change in course. By contrast, where inquiry reveals that an agency action is consistent in discernible principle with prior rulings, a court must uphold the action so long as it is clear that the agency is traveling the same path and the path is a reasonable one. Hall Enterprises falls into the latter category of cases; while the road signs are not unambiguous, the agency's path is still discernible. The denial of labor certification for Eric Hall was neither arbitrary nor capricious.

Affirmed.

EXERCISES

1. In order for a person to enter the country as the spouse of a U.S. citizen, the couple must demonstrate that the marriage is not a sham relationship. Indicate how you would demonstrate the fact of the marriage to an immigration officer.

2. Religious workers are permitted to enter the country, subject to numerical limitations, as special immigrants. What if the religion is counter to general U.S. sensibilities? Should the religious worker be denied entry? If a Moslem muezzin who advocates polygamy as part of the Islamic faith wishes to enter the country, should he be granted or denied entry? Why or why not?
3. The category of immigrants subject to numerical limitations is in fact a quota system. What is your opinion of quotas? Do you believe that the categories within this group are appropriate? Why or why not? Which, if any, other groups would you want added to this list?
4. Why should the unmarried sons and daughters of U.S. citizens be subject to numerical limitations for entry, while their younger siblings are not? Why should the marital status of these persons be taken into consideration?
5. A gay couple legally marries under the laws of a foreign country. One of the spouses is an American citizen, the other the citizen of the country in which the marriage took place. Should the alien be permitted entry to the United States as the spouse of a U.S. citizen? Why or why not?

Chapter Four

NONIMMIGRANT CATEGORIES

CHAPTER PREVIEW

The largest number of visas issued by the United States government each year are to those persons who are classified as nonimmigrants. A **nonimmigrant** is an alien who wishes to enter the United States for a terminable period of time. The person does not intend to become a permanent resident of the country, nor does the person seek U.S. citizenship.

Pursuant to the INA, the Immigration and Nationality Act of 1952 as amended, there are currently 19 categories of nonimmigrants, and many of these categories contain subdivisions as well. Each of these classifications will be discussed in turn, in the order in which they appear in the INA. This chapter focuses on the requirements to apply for a nonimmigrant visa; the next two chapters will detail the procedures for applying for a visa, both for nonimmigrant and for immigrant categories. Note there is a special category for NATO personnel that will not be discussed in this chapter.

NONIMMIGRANT CATEGORIES

Nineteen nonimmigrant categories of visas are enumerated in the INA, indexed by letter. Each will be discussed in order.

A: Diplomatic Personnel

This category is designed to include ambassadors, public ministers, career diplomats, consular officers, and members of their immediate families. These persons are stationed in the United States as representatives of their countries to the United States government. Other diplomatic personnel who are posted to international organizations, such as the United Nations, which are located within the geographic boundaries of the United States come under a different classification (See G: Representatives of International Organizations; below).

This category is subdivided into three groups:

- A-1: This group consists of the ambassadors, ministers, consuls, career diplomats, and their families. (INA §101(a)(15)(A)(i))
- A-2: This grouping is for other diplomatic members of foreign ministries stationed in the United States, and their families, who do not qualify as ambassadors, consuls, etc., under the A-1 group. (INA §(a)(15)(A)(ii))
- A-3: This is the grouping for the personal employees, attendants and servants of the persons who qualify under the A-1 and A-2 classifications. (INA §101(a)(15)(A)(iii))

Example: The government of Turkey sends an ambassador to represent its interests in Washington, DC. The ambassador, his wife, and their children would qualify for A-1 visas.

Example: The wife of the Turkish ambassador wants to bring her children's nursemaid to Washington to care for the children while the couple is stationed in the District of Columbia. The nursemaid would be able to enter the country on an A-3 visa.

Example: Once in the United States, the Turkish ambassador realizes that he could use the services of a financial officer to assist him with his official duties. The Turkish government agrees to send a financial attaché to the embassy in Washington. This person, assuming that she was a career diplomat, could qualify for an A-2 visa.

Persons who have been issued an A-1 or A-2 visa may remain in the United States for as long as the U.S. secretary of state recognizes their status. Persons in the United States on an A-3 visa are only granted entry for three years, but the visa may be renewed for two-year increments.

B: Temporary Visitors

This classification is intended to provide visas for those persons who wish to come to the United States for a short period of time for business or pleasure.

B-1: This classification is for people entering for a short business visit, and labor certificates are not required for these people. Other business visitors, here for specialized programs, come under separate classifications. (INA §(a)(15)(B))

Example: The head of a Singapore company wants to come to the United States for three weeks to attend a trade show and to travel to visit several American customers to increase his business. This person would qualify for a B-1 visa.

B-2: This category is for people coming to the U.S. primarily as tourists, for medical treatment, or as potential students who want to visit educational institutions.

Example: A family from Chile buys a package tour to the United States to spend one week in Miami and one week in New York to sightsee. This family could be issued a B-2 visa.

Example: A young girl from Afghanistan needs medical treatment that can only be provided in the United States. This girl, and her immediate family, could be issued a B-2 visa to enter the United States for medical treatment.

C: Visitors in Transit

This is a specialized category designed for very short-term needs.

C-1: is for persons in transit who are permitted to enter the country for a maximum of eight hours.
C-2: is for persons who are given the right of transit to the United Nations, and the C-2 nonimmigrant may only stay in the United States for a maximum of 29 days.

C-3: This category exists for foreign government officials who are not posted to the United States but who wish to travel through the United States either to their posted country or to their home country. A C-3 visa is valid for 29 days. No visa in this category is renewable. (INA §101(a)(15)(C))

Example: A British subject is en route to London, England, from Sydney, Australia. His flight has a six-hour layover in New York, and rather than stay at the airport, this alien wants to visit the Statue of Liberty. The Britisher may be given a C-1 visa at the airport for an eight-hour visit.

Example: A person representing rebel forces in Bosnia wishes to address the United Nations in order to alert the media to the plight of his people. He is not a diplomat from a government recognized by the United States, nor is he a tourist. He may apply for, and may be granted, a C-2 visa that would allow him to address the General Assembly of the United Nations.

Example: The French ambassador to New Zealand is on his way home to France. En route he stops in the United States for a two-week visit. The diplomat would be entitled to a C-3 visa.

D: Crew Members

This category covers foreign persons working on vessels docked in a United States port.

D-1: applies to crew members who are returning with their vessel when it leaves the U.S.

D-2: applies to crew members who are leaving one vessel and who intend to start work on a different vessel. These persons are generally prohibited from working while they are actually in the United States, and they cannot enter the U.S. if there is a strike or lockout in the U.S. involving their employers. However, certain exceptions may be made by the attorney general in the interest of national security or because the crew member had worked for the employer for at least one year prior to the labor action. The visas are limited to a stay of 29 days and are not renewable. (INA §101(a)(15)(D))

Example: A flight attendant working on Garuda Airlines has a two-day layover in New York before the flight returns to Bali. The flight attendant would be eligible for a D-1 visa to allow entry to the United Sates for the period of the layover.

E: Treaty Traders and Investors

The E classification is designed for persons who are engaged in business in the United States pursuant to a treaty the U.S. has with the alien's homeland.

E-1: A **treaty trader** is an alien who is actively engaged in operating a business. (INA §101(a)(15)(E)(i))

E-2: A **treaty investor** is an alien who is investing funds in a U.S. enterprise. (INA § 101(a)(15)(E)(ii))

In order to be entitled to a visa in this category, a commercial treaty must be in force between the United States and the alien's homeland.

> **Example:** The United States has a Treaty of Friendship, Commerce and Navigation with Spain. A Spanish citizen wishes to investigate the possibility of starting a joint venture in the United States with an American company. Pursuant to the terms of the treaty, the Spanish citizen may be entitled to a visa under the E category.

In order to obtain a visa in this category, it must be demonstrated that the trade in question will be "substantial," both in terms of size and monetary value.

If the United States does not have a treaty with the alien's homeland, but that foreign country affords U.S. citizens reciprocal benefits, the alien may still be entitled to an E category visa. Countries that come under this exception include Australia and Canada.

F: Academic Students

The student category of nonimmigrant visa is one of the most frequently sought means of entry to the United States. The INA recognizes two categories of student: academic and vocational. The students pursuing academic studies fall under the F category; students pursuing vocational studies fall under the M category discussed later.

In order to qualify for student visa status under the F classification, the student must be enrolled in a full course of study, and the study must be completed within eight years of entry. Even though the student is required to be enrolled in school full time, the student is still permitted to work on campus up to 20 hours per week, provided that the alien student does not displace a U.S. student for the job. The employment may include off-campus work, provided that the work is in some way connected with the course of study. The student may work more than 20 hours per week during periods of vacation and school holidays.

> **Example:** An alien in the United States under a student visa is enrolled in Stanford's MBA program as a management major. The alien student is offered a part-time job as an assistant manager in an American company that engages in business in the alien's homeland. The company wishes to integrate the alien's knowledge into its sales strategy. The student's work will be monitored by Stanford, and the student will receive some academic credit for the work performed. The student, under these circumstances, may work for the company.

The F category contains two subdivisions:

F-1: is for the actual student. To qualify for F-1 status the alien student must be enrolled in an academic program in a high school, college, university, seminary, conservatory, or language institute. This category does not apply for vocational and nonacademic programs. (INA §101(A)(15)(F)(i))

> **Example:** A foreign lawyer wishes to obtain a master of laws degree at a U.S. law school. If accepted into a master's program by an American university, the alien attorney can qualify for an F-1 visa.

An F-1 visa is valid for the period of study, plus a period of practical training, plus sixty days. The student may change the course of study, and/or transfer to different schools or seek additional education by applying for an extension based on compelling academic or medical reasons.

> **Example:** Eighteen months after enrolling in a bachelor's degree program at an American university, an alien student becomes seriously ill and must drop out of school for nine months. The alien may have the F-1 visa extended, even though the full course of study was temporarily abandoned because of a compelling medical need.

Students in the United States under an F-1 visa may be accompanied by their spouses and children who would qualify for an

F-2 visa: The provisions of the law dealing with marriage fraud and proof of family relationship previously discussed apply to the student's spouse and children seeking entry under the F-2 classification. (INA §101(a)(15)(F)(ii)).

The spouse and children of the F-1 student are completely prohibited from working while in the United States.

When an alien is granted an F-1 classification, the student is issued a Form I-20 that includes the date on which the course of study must be completed. If, as in the above example, circumstances prevent the student from completing the course of study by the date appearing on the I-20, the educational institution can notify the INS for an extension on Form I-538, which is submitted with a new I-20A-B Form to indicate the new completion date.

G: Representatives to International Organizations

This category of nonimmigrant is divided into five subsections:

G-1: Principal representatives of governments that are recognized by the United States, plus their staff and families. (INA §101(a)(15)(G) (i))

G-2: Other, nonprincipal representatives to international organizations sent by governments recognized by the United States. (INA §101(a)(15)(G) (ii))

G-3: Persons who would be classified under G-1 or G-2 but for the fact that their governments are not recognized by the United States. (INA §101(a)(15)(G) (iii)

G-4: Persons directly employed as officers or other employees of the international organization. (INA §101(a)(15)(G) (iv))

G-5: Attendants, servants, and other personal employees of persons who are granted entry under the G-1, G-2, G-3 or G-4 categories. (INA §101(a)(15)(g) (v))

All of the visas issued under this classification are valid for one year, and are renewable, and only family members of the G-4 category may accept work in the United Sates, subject to INS approval.

Example: The government of Israel wants to send an ambassador to represent its interests to the U.N. Because the United States recognizes Israel, the ambassador would be entitled to a G-1 visa.

Example: The leader of the Palestine Liberation Organization wants to send an ambassador to represent its interests to the U.N. The United States does not officially recognize the PLO as a state, but its representative to the U.N. may be afforded a G-3 visa.

Example: The United Nations employs an Iranian citizen as a public relations officer. This person would be entitled to a G-4 visa as an employee of an international organization.

Example: The Iranian public relations officer employed by the U.N. wants to bring an Iranian nanny over to the U.S. to take care of his children. The nanny may qualify for a G-5 visa.

The classifications G-1 through G-4 include the alien's family members as well as the subject alien.

Pursuant to the Immigration Reform and Control Act of 1986 (see Chapter One), certain G-4 nonimmigrants who had been physically present in the United States for a specified period of time could have their status adjusted to special immigrant status. They could then reside in the United States permanently. Furthermore, this act permits certain parents and children of aliens who qualify for this special treatment to enter the country under a nonimmigrant N classification visa (see below).

H: Temporary Workers

This category is designed to help American employers meet certain temporary employment needs by hiring foreign workers because of a shortage of qualified American workers. There are six subcategories of temporary workers: (INA §101(a)(15)(H))

H-1A: This category is for registered nurses. To qualify for this status, not only must the requisite educational background exist, but the secretary of labor must certify that an unexpired attestation is on file for each facility (other than a private home) for which the alien will work.

Example: A hospital in Fort Lauderdale has a shortage of experienced nurses, and seeks to employ, temporarily, registered nurses from the Dominican Republic. Provided that the secretary of labor has an unexpired attestation as to that hospital, the hospital may be able to have nurses from the Dominican Republic enter the United States on an H-1A visa.

H-1B: This category exists for temporary workers who qualify as professionals. Persons of exceptional ability in the arts or sciences, or persons who work in **specialty occupations** (a job requiring theoretical and practical application of a highly specialized body of knowledge). To meet these requirements, the person seeking H-1B status must either

a) obtain a state license, if such license is required to practice;
b) have obtained a bachelor's or higher degree in the specific field; or
c) have attained experience in the specialized area equivalent to a bachelor's degree, and must have broad practical experience in the specialty.

There is a yearly numerical limit of 65,000 visas that may be issued under the H-1B classification, and both the H-1A and H-1B nonimmigrants are required to have a **labor condition** application filed with the secretary of labor that specifies

a) the wages the alien will receive do not exceed prevailing wages;
b) the alien's job will not have an adverse effect on American labor;
c) no labor dispute exists between the employer and U.S. labor organizations.

An H-1A or H-1B visa is valid for three years and may be renewed for up to three years.

Recently there has been much debate regarding the effect of the North American Free Trade Agreement (NAFTA) on the H-1B visa. Applications for H-1B visas have been steadily increasing, and obtaining a TN visa pursuant to the provisions of NAFTA has become more widespread. This is because the H-1B visas are difficult to obtain, and the TN visa applies to a similar classification of alien. As of the writing of this text, Congress is discussing possible changes in the H-1B classification to address this situation.

Example: An American medical products manufacturing company needs an engineer with a specialized knowledge of particular medical equipment. The company knows of a German engineer who would be perfect for the job. The American company files a Labor Condition application with the secretary of labor and is able to obtain an H-1B visa for the German engineer.

H-2A: These visas are limited to persons entering the United States as temporary agricultural workers.

H-2B: These visas are intended for aliens who enter the United States to fill a *temporary* position. H-2 visas are limited to 25,000 annually, and the employer must obtain a labor certificate in order for the alien to be able to enter the country (see Chapter Five).

H-3: This category covers aliens who come to the United States for special training programs. In order to qualify, the training program must be unavailable in the alien's home country, and the visa is limited to two years.

H-4: This visa is for the spouse and children of the H-1, H-2, and H-3 nonimmigrants, and H-4 visa holders may not accept employment while in the United States.

The H visas, except as noted above, are valid for the period of employment, and all H status visa holders are permitted to apply for an adjustment of status to an immigrant classification, provided they meet the requirements for immigrant status as discussed in the previous chapter.

I: International Media Representatives

Representatives from recognized media organizations, such as newspapers, television stations, journals, etc., are permitted entry to the United States in order to cover news events happening here, provided, however, that U.S. citizens are granted similar privileges in the alien's homeland. This visa includes the representatives spouse and children, and it is valid as long as the representative is employed by the media agency. (INA §101(a)(15(I))

> **Example:** A newsperson from *France Soir* is assigned to the United States to cover the presidential election. This newsperson, including the alien's spouse and children, are permitted to enter the United States on an I classification visa.

J: Exchange Visitors

There are two categories enumerated under the J visa:

J-1: for the exchange visitor
J-2: for the spouse and children of the exchange visitor.

An **exchange visitor** is a student, scholar, teacher, or a specialist or leader in a field of specialization, who has been invited to participate in an exchange program by the United States Information Agency (USIA). The term of the visa is dependent upon the time period of the exchange program. The J-1 nonimmigrant is permitted to work in the United States, and the J-2 accompanying family members *may* be permitted to work with government approval. (INA §101(a)(15)(J))

> **Example:** A research scientist from Sri Lanka is invited to participate in a special research project sponsored by the USIA. The research scientist, the scientist's spouse and children, may come to the United States as J visa nonimmigrants.

If the J category nonimmigrant wishes to reside permanently in the United States, or to change status to an H or L nonimmigrant visa, the alien must first return to his or her homeland for a period of two years before applying for the new status if

a) the alien participated in a program financed by the U.S. or foreign government;
b) the alien is a native or resident of countries designated by the USIA as requiring the alien's specialized knowledge;
c) the alien came to the U.S. to receive graduate medical training. Persons in this subdivision may not change their status to any other nonimmigrant classification.

> **Example:** A physician from Paraguay comes to the United States for graduate medical training at Johns Hopkins University. After completing the training, the physician wishes to be employed by a hospital in Baltimore. The physician must return to Paraguay for two years before applying for reentry, and may only reenter on an immigrant basis.

Waivers of the two-year reentry requirement may be granted when:

a) not granting the waiver would cause a hardship to a U.S. citizen or permanent resident spouse or child of the nonimmigrant

> **Example:** A nonimmigrant in the United States on a J visa gives birth to a child while here. The child is a U.S. citizen, and is in need of pediatric medical care that can only be obtained in the U.S. This nonimmigrant may be able to have a status change without returning home for the two-year period because of the hardship it would create for the child.

b) persecution against the alien in the alien's homeland based on race, religion, nationality, political opinion or membership is likely. This may constitute a change to refugee status, as will be discussed in Chapter Eight
c) the alien's homeland does not object to the change
d) a U.S. government agency requests the change.

Example: A foreign bacteriologist is in the United States on a J visa to participate in a special training program. The National Institute of Health wishes to employ the nonimmigrant because of the bacteriologist's particular background. The nonimmigrant's homeland, although in need of the bacteriologist, believes that the research project at the NIH would have worldwide application. Therefore the homeland does not object to allowing the bacteriologist to remain in the U.S. In these circumstances, the bacteriologist may receive an immediate change of status.

K: Fiancé(e)s of U.S. Citizens

The fiancé or fiancée of a U.S. citizen is permitted to enter the United States for a 90-day period in order to celebrate a valid marriage. The U.S. citizen must file a petition in the district where the citizen resides, which is then forwarded to the U.S. consulate in the country where the alien lives. A K-status nonimmigrant is required to submit to a medical examination before entry. Any children of the alien fiancé or fiancée may enter under a K-2 status. If the marriage is not celebrated within the 90 days, the nonimmigrant must leave the country, and this classification cannot be changed to any other status. (INA §101(a)(15)(K))

L: Intra-Company Transferees

Multinational corporations are permitted to transfer personnel to U.S. offices and these persons may enter the United States as L-status nonimmigrants.

L-1: the employee classification,
L-2: the employee's accompanying spouse and children classification.

The alien must have been employed by the company for at least one year prior to the transfer, and must be employed in an executive or managerial capacity with specialized knowledge of the company's products and procedures. These visas are valid for up to five years. The L visa is renewable, and the L-2 visa holders may not be employed while in the United States. Aliens are permitted to enter the U.S. under an L visa while intending to seek status as permanent residents. (INA §101(a)(15)(L))

Example: An American corporation with worldwide offices wants to transfer its vice president of European operations to the United States so he can become familiar with the American market. The executive may be permitted to enter for up to five years under an L-1 classification.

M: Vocational and Nonacademic Students

Students who wish to come to the United States for nonacademic study must seek entry under an M status visa.

M-1: for the student
M-2: for the spouse and children of the student.

The student may be employed while in the United States to aid in the training the student is receiving; the M-2 family members may not work while in the United States. (INA §101(a)(15)(M))

Example: An alien wishes to come to the United States to be trained in computer repairs. This course of study is considered to be vocational rather than academic, and the student may be entitled to an M-1 visa to study in the U.S.

N: Parents of G-4 Nonimmigrants

Certain nonimmigrants who are in the United States as officers and employees of international organizations are classified as G-4-status nonimmigrants. The parents of these nonimmigrants can receive a special visa that is valid only while the G-4-status nonimmigrant is considered to be a child. (INA §101(a)(15)(N))

O: Aliens With Extraordinary Ability

Since 1990 aliens who have extraordinary ability in the arts, sciences, education, business or athletics may enter the United States, along with accompanying personnel and family members, for the duration of the event for which the alien is admitted. In order to qualify for this category, the nonimmigrant must be recognized as having extraordinary ability in the national or international arena, and the attorney general must determine that the alien's entry will provide substantial benefit to the United States.

The O category is subdivided into three classifications:

O-1: the nonimmigrant of extraordinary ability. (INA §101(a)(15)(O)(i))
O-2: persons accompanying the nonimmigrant solely for the purpose of assisting the O-1 nonimmigrant in the event for which entry was granted. (INA §101(a)(15)(O)(ii))
O-3: the spouse and children of the O-1 and O-2 nonimmigrants. (INA §101(a)15)(O)(iii))

Example: A Bulgarian gymnastic coach is considered to be one of the best athletic coaches in the world. An international gymnastic competition is being held in the United States, and several of the coach's students are competing. Because of her acknowledged extraordinary ability, the coach, her two assistants and her spouse, may enter the U.S. under O visas for the competition.

P: Internationally Recognized Athletes and Artists

The P-1 category was established to permit internationally recognized athletes and artists to enter the United States for a competition or performance. If a group is seeking entry, each member, in order to be granted a visa under this category, must have had a substantial relationship with the group for at least one year. The P classification is usually sought by groups rather than individuals who would qualify under the O status discussed above. (INA §101(a)(15)(P))

P-1: Persons who enter under this classification are permitted to stay in the United States for up to five years.
P-2: Classification exists for persons who are part of an entertainment group participating in an exchange program with a United States organization.
P-3: Artists who perform "culturally unique" programs may be granted this visa. Generally "culturally unique" would refer to work typical of the alien's homeland.

Example: A group from South America performs traditional Incan and Native South American music. This group wishes to enter the United States to introduce its unique program to North America. The group, which has received international recognition, is the only group of its kind, and may be entitled to a P-3 visa.

The spouse and children of the group members who enter under one of the first three P subclassifications may enter with P-4 visas to accompany the entertainer.

Q: Participants in International Exchange Programs

This category was added in 1990 for persons participating in international exchange programs such as the Experiment in International Living. (INA §101(a)(15)(Q))

R: Religious Workers and Their Children

In 1990 this category was added for persons working for recognized religious organizations who come to the United States to work for the organization on a temporary basis. Compare this category with the immigrant category of religious worker discussed in the previous chapter. (INA §101(a)(15)(R))

V: Spouses and Children of Permanent Resident

Pursuant to the Legal Immigration and Family Equity Law Act, a new category of visa was created in 2001 permitting spouses and children of permanent residents to work in the United States

ETHICAL CONSIDERATIONS

One of the growing concerns identified by the United States government is that aliens entering the country under a nonimmigrant status visa may remain in the country after their visas have expired. For almost all of the nonimmigrant classifications, in order to qualify, the alien must affirmatively state that he or she does not intend to take up permanent residence in the United States. Consequently, aliens who enter on a nonimmigrant visa just to be able to enter the U.S. legally, but who have no intention of returning to their homelands, have perjured themselves and have in effect entered the country illegally. Also, since the events of September 11, 2001, the government is more closely scrutinizing aliens wishing to enter the country to determine whether they have terrorist affiliations.

Many of the nonimmigrant visa categories severely limit or totally prohibit the nonimmigrant from working while in the United States (obviously not for the work-related nonimmigrant classifications). If these persons work while in the country, not only are they violating the terms of their visas, but the U.S. citizens who knowingly hire them are also violating the law. In most instances, because the nonimmigrant is willing to work for very low wages, the employer is attempting to benefit financially by violating U.S. law. U.S. citizens and legal permanent residents are thereby injured by having jobs taken away and given to persons who are legally prohibited from working.

The provisions for permitting entry to aliens on a temporary basis were not intended to provide a loophole in meeting the immigrant entrance requirements, and persons who use these provisions as such are involved in a clear legal and ethical violation of the spirit and letter of the law.

CHAPTER REVIEW

The Immigration and Nationality Act of 1990 provides for nineteen categories for entry to the United States for nonimmigrants. A nonimmigrant is an alien who wishes to enter the United States for a temporary period and who has the intention of returning home after the period of the visa has expired. The nineteen categories of nonimmigrant are

1. diplomatic personnel
2. temporary visitors
3. visitors in transit
4. crew members
5. treaty traders and investors
6. academic students
7. representatives to international organizations
8. temporary workers
9. international media representatives
10. exchange visitors
11. fiancé(e)s of U.S. citizens
12. intra-company transferees
13. vocational and nonacademic students
14. parents of G-4 nonimmigrants
15. aliens with extraordinary ability
16. internationally recognized athletes and artists
17. participants in international exchange programs
18. religious workers and their families
19. spouses and children of lawful permanent residents

Many of these nonimmigrant categories permit the nonimmigrant to be accompanied by his or her spouse and children.

The purpose of the nonimmigrant classifications is for temporary stays in the United States. If the nonimmigrant remains in the United States after his or her visa expires, the nonimmigrant becomes an undocumented alien subject to the provisions of the 1996 Act, which will be discussed in later chapters.

CHAPTER VOCABULARY

Culturally unique —Typical of a particular country or ethnic group.

Exchange visitor — A student, scholar, teacher or specialist who has been invited to participate in an exchange program by the U.S. Information Agency.

Extraordinary ability — Being recognized either nationally or internationally as having specialized knowledge or skill.

INA — The Immigration and Nationality Act (see Chapter One).

Labor condition application — Document to be filed by H-category employers.

Nonimmigrant — Alien who wishes to enter the country for a terminable period of time.

Specialty occupation — Job requiring theoretical and practical application of a highly specialized body of knowledge.

Treaty investor — Person who, subject to a valid U.S. treaty, plans to invest funds in a U.S. enterprise.

Treaty trader — Person who, subject to a valid U.S..treaty, plans to participate in an enterprise in the United States.

EDITED JUDICIAL DECISIONS

The following two cases have been included to highlight material discussed in the body of the chapter. *International Auto Exchange, Inc. v. The Attorney General* discuses intra-company transfers, and *Romero v. Consulate of the United States* concerns an alien's right to judicial review of a denial of a nonimmigrant visa.

INTERNATIONAL AUTO EXCHANGE, INC. v. The ATTORNEY GENERAL
643 F. Supp. 616 (D.D.C. 1986)

This matter is before the Court on Cross-Motions for Summary Judgment on plaintiff's Action for Declaratory Judgment and Injunction.

Plaintiff Rajab established International Auto Exchange, Inc. (also a plaintiff), which is a subsidiary of a Saudi Arabian Company. Plaintiff was authorized to enter the United States for this purpose under intracompany transferee ("L-1") status granted by the Immigration and Naturalization Service (INS). Plaintiff Rajab's initial approval was for one year, and he thereafter was granted three one-year extensions, the last of which expired on November 1, 1984. Plaintiff sought and was denied an additional two-and-one-half-year extension. The ultimate reason supporting the denial was that the record no longer established that Rajab's services were needed on a temporary basis only, which was a prerequisite to L-1 status.

INS is authorized to grant L-1 status and extensions pursuant to the Immigration and Naturalization Act, 8 U.S.C. 1101(a)(15) and 1184(a). The act was liberally applied by INS which granted extensions routinely upon a statement that the status was necessary for a specific time period. At the time Rajab applied for a 2 1/2 year extension, INS had established regional adjudication's centers (RACs) and a centralized Administrative Appeals Unit (AAU). These offices adopted a more restrictive application of the statute in examining whether a petition satisfied the temporary basis requirement. The offices decided that since Rajab was granted four one-year periods and then requested a 2 1/2 year extension without providing a rationale for the necessity, the application no longer supported status as a temporary employee. Subsequent to the denial of plaintiff's petition, INS issued a policy directive indicating that an employer's statement that the services are needed temporarily would be sufficient for an initial grant of three-year status and an extension of two more years. If extraordinary circumstances exist, an additional extension of one year could be granted, however, this sixth year would be the maximum. This directive was applicable to new or pending petitions only, so Rajab was not eligible for this new policy.

The Court recognizes the discretion given to INS to enforce the provisions of the Act and will overturn an INS determination "only if the decision is found to have been arbitrary, capricious, or an abuse of discretion." *Chavan v. Drysdale*, 513 F. Supp. 990, 913 (N.D.N.Y.1981). See, *Foti v. INS*, 375 U.S. 217, 228, 84 S. Ct. 306, 313, 11 L. Ed. 2d 281 (1963). The Court may only determine whether the decision was

"made without a rational explanation, inexplicably departed from established policies, or rested on an impermissible basis such as invidious discrimination against a particular race or group, or, in Judge Learned Hand's words, on other "considerations that Congress could not have intended to make relevant."

Wong Wing Hang v. INS, 360 F.2d 715, 719 (2d Cir.1966), citing U.S. ex rel. *Kaloudis v. Shaughnessy*, 180 F.2d 489, 491 (2d Cir.1950).

Plaintiffs contend it is arbitrary, capricious and an abuse of discretion for INS to have adopted a more restrictive attitude. Plaintiffs assert it is further arbitrary for INS to have issued a new policy directive without making it retroactive.

Defendant has cited several INS decisions from the restrictive period, which also denied petitions which did not support a statement of temporary need. The Court concludes that the restrictive approach was uniformly and consistently applied during that period, and, therefore, was not arbitrary and capricious as to this plaintiff. The Court also concludes that the denial of plaintiff's petition was not based on an attempt to discriminate against plaintiff's race or other association.

The Court must therefore focus on whether it was an abuse of INS' discretion to restrictively interpret the Act's requirement that the employment be of a temporary nature, during the period prior to the INS policy directive. "From the Administrative Appeals Unit's perspective, [INS] is obliged to prevent the 'H' or 'L' statuses from being routinely used as intermediary steps to residence." In the decisions rendered under the stricter interpretation, the AAU regularly cites Matter of University of California Medical Center, 10 I & N Dec. 715 (Reg.Comm'r 1964), for the proposition that "H" or "L" extensions may not be used as a substitute for residence status while the alien awaits the availability of a visa number.

The Act's legislative history envisioned a three-year period as being sufficient for the L-1 status employee, with reasonable extension for bona fide requests. Congress also recognized that it was valid for L-1 employees to have a dual intent of working in a temporary capacity, while simultaneously seeking permanent residence. The L-1 employees should have the same "opportunity available to other non-immigrants." H.R.Rep. No. 851, 91st Cong., 2d Sess. 6-7 (1970), U.S.Code Cong. & Admin.News 1970, pp. 2750, 2755.

The Court concludes Congress did not intend the L-1 status to be extended continually without a supporting basis for requesting the temporary status. The L-1 status was created to allow "foreign nationals to learn American management techniques . . . and thus more effectively manage the affiliate operations of U.S. companies when they return overseas." Id. at 4, U.S.Code Cong. & Admin.News 1970, p. 2752. It also enables foreign nationals to render managerial, executive or other specialized knowledge to affiliate businesses in the United States on a temporary basis. See, 8 U.S.C. 1101(a)(15)(L).

The Court concludes it was not an abuse of INS's discretion to strictly require a temporary basis of employment in reviewing extension applications, given Congress's intent expressed in the Act's legislative history as well as INS' need to prevent abuse of the L-1 status. Although the new policy directive eases the degree of proof of temporary employment, it has the same effect as the restrictive policy by setting a five-year limit on the duration of status (with a potential one-year extension for extraordinary circumstances). The fact that INS is now applying a new approach does not invalidate the interim approach per se. The result to an L-1 status employee is roughly equivalent. The Court concludes for this reason that it is also not arbitrary for INS to refuse to apply the new policy retroactively.

ORDERED that Defendant's Motion for Summary Judgment is GRANTED.

ROMERO v. CONSULATE OF THE UNITED STATES

860 F. Supp. 319 (E. D. Va. 1994)

OPINION: These separate but essentially similar cases raise the issue, seldom presented in this circuit, whether off-shore aliens have the right of judicial review of a consular officer's decision denying their requests for non-immigrant visas to visit the United States. Plaintiffs Ines Elvira Navarro de Cuello ("Navarro") and Carlos Romero ("Romero") were denied non-immigrant visitor visas for entry to this country by consular officers in Barranquilla, Columbia, on the ground that plaintiffs were suspected of having participated in drug trafficking. Plaintiffs deny any involvement in drugs and sue the United States and various entities of the United States, seeking judicial review of the consular officers' decisions, as well as damages for emotional distress stemming from the government's allegedly "negligent investigation" that implicated plaintiffs in drug trafficking. Because the decision whether to grant or deny non-immigrant visitors visas is in the sole discretion of consular officers and is not subject to judicial review, and because the negligent investigation allegation does not state a claim upon which relief can be granted, plaintiffs' actions must be dismissed with prejudice.

I.

Romero, a native and citizen of the Republic of Colombia, applied for a non-immigrant visa in March 1992. A United States consular officer in Barranquilla denied Romero's request on the ground that there was reason to believe that Romero was engaged in drug trafficking. The letter informing Romero of the consular officer's decision stated that:

After a careful investigation, it has been concluded that you were found ineligible to receive a visa for the United States, in July 1989, under Section 212 (a)(2)(C) of the Immigration and Nationality Act. This section prohibits the issuance of a visa to anyone:

"Who the consular or immigration officer knows or has reason to believe is or has been an illicit trafficker of controlled substances; who is or has been a known aider, conspirer, or assister with other in the illegal trafficking or any controlled substance."

The determination was based on information of a confidential nature, and for that reason it is not possible to divulge it, according to the laws of the United States that protect confidential information. Nevertheless, the Consulate would have the pleasure to consider and reexamine whatever information you may wish to present on your case after one year from the date of this letter.

It is unfortunate that it was necessary to make this decision.

Letter of March 6, 1992 from Maria Otero, United States Consul, Barranquilla, Colombia, to Carlos Horacio Romero Paez.

Navarro, also a Colombian citizen and resident, requested a non-immigrant visa to the United States in October 1992. As with Romero, a United States consular officer in Barranquilla, Columbia refused to issue the requested visa on the ground that Navarro was suspected of involvement in drug trafficking. The letter sent to Navarro was essentially similar to the Romero letter and stated, in part, as follows:

Permit us to inform you that in accordance with the information that we have in our records, you are permanently ineligible to receive a tourist visa under section 212()(2)(c) of the Immigration and Nationality Act of the United States.

Section 212(a)(2)(C) establishes that the consular section cannot approve a visa for any person who the consular or immigration officer knows or has reason to believe is or has been an illicit trafficker of controlled substances; who is or has been a knowing collaborator, instigator, conspirator or has been colluding with other persons for the illegal trafficking of said substances.

According to the information furnished by the Department of State and the information supplied in the interviews you are not eligible to receive a visa. We regret that our response could not be more favorable.

Letter of October 19, 1992, from Maria Otero, United States Consul, Barranquilla, Colombia, to Ines Elvira Navarro.

Plaintiffs filed their respective actions in February 1994, naming as defendants the United States, the United States Consulate in Barranquilla, the Attorney General, and the Drug Enforcement Administration. Specifically, plaintiffs assert that consular officers in Barranquilla failed adequately to specify the factual bases for denying plaintiffs' visa applications. Based on this contention, plaintiffs seek discovery of the records and specific facts upon which the denials were purportedly based. Next, plaintiffs assert that the government failed to provide them with an opportunity for administrative review of consular officers' denial of their visa applications. Accordingly, plaintiffs now seek review under both the Immigration and Nationality Act of 1952 (hereafter "INA"), 8 U.S.C. §1181 et. seq., and the Administrative Procedure Act (hereafter "APA"), 5 U.S.C. §§701-706 (1946). Finally, plaintiffs seek damages against the Drug Enforcement Administration for infliction of emotional distress stemming from a "negligent investigation." Citing the principle that consular officers' visa determinations are "beyond the province of the Court," the government contends that plaintiffs lack standing to pursue.

Though no constitutional provision explicitly vests Congress with the power to determine the admission of aliens into the United States, there is no doubt that this power exists. And courts have broadly construed this Congressional power, finding that it extends not only to which classes of aliens may enter the United States, but also to the terms and conditions of their entry. *Kleindienst v. Mandel*, 408 U.S. 753, 766, 33 L. Ed. 2d 683, 92 S. Ct. 2576 (1972); see *Anetekhai v. INS*, 876 F.2d 1218, 1221 (5th Cir. 1989); *Li Hing of Hong Kong, Inc., v. Levin*, 800 F.2d 970, 971 (9th Cir. 1986). Exercising this power, Congress, in the INA, has given United States consular officers exclusive authority over the issuance of non-immigrant visas for visits to the United States. 8 U.S.C. §1201 (1987 and Supp. 1994), see 8 U.S.C. §1101(a)(9). And both prior to and since the INA's enactment, courts have consistently held that a consular officer's decision to grant or deny a visa is not subject to judicial or administrative review.

Importantly, the doctrine of nonreviewability of consular officers' visa determinations is essentially without exception. Thus, even where a consular judgment rests on allegedly erroneous information, courts generally will not intervene. See *Loza-Bedoya v. Immigration*

& Naturalization Service, 410 F.2d 343, 346-47 (9th Cir. 1969); see also *Garcia v. Baker*, 765 F. Supp. 426, 428 (N.D. Ill. 1990). Likewise, the fact that a consular officer may have erroneously interpreted and applied the INA, see *Grullon v. Kissinger*, 417 F. Supp. 337, 339-340 (E.D.N.Y. 1976), aff'd 559 F.2d 1203 (2d Cir. 1977), or indeed the fact that a consular officer's decision was not authorized by the INA, see *Centeno v. Shultz*, 817 F.2d 1212, 1213, (5th Cir. 1987), cert. denied, 484 U.S. 1005, 98 L. Ed. 2d 648, 108 S. Ct. 696 (1988), does not entitle visa applicants to relief. Finally, visa applicants like plaintiffs cannot assert cognizable claims based on the contention that the State Department and Attorney General, in denying an applicant's visa request, failed to follow their own regulations. See *Burrafato v. United States* Dep't of State, 523 F.2d 554, 557 (2d Cir. 1975), cert. denied, 424 U.S. 910, 47 L. Ed. 2d 313, 96 S. Ct. 1105 (1976). In sum:

> whether the consul acted reasonably or unreasonably, is not for [the courts] to determine. Unjustifiable refusal to vise a passport may be ground for diplomatic complaint by the nation whose subject has been discriminated against. . . . It is beyond the jurisdiction of this court.

Id. at 556 (quoting United States ex rel. *London v. Phelps*, 22 F.2d 288, 290 (2d Cir. 1927), cert. denied, 276 U.S. 630, 72 L. Ed. 741, 48 S. Ct. 324 (1928)).

Faced with this daunting array of authority, plaintiffs attempt to carve out an exception to the principle of nonreviewability by arguing that while federal courts may not have jurisdiction to review a consular officer's substantive decision, courts may nonetheless review an officer's decision for alleged procedural irregularities. Thus, plaintiffs contend that consular officers must specify the factual predicates for their visa determinations, and assert that consular officers in Barranquilla failed to do so. Plaintiffs' argument is meritless; no such exception to the doctrine of consular nonreviewability exists. It is true that a visa may be refused "only upon a ground specifically set out in the law or regulations thereunder," and that the factual predicate for such a denial must be based on "a determination based upon facts or circumstances which would lead a reasonable person to conclude that the applicant is ineligible to receive a visa as provided in the INA and as implemented by the regulations." 22 C.F.R. §40.6 (1993). But offshore aliens have no right to judicial enforcement of these provisions, or to judicial review of administrative compliance with them. Further, neither the INA, relevant regulations, nor applicable case law require a consular officer to disclose the particular facts relied on in denying a visa request. Rather, consular officers are merely required to inform the unsuccessful applicant "of the provision of law or implementing regulation on which the refusal is based," and of any statutory provisions under which administrative relief may be available. 22 C.F.R. §42.81(b) (1993). These requirements were met here; consular officers in Barranquilla clearly indicated to Romero and Navarro that their visa applications were denied based on the officers' suspicions that plaintiffs were involved in narcotics trafficking, making them excludable aliens pursuant to 8 U.S.C. §1182 (a)(2)(c). In any event, as offshore aliens, plaintiffs have no right to judicial review of the consular officers' decisions, nor are they entitled to discovery of the documents and particular facts upon which consular officers relied in denying their visa applications.

Also meritless is plaintiffs' contention that they are entitled to an administrative review of the consular officers' decisions pursuant to 22 C.F.R. §41.121. Their reliance on this regulation is simply misplaced. Section 41.121 outlines the internal procedures that consular officers are required to follow after the denial of an applicant's visa request. Nothing in the regulation provides an offshore visa applicant with the right to seek administrative review of the consular officer's factual determination.

Nor can plaintiffs rescue their claims from the doctrine of consular nonreviewability by citing the APA. The APA provides no implied grant of subject matter jurisdiction to review consular decisions. Cf. *Califano v. Sanders*, 430 U.S. 99, 105, 51 L. Ed. 2d 192, 97 S. Ct. 980 (1977). And in general, disputes regarding an alien's right to enter and remain in the United States are governed by the special judicial review provisions of the INA, not the APA. See, e.g., *Marcello v. Bonds,* 349 U.S. 302, 310, 99 L. Ed. 1107, 75 S. Ct. 757 (1955) (hearing provisions of APA, with certain enumerated exceptions, inapplicable to deportation proceedings); *Heikkila v. Barber*, 345 U.S. 229, 235-37, 97 L. Ed. 972, 73 S. Ct. 603 (1953). Moreover, reading the APA to include the right to seek administrative review of consular decisions violates the doctrine of consular nonreviewability and "would be inconsistent" with the language and spirit of both the INA and APA. *Haitian Refugee Ctr. v. Baker*, 953 F.2d 1498, 1507 (11th Cir.), cert. denied, 117 L. Ed. 2d 477, 112 S. Ct. 1245 (1992).

In sum, exercising jurisdiction over the claims of these aliens would violate the long-standing doctrine that a consular officer's visa determination is nonreviewable, Although the doctrine of consular non-reviewability is not without its critics, it is well-grounded in established principles of national sovereignty and in sensible public policy. Were the rule to be otherwise, federal courts would be inundated with claims of disappointed and disgruntled off-shore aliens seeking review of consular officers' denials of their requests for non-immigrant visitors' visas. The doctrine of consular nonreviewability has been well-established for over seventy years, and the facts of this case warrant no departure from it.

An appropriate Order shall issue.

EXERCISES

1. A client of your firm is a major U.S. corporation that wants to bring the following people over to the United States for a temporary period. Indicate under which visa classification, if any, the following would qualify:
    a) A French paralegal to assist in drafting contracts with French companies
    b) An Indian manager from the client's Calcutta office to be trained for a higher management position
    c) A Japanese filmmaker to produce a trade film for the company.
2. The only nonimmigrant category that requires a medical examination is for the fiancé(e) of an American citizen. What is your opinion of this requirement? Do you think it is fair? Could you argue that it is unconstitutional? Why or why not?
3. While studying in the United States, a Chilean student fathers a child with an American citizen. The Chilean wants to remain in the United States after his student visa expires, but does not want to marry the child's mother. Should he be permitted to remain in the United States? Why or why not?
4. An Australian citizen entered the United States to receive training as a paralegal and has now been hired by a law firm for practical training. The Australian is willing to work for less money and, therefore, was hired instead of an American paralegal. What is your opinion of this situation? Explain.
5. Do you think there is a necessity for having 19 nonimmigrant classifications? Aren't some of the classifications fairly similar? Argue for or against maintaining the current nonimmigrant categories. If you are opposed to the current categories, explain how you would change them. Is your answer affected by the events of September 11, 2001?

Chapter Five

ADMISSION TO THE UNITED STATES

CHAPTER PREVIEW

The two preceding chapters discussed the requirements for aliens to enter the United States, either as immigrants or nonimmigrants. In order to enter the country legally, the alien must acquire a visa from the U.S. government. A **visa** is the government grant of entrance to the United States for aliens for the purpose and duration expressed in the document. This chapter will focus on the procedures that the alien must follow in order to obtain the visa.

The Immigration and Naturalization Service (INS) provides various forms and documents that must be completed by the alien, and sometimes by U.S. government agencies and/or U.S. citizens or legal permanent residents, in order for the alien to be able to obtain the appropriate visa. These forms are provided free of charge by the INS, and several appear in this chapter to exemplify the procedures discussed.

This chapter will detail the procedures for obtaining a visa for an immigrant, a nonimmigrant, and for the **adjustment of status** from a nonimmigrant to an immigrant classification.

PROCEDURES FOR OBTAINING IMMIGRANT VISAS

The procedures for obtaining an immigrant visa vary dependent upon the classification of immigrant visa the alien is seeking.

Spouse (INA §101(a))

If the alien spouse of a U.S. citizen is seeking entry to the United States as a permanent resident, the spouse is permitted immediate entry but remains in the United States for two years on a **conditional status** (see *Azizi v. Thornburgh* at the end of Chapter Three). This waiting period is mandated in order to ensure that the marriage was not entered into fraudulently.

Within the last 90 days of this two-year conditional status period, the spouse must file a petition with the INS requesting permanent resident status (INA §216). The INS will then schedule an interview to ascertain:

1. that the marriage was not entered into for a sham or fraudulent reason;
2. that the marriage has not been judicially terminated (divorce or annulment); and
3. that no fee has been paid to the U.S. citizen spouse for the purpose of filing the petition.

> **Example:** The husband of a U.S. citizen enters the United States with an immigrant visa not subject to numerical limitations. After the couple resides together in the United States for 22 months, the alien spouse files a petition with the INS to have his status changed from a conditional resident to a permanent resident. INS schedules an interview with him and his wife to determine that they are in a legitimate marital relationship.

After the interview, the Attorney General decides whether or not to grant the petition. If the petition is granted, the spouse's status is changed to that of a permanent resident. If the petition is denied, or the couple does not file a petition, the alien spouse's status is terminated and removal proceedings are instituted.

Example: During the interview the INS officer determines that the marriage was not a true marriage and was entered into for the purpose of permitting the alien to enter the United States. Under these circumstances, the attorney general will deny the petition for permanent resident status, and removal proceedings will be instituted.

The attorney general may grant a **hardship waiver** (INA §216(c)(4)) of removal if

1. the alien can prove that extreme hardship will result if he or she is removed from the country;
2. the marriage had been entered into in good faith but was terminated, and the alien was not at fault for not filing a petition; or
3. the marriage was entered into in good faith but was terminated because of extreme cruelty which was not the fault of the alien.

Example: The alien enters into a legitimate marriage with a U.S. citizen. After entering the United States, the citizen spouse continually beats the alien spouse, who finally seeks a judicial termination of the marriage. Under these circumstances the attorney general may grant a hardship waiver and permit the divorced alien spouse to remain in the United States.

These procedures for obtaining visas for alien spouses apply to the children who accompany the spouse as well.

Immediate Relatives of U.S. Citizens or Permanent Residents (INA §203(c))

A four-part procedure must be followed for immediate relatives of U.S. citizens or permanent residents seeking immigrant status:

1. The U.S. citizen or permanent resident must file **Form I-130, Petition for Alien Relative,** with the INS officer having jurisdiction over the alien (if the alien is already in the United States) or with the U.S. consular office in the country where the alien relation resides. (**Form I-600** must be completed for adopted children.) The INS officer has jurisdiction over the petition. (A provision in the INA permits the alien or any other person to file the petition on behalf of the alien for Amerasian children.)
2. The petitioner must submit proof of his or her U.S. citizenship or permanent resident status, as well as proof of the relationship to the alien in question.
3. The petition is dated when it is filed, which creates a priority date.
4. If the petition is intended for adopted children, the petition must include proof of the authorization of the adoption by an authorized or licensed public adoption agency.

Visa petitions are made under oath, and the burden of proof rests with the petitioner.

If the alien is residing outside the United States at the time the petition is filed, the petition is filed with the consular office. If the petition is approved, a visa is issued which is valid for four months, meaning that the alien must enter the United States within this period of time (three years for adopted children). Once in the United States, the immigrant is issued a **Form I-151**, known as a green card, which is documented proof that the alien is a permanent resident and is entitled to work in the United States. The green card is valid for ten years from the date of issuance.

Employment-Related and Diversity Visas

The procedures for obtaining immigrant visas for the employment-related category depend upon whether the visa is applied for inside or outside the United States.

Inside the United States

If the application for the visa is filed inside the Untied States, the following steps must be followed:

1. The U.S. employer files **Form I-140, Immigrant Petition for Alien Worker,** in the INS office closest to the location to where the job will be. (See Appendix 5-1.) If the alien qualifies as a person of extraordinary ability (see Chapter Three), anyone may file the petition. For diversity aliens and those in the fifth preference category, the alien may file his or her own petition.

2. The attorney general *may* waive the job offer requirement for those persons in the second employment-related preference category.

3. The Department of Labor must issue a labor certificate indicating that the alien's skills are needed for persons in the second and third employment-related preference category. Two types of labor certificates may be issued:

    a) Schedule A for doctors, nurses, and ministers.
    b) Schedule B for unskilled labor.

    If the alien's occupation falls into Schedule A, **Form ETA 750** must be filed with the INS office or the U.S. consular office. If INS determines that the alien qualifies for Schedule A, a certificate is granted. For those on Schedule B, a certificate will only be granted if a waiver is obtained from the DOL Regional Certifying Office indicating a shortage in the alien's work area. These waivers are rarely given.

    If the alien's occupation is not listed on either schedule, **Form ETA 750** must be submitted to the local state job office where the alien will be working. The U.S. employer must submit evidence of its unsuccessful attempt to find U.S. workers to fill the position. The regional office will process the application and then forward it to the DOL for determination.

4. If the INS determines that the application is valid, a visa will be issued. If the INS denies the application, it will issue a **Notice of Findings**, which is considered a preliminary denial. The employer must meet the requirements indicated in the DOL's finding or submit an opposition argument within 35 days of the issuance of the Notice. If the INS still decides to deny the petition, it must file a **Final Determination,** at which point the employer may seek review with the **Board of Alien Labor Certification Appeals**. This

review can take several years. An employer who is still unsatisfied with the result may seek judicial review in federal court.

Outside the United States

If the alien is applying for an employment-related or diversity visa from outside the territorial boundaries of the United States, a five-step process must be followed (after the labor formalities within the United States have been met for the employment related group):

1. The alien files **Form OF-222** with the U.S. consular office in the country where the application is being made in order to establish the alien's *prima facie* evidence of eligibility to receive an immigrant visa.

2. If the consular office determines that the alien has established a *prima facie* case for eligibility, the alien will receive **Form OF-169** to complete. This form requires the alien to submit the following:

   a) any police or military records that have been maintained about the alien
   b) birth and marriage certificates
   c) valid passport issued by the alien's homeland
   d) photographs of the alien
   e) for diversity immigrants, evidence that the alien will not become a public charge. This requirement may be met by evidence of bank accounts or statements by U.S. citizens or legal permanent residents who agree to be financially responsible for the alien. (See Appendix 5-2, Affidavit of Support.)

3. When all of the preceding information has been submitted, the alien will receive **Form OF-230** to complete. This is the actual application for the immigrant visa.

4. A hearing is conducted at the consular office that will include taking the alien's fingerprints and a medical examination, if one is required.

5. Finally, the consular office will grant or deny the application. If the application is denied, the alien has one year in which to overcome any objection the consular office has indicated with respect to the application. If the application is approved, the alien receives **Form OF-155**, the visa, which is valid for four months (three years for adopted children). This means that the alien must enter the United States within four months after the issuance of the visa or the visa expires and cannot be renewed. Once in the United States, the alien will receive a green card (see above) enabling the alien to work.

PROCEDURES FOR OBTAINING NONIMMIGRANT VISAS

For persons seeking entry into the United States as nonimmigrants, the procedures vary depending upon which category of nonimmigrant visa the alien wishes to receive.

Academic Students (F Classification)

For persons seeking entry under the F nonimmigrant classification, the academic institution where the alien wishes to study must complete a Certificate of Eligibility for the alien to receive the F-1 student visa. This certificate, **Form I-20-A-B**, Petition for Approval of School for Admission by Nonimmigrant Student, is sent to the prospective alien student. The student alien applies for the student visa by submitting the Form I-20-A-B to the U.S. consular office in the alien's homeland. With the I-20-A-B the alien must also submit evidence that

- the alien will have sufficient funds to support him- or herself while studying in the United States;
- the alien will maintain a home residence in the homeland to which the alien will return after completing his or her studies;
- the alien will return to his or her homeland (proof may take the form of a job offer in the foreign country).

Example: A student from Thailand wishes to receive a bachelor's degree in American history from an American university. She applies and is accepted as an undergraduate student at the University of St. Louis. The University completes Form 20-A-B, which it sends to her in Bangkok. The student submits this form to the U.S. consular office in Bangkok, along with a statement from her family, including bank records, that they will be responsible for all of her expenses while in the United States. She also needs a statement that she will continue to live with her parents on her return to Thailand, and documentation from the Thai Ministry of Education that her skills will be needed for Thai schools. The student will need to meet all the requirements to obtain a student visa.

If the student is going to be accompanied by family members (spouse and/or children) to the United States, these family members must be included the Form I-20-A-B. If a family member plans to join the student once the student is in the United States, the family member needs to have a copy of the Form I-20-A-B, which must be submitted separately to the consular office to obtain a visa prior to departure.

If the student is granted the visa, the visa is valid for the duration of the student's course of study, plus any practical experience needed to complete the education, plus 60 days. Restrictions with respect to employment and leaves of absence have been discussed in the previous chapter. Once in the United States, the student may apply for an adjustment of status to an immigrant classification (see below).

Fiancé(e)s (K Status)

The U.S. citizen who plans to marry the alien must file **Form I-129F, Petition for Alien Fiancé(e),** with the INS office in the district that has jurisdiction over the geographical area in which the citizen lives. The INS then sends this form to the U.S. consular office in the alien's homeland. The alien must submit to a medical examination (the only nonimmigrant category requiring a medical examination), and then the consular office will issue the visa that is valid for 90 days.

Example: A U.S. citizen wishes to marry a man from Guatemala. The U.S. citizen files Form I-129F with the INS office in the district where she lives, and the INS office sends this form to the U.S. consular office in Guatemala. The consular office informs the alien of the application, and the alien must submit to a medical examination. If the alien passes the medical exam, he will be issued a nonimmigrant visa as the fiancé of an American citizen. This visa permits his entry to the United States for a 90-day period.

Other Nonimmigrant Categories

The other categories of nonimmigrants fall into three classifications for procedural purposes in order to obtain a visa:

Group 1:

A. diplomatic personnel
B. temporary visitors
C. visitors in transit
D. crew members
E. treaty traders and investors
G. representatives to international organizations
I. international media representatives
N. parents of G-4 nonimmigrants
O. aliens with extraordinary ability.

The aliens who fall into this classification do not have to show any prior contact with U.S. citizens or legal permanent residents. The aliens file **Form OF-156** with the U.S. consular office and the applicants are inspected by an immigration officer (the inspection is generally not very detailed).

Group 2:

J. exchange visitors
M. vocational and nonacademic students
Q. participants in international exchange programs.

For persons who seek visas under this grouping, proof of acceptance into the specific program must be submitted to the consular office, along with **Form I-20,** which must be completed by the educational institution, or **Form IAP-66**, which is completed by the exchange program sponsor. If the consular office is satisfied that the alien has sufficient knowledge of English, the application will be approved and the visa issued.

Group 3:

H. temporary workers
L. intra-company transferees
P. internationally recognized athletes and artists
R. religious workers.
V. spouses and children of lawful permanent residents

In order to obtain visas for persons within these groupings, the prospective employer must submit proof of the need for the alien to be in the United States. The employer completes **Form I-129** that, if approved, provides the basis for the alien's visa.

On arrival to the United States, the alien is inspected by an immigration officer and is given **Form I-94** indicating the length and terms of the alien's stay in the United States.

ADJUSTMENT OF STATUS

Adjustment of status refers to the procedures whereby a nonimmigrant may change his or her status to an immigrant category. This adjustment procedure is available for all nonimmigrants except for crew members (D classification).

In order to adjust one's status, the alien must file **Form I-485, Application to Register Permanent Residence or Adjust Status,** with the INS District Office where the alien is residing. (See Appendix 5-3.) In order to be approved, the following criteria must be met:

a) The alien must have been inspected and legally admitted to the United States. Except where the government has permitted amnesty for persons who had unlawfully entered the country but who have lived here for a number of years, an alien who has illegally entered the United States is not eligible for adjustment of status.

> **Example:** A migrant worker from Mexico unlawfully entered the United States over seven years ago and wishes to remain in the country as a lawful permanent resident. Because he was neither inspected nor lawfully admitted to the country, he would not be permitted to become a permanent resident.

b) The alien must meet the statutory eligibility requirements necessary for all persons who wish to become immigrants. This means that if the nonimmigrant wishes to qualify as a priority worker in the employment-related classification of immigrant (see Chapter Three), the alien must be able to document the extraordinary ability required of all persons seeking admission under this classification.

> **Example:** An alien student has completed an entire doctoral program in the United States and has participated in extensive postdoctoral research. This alien student would probably be able to demonstrate the extraordinary ability required to permit an adjustment of status to an employment-related immigrant classification.

c) The immigrant visa must be immediately available. This means that if the adjusted status is one with a numerical limitation, there must be a visa spot available within this numerical limit.

> **Example:** In the preceding example, once the alien has demonstrated "extraordinary ability," the INS must determine that there are still employment-related visas available so that the alien may be granted one immediately. If none is available, the alien's status cannot be adjusted at this time.

d) The alien cannot have been in any unlawful status in the United States after November 6, 1986, or have accepted any unauthorized employment after January 1, 1979, unless the alien is the immediate relative of a U.S. citizen, the graduate of a foreign medical school who is licensed in the United States since 1978, or the violation is technical in nature. The purpose of this requirement is to limit or exclude persons unlawfully in the United States from obtaining immigrant status. "Technical violations" are determined on a case-by-case basis.

Example: A doctor from Egypt came to the United States under a student visa to engage in postgraduate study. While in the United States she passed a medical licensing exam in Virginia. After the expiration of the student visa, the doctor remained in the United States, accepting employment at a clinic in Virginia. She may still qualify for an adjustment of status, even though she has been in the United States in an undocumented state since the student visa expired and has accepted employment. She falls into the exception as a graduate of a foreign medical school who is licensed in the United States.

Pursuant to the Legal Immigration and Family Equity Law which came into effect on December 31, 2000, undocumented aliens may apply for an adjustment of status and be considered for such adjustment while they are in the United States. This provision for the adjustment of status applied to persons who are claiming status as an immediate family member of a United States citizen who entered the country lawfully but who are undocumented, and for persons who claimed an employment-based visa, provided the alien employee obtains a labor certificate from a U.S. employer and was in the United States for at least 180 consecutive days. These persons must pay a $1,000 fee to be interviewed. Applications for adjustment of status under this provision must have been filed by April 30, 2001.

PRIVATE LEGISLATION

For persons who are unable to obtain a visa by means of the procedures discussed above because of an inability to meet the statutory requirements, an option is still available for possible entry to the United States.

If the alien can interest a member of Congress in his or her case, the congressperson may initiate a **private bill** in Congress, and the legislature could pass a law permitting this particular named individual to enter or remain in the United States. Although this procedure is unusual, it is not as rare as one might think.

Example: An alien couple has lived in the United States without lawful documents for a number of years and has given birth to several children while living in the country. Under the law, this couple must now be removed to their homeland. The Congressman in the district where the family lives has become interested in their case. The family has always been hardworking, paid taxes, and has contributed to the community. The Congressman submits a bill to Congress to permit this family to remain in the U.S. as lawful permanent residents. If the bill passes, the family may remain in the country.

ETHICAL CONSIDERATIONS

Two main areas of ethical concern may be involved in the obtaining of visas: one on the part of the alien, and the other on the part of the U.S. government.

In order to obtain legal entry to the United States, many aliens have falsified records and information so that they may obtain a visa, either as an immigrant or as a nonimmigrant. For those seeking immigrant status, marriage and birth certificates have been forged, and health and educational backgrounds have been misrepresented. Those persons may in fact receive a visa, but because the basis upon which the visa was granted was false, the visa itself is invalid and the recipient is subject to removal. Many U.S. citizens or permanent residents who assist an alien in falsifying information in order to obtain a visa may also be subject to sanctions and/or removal proceedings.

With respect to the government, the INS officer is usually the person who has initial power to grant or deny a visa application, and the officer's own prejudices may affect the ultimate decision that is reached. The immigration laws are supposed to be uniformly and fairly applied to all persons, but the individual idiosyncrasies of INS officers are often the determining factors in application decisions. This is not to say that immigration officers are unfair or discriminatory, just that the possibility exists, and the burden is on the alien seeking admission to demonstrate that the officer's disposition of the application was unjustified. In early 1998, news reports surfaced that INS officers were denying visas to persons because of the clothes the applicant wore or the way the applicant wore his or her hair.

CHAPTER REVIEW

The procedures for obtaining a visa to enter the United States vary depending upon the nature of the desired visa. For persons seeking immigrant visas, the procedures generally require certification or statements from U.S. citizens or lawful permanent residents with respect to the prospective immigrant's family relationship or potential employment. Also, the forms that must be completed will vary depending upon whether the visa is applied for inside or outside of the United States.

For persons seeking entry as nonimmigrants, the procedures generally include submitting applications to the U.S. consular office and being inspected for eligibility. Once in the United States as a lawful nonimmigrant, the nonimmigrant may have his or her status adjusted to an immigrant status (except for crew members) upon a showing of eligibility under an immigrant classification, if a visa under that classification is immediately available. Adjustment of status procedures are generally for those persons who are filing for immigrant status once they are lawfully in the United States under a nonimmigrant classification, but also includes changing from one nonimmigrant category to another.

In very limited circumstances, an alien may be admitted to the United States, or be permitted to remain in the country, by means of a private bill passed in Congress specifically for the benefit of the named alien.

CHAPTER VOCABULARY

Adjustment of status — Changing an alien's classification from one category to another.

Conditional status — Basis on which an alien who marries a U.S. citizen and obtains permanent resident status can remain in the U.S. for two years.

Hardship waiver — Waiver granted by the attorney general if removing an alien would result in undue hardship to a U.S. citizen.

Immigration and Naturalization Service (INS) — Federal agency under the Department of Justice authorized to implement the immigration laws.

Private bill — Legislation intended to affect only the person named in the law.

Visa — Government grant of entry to the country for aliens.

EDITED JUDICIAL DECISIONS

The first case discusses procedures involved in an adjustment of status, and the second decision analyzes what is considered a "material misrepresentation" on an immigrant visa application.

SANGHAVI v. IMMIGRATION AND NATURALIZATION SERVICE
614 F.2d 511(5th Cir. 1980)

Appellant Manoj Manilal Sanghavi is a native and citizen of India who last entered the United States in December 1973 as a nonimmigrant student with authority to remain in this country until June 30, 1975. Sanghavi concedes deportability but asserts that the Immigration and Naturalization Service (the "Service") improperly rejected his application for permanent residency on account of his eligibility for investor status under the Service's regulations. See 8 C.F.R. §212.8(b)(4) (1976). We find that the Service was justified in rejecting appellant's application for investor status, and accordingly affirm.

Section 245(a)(2) of the Immigration and Nationality Act (the "Act"), 8 U.S.C. §1255(a)(2), provides that the status of an alien may be adjusted to that of a permanent resident by the Attorney General in his discretion and under such regulations as he may prescribe if the alien is eligible to receive an immigrant visa and is admissible to this country for permanent residence. Under section 212 of the Act, 8 U.S.C. §1182, a nonimmigrant alien is ineligible to receive a visa unless he possesses a labor certificate issued under section 212(a)(14) of the Act, 8 U.S.C. §1182(a)(14), but Sanghavi did not qualify under that section. However, the Attorney General has promulgated regulations providing an exemption from the labor certificate requirement for any alien who establishes on Form I-526 that he is seeking to enter the United States for the purpose of engaging in a commercial or agricultural enterprise in which he has invested, or is actively in the process of investing, capital totaling at least $10,000, and who establishes that he has had at least 1 year's experience or training qualifying him to engage in such enterprise. 8 C.F.R. §212.8(b)(4) (1976). Sanghavi contends that he was qualified under this regulation to obtain a visa to satisfy the eligibility requirement of section 245(a)(2) and thus becomes entitled to permanent resident status.

Appellant applied for investor status on February 26, 1976. On February 28, 1977, the District Director found that Sanghavi had not met the requirements and an order to show cause why he should not be deported was subsequently issued. After a series of hearings, an immigration judge, in a decision dated February 1, 1979, affirmed the denial of adjustment of status. Appellant was given until April 1, 1979 to depart the country voluntarily. Prior to the deadline, he filed an appeal with the Board of Immigration Appeals. After oral argument, the Board dismissed the appeal and issued a written order dated September 4, 1979 giving appellant 30 days to leave the country voluntarily. Appellant then petitioned for review in this court pursuant to section 106 of the Act, 8 U.S.C. §1105a.

In assessing appellant's claim for investor status, we note that an alien bears the burden of proving that he is eligible for relief from deportation. *Pelaez v. INS*, 513 F.2d 303, 305 (5th Cir. 1975), cert. denied, 423 U.S. 892, 96 S. Ct. 190, 46 L. Ed. 2d 124 (1975); *Vosough-Kia v. INS*, 441 F.2d 545 (9th Cir. 1971). Therefore, in the context of this case, appellant had the burden of proving that he had invested or was actively in the process of investing capital totaling $10,000 or more. At each step of the administrative proceeding, the appropriate authority found that appellant had not met this burden. We agree.

On his application, appellant purported to have invested the requisite amount in a business known as Kathy's Office Supply which was involved in office furniture sales. The business was operated from appellant's home and had no other employees besides appellant. The record shows that appellant testified that his business was only worth $2,000 and $3,000 as of August 1977, more than a year after the date of his initial application. Indeed, it was not until the middle of 1978 that appellant's business allegedly had a net worth greater than $10,000. Appellant asserts two reasons justifying his claim of investor status. First, he argues that the record shows that he obtained an $8,000 loan prior to his application which should have been aggregated with his capital investment to reach the $10,000 figure. Second, appellant relies on the language "actively in the process of investing" used in the regulation for the proposition that the alleged subsequent investment in 1978 was sufficient to qualify him for investor status at the time of his application.

With respect to the $8,000 loan, the evidence adduced during the administrative proceeding is exceedingly sparse. The District Director found that of appellant's initial investment, $8,000 was in the form of a loan which was used to purchase office furniture for a specific job. When payment was received from the customer in question, the loan was repaid. While appellant stated that he made the loan "to establish his credit" and to purchase inventory, there is no documentary evidence concerning the loan. More importantly, there is no evidence concerning whether the money was permanently invested in appellant's business. Even accepting appellant's assertion that he used the money to purchase furniture, it is not clear whether this money was in fact "invested" in the business or merely used to finance a one-time purchase of furniture for sale as opposed to permanent investment in inventory. As a result, appellant has not met his burden of proving that the proceeds of the loan were invested in his business.

Appellant's second argument fares no better. To be sure, the language "actively in the process" of investing indicates that the regulation envisions a future-oriented examination of an alien's investment. Thus, the mere fact that $10,000 was not invested at the date of application would not be determinative of an alien's claim of investor status. Even though the regulation embraces future investment, this does not require the conclusion that appellant's alleged investment more than two years after his application was sufficient to meet the $10,000 requirement. Indeed, the regulation calls for the alien to be actively in the process of investing which necessarily means that he must have the actual intent to invest the required funds and be pursuing a plan of investment. There is no evidence in the record that appellant had any definite plan or actual intent to invest additional capital at the time of his application. See Matter of Heidari, Interim Dec. 2581 (BIA 1977). Appellant's unsupported statement of his subjective intent to invest additional capital at some undetermined future time, especially in light of the fact that subsequent investment, if it actually occurred, did not take place until well over two years from the date of his application, is insufficient to meet his burden of proving that he was "actively in the process of investing." A holding to the contrary would eliminate the objective requirement of the investor status regulation by permitting an alien to allege in the most conclusory terms his future intent to meet the dollar amount of investment under the regulation without any specific plan for actually doing so.

Since appellant's contentions are without merit, we affirm.

AFFIRMED.

FORBES v. IMMIGRATION AND NATURALIZATION SERVICE

48 F.3d 439 (9th Cir. 1995)

The Board of Immigration Appeals (BIA) dismissed the appeal of the Forbes family. It upheld the findings of the Immigration Judge (IJ) that the principal petitioner, Dr. Ronald Ingle Forbes, willfully made a material misrepresentation on his immigration application and was therefore deportable, and that the eligibility of the other family members depended on Dr. Forbes' status. The Forbes family petitions this court to review the BIA's decision.

I.

Petitioners, a husband, wife, and their eight children, are citizens of Canada. Most of the facts relevant to this case involve the husband, Ronald Ingle Forbes, who was born in Jamaica on October 8, 1921, and is a medical doctor licensed to practice in Canada and the United States. On September 1, 1977, Dr. Forbes, his wife, and seven of the children were granted immigrant visas by the United States Consul in Vancouver, British Columbia based on investments made in the United States. Later that day, they were admitted into the United States at Blaine, Washington as permanent residents. The INS subsequently granted a second preference immigrant visa petition that Dr. Forbes submitted on behalf of his son, Martin Stuart Forbes.

On December 15, 1978, ten Orders to Show Cause were issued charging the family with deportability under section 241(a)(1) of the Immigration and Nationality Act (INA). The orders alleged that Dr. Forbes had been arrested and charged with conspiracy to commit an indictable offense, and was ineligible to receive a visa as he willfully neglected to tell the consular officer that he had been arrested and criminal charges against him were pending at the time he applied for a visa[;] therefore his visa was procured by fraud or by willfully misrepresenting a material fact.

The orders alleged that the other family members were ineligible because they were admitted based on Dr. Forbes' application.

The basis for the allegation involves an incident that occurred on May 13, 1977. On March 20, 1977, Dr. Forbes was charged in Vancouver, British Columbia with obtaining credit by false pretenses. He did not appear as scheduled in Vancouver Provincial Court on April 29, 1977 due to illness. A bench warrant was then issued in order to preserve the court's jurisdiction, but Crown Counsel and the court agreed that the warrant would not be executed provided that Dr. Forbes appeared on May 13, 1977. Although Dr. Forbes did appear on May 13, the Sheriff's Department erroneously executed the warrant. Dr. Forbes was apprehended while in the courthouse. He was booked and fingerprinted. The court and Crown Counsel commented that the incident was unfortunate and should not have occurred. On May 24, 1977, Dr. Forbes' attorney sent Dr. Forbes a letter stating that the "arrest was not proper and [was] illegal," and that Crown Counsel "agreed that you should never have been arrested and he apologized on behalf of the Crown."

On August 16, 1979, a stay of proceedings was entered with respect to the criminal charges pending against Dr. Forbes in Canada. Evidence in the record indicates that such a stay is equivalent to a dismissal. See Canada Crim. Code §579.

On his visa application, which he completed on June 9, 1977, Dr. Forbes answered no to question 34, which reads, "Have you ever been arrested, convicted or confined in a prison, or have you ever been placed in a poorhouse or other charitable institution? (If answer is Yes, explain)."

At the deportation hearing on February 3, 1979, Dr. Forbes testified that because the arrest was improper and he received an apology, he resolved in his mind that it was not an arrest. He said that he had no doubt that he had not been arrested, but was unsure of how to answer the question on the application. He consulted his attorney, who told him to answer no. He stated, "I had resolved it, that my answer was correct. Not that I was avoiding anything, but that my answer was correct." At the hearing on August 19, 1986, Dr. Forbes answered yes to the question, "So you had actually been arrested and the Court apologized for the fact that you were arrested, isn't that what happened?"

The government introduced the affidavits of two INS investigators who had spoken with Mr. Burgoon, the U.S. Consular Officer who interviewed Dr. Forbes regarding his application. Mr. Burgoon "stated that he had not been made aware of the criminal proceedings pending against Mr. Forbes when the visa was issued and if he had been the visa would not have been issued at that time."

The Immigration Judge ("IJ") found that Dr. Forbes and his family were deportable. He stated:

I am satisfied . . . that Ronald Forbes, either willfully or deliberately, failed to reveal to the Consular Officer that he had been arrested and that charges were pending. I find that the failure of the respondent to truthfully answer the questions on the application for the visa cut off a line of inquiry which could have resulted in a denial of the application for immigrant visas.

The IJ further found that the other family members would not have been eligible for issuance of immigrant visas because their eligibility depended on Dr. Forbes' eligibility. Petitioners appealed to the BIA, arguing that there was no fraud or willful misrepresentation of any material fact in applying for the immigrant visas. The BIA concluded that Dr. Forbes willfully made a material misrepresentation on his application and was therefore deportable. The Forbes family petitions this court to review the BIA decision. We grant the petition because we hold that Dr. Forbes' misrepresentation was not material.

II.

To find Dr. Forbes excludable under section 212(a)(19) of the INA, the BIA must have found by clear, unequivocal, and convincing evidence that Dr. Forbes procured his visa by willful misrepresentation of a material fact. *Hernandez-Robledo v. INS*, 777 F.2d 536, 539 (9th Cir. 1985). See 8 U.S.C. §1182(a)(19) (1977). We must determine whether there is reasonable, substantial, and probative evidence in the record as a whole to support the BIA's conclusion. *Gameros-Hernandez v. INS*, 883 F.2d 839, 841 (9th Cir. 1989). The issue of materiality is a legal question. *Kungys v. United States*, 485 U.S. 759, 772, 99 L. Ed. 2d 839, 108 S. Ct. 1537 (1988). "In determining whether an alien has procured his visa by fraud or willful misrepresentation of a material fact within the meaning of section 212(a)(19), it is appropriate to examine the circumstances as they existed at the time the visa was issued." Matter of Healy and Goodchild, 17 I&N Dec. 22, 28 (BIA 1979).

A.

The requirement in §212(a)(19) of fraud or willful misrepresentation is satisfied by a finding that the misrepresentation was deliberate and voluntary. *Espinoza-Espinoza v. INS*, 554 F.2d 921, 925 (9th Cir. 1977). Proof of an intent to deceive is not required. Id. Rather, knowledge of the falsity of a representation is sufficient. Id. (citing Matter of Hui, 15 I&N Dec. 288 (BIA 1975)).

It is clear from the record that Dr. Forbes was arrested. He acknowledged as much in his own testimony. Moreover, his attorney referred to the incident as an arrest in the letter explaining why it happened. Dr. Forbes contends that any misstatement was not willful because he had strong rational bases for concluding that no arrest had occurred. His argument is essentially that he was not aware of the falsity of his statement when he made it.

The BIA disagreed, noting that Dr. Forbes conceded at his hearing that he had been arrested. It stated:

The question on the visa application is not circumscribed or limited nor does it legitimately permit interpretations of the term "arrest." We find therefore the principal respondent's interpretation of that question unwarranted and unreasonable in view of the unambiguous question contained in the visa application. . . . By permitting [an explanation of any affirmative answer], the visa application clearly encompasses an event such as this respondent experienced even if we accept that he honestly believed his interpretation of such event. . . . Clearly, in light of the broad nature of the visa inquiry on this issue and the fact that a visa applicant is requested to explain an affirmative answer on this issue, it is not credible for the principal respondent to assert that he did not believe an affirmative reply was required in his case.

The BIA also refused to excuse Dr. Forbes' misstatement based on his testimony that he followed his attorney's advice. The BIA assumed that Dr. Forbes testified truthfully regarding his interpretation of the event when he stated that at the time he filled out the application, he had resolved in his mind that the incident was not an arrest. However, it rejected Dr. Forbes' testimony that he believed when he completed the application that his answer to the question was correct.

There was substantial evidence supporting the BIA's conclusion that Dr. Forbes' misstatement was willful. It may have given undue weight to Dr. Forbes' acknowledgment at the August 19, 1986 hearing that he had actually been arrested. Dr. Forbes' concession that he was arrested is not necessarily inconsistent with his earlier testimony that, at the time he completed the application, there was no doubt in his mind that he had not been arrested. Nevertheless, Dr. Forbes was apprehended and fingerprinted. He signed a booking sheet. The letter he received from his attorney referred to the incident as an arrest. And the question on the application allows for an explanation. Even if Dr. Forbes believed he had not been arrested because the warrant should not have been executed and the court apologized, the BIA did not err in concluding that he was aware that he should have answered yes.

B.

The test of whether "concealments or misrepresentations [are] material is whether they have a natural tendency to influence the decisions of the Immigration and Naturalization Service." Kungys, 485 U.S. at 772. "A misrepresentation or concealment can be said to have such a tendency . . . if honest representations 'would predictably have disclosed other facts relevant to [the applicant's] qualifications.'" Id. at 783 (Brennan, J., concurring) (quoting id. at 774 (opinion of Scalia, J., joined by Rehnquist, C.J., and Brennan, J.)). The government must "produce evidence sufficient to raise a fair inference that a statutory disqualifying fact actually existed." Id. at 783 (Brennan, J., concurring). See *United States v. Puerta,* 982 F.2d 1297, 1303-04 (9th Cir. 1992) (reviewing opinions in Kungys and concluding that "Justice Brennan's view of materiality controls").

Disclosure of the arrest incident would predictably have revealed the charges pending against Dr. Forbes, which were relevant to his qualifications. Thus the misrepresentation had a natural tendency to influence the decision of the INS. We must therefore determine whether the government's evidence was "sufficient to raise a fair inference that a statutory disqualifying fact actually existed." Kungys, 485 U.S. at 783.

As evidence that the misrepresentation was material, the government introduced affidavits of two INS investigators who spoke with Mr. Burgoon, the consular officer who had interviewed Dr. Forbes. The INS investigators related Mr. Burgoon's description of his policy regarding immigrant visas:

Burgoon stated that it was his policy to hold issuance of an immigrant visa in abeyance with regard to any applicant who had criminal proceedings pending against him until final disposition of the proceeding was determined. He stated that had he known that criminal proceedings were pending against Forbes at the time the visa was issued he would not have issued the visa until final disposition of the pending proceeding had been made.

Petitioners argue that they would not have been disqualified if Dr. Forbes had disclosed the pending charges. While Mr. Burgoon may have delayed issuance of their visas, he would not have denied the application. They contend that the visas would have been issued when the charges were subsequently dropped. The BIA found that Dr. Forbes' misrepresentation was material because it determined that the Consul would not have issued the visas had it known of the charges. The BIA was "unwilling to conclude . . . that the action of the prosecutor in the criminal matter is a dismissal of the charges even if the practical effect may be the same."

We hold that the charges against Dr. Forbes had been dismissed by the time the IJ rendered his decision. The record contains substantial, uncontradicted evidence that under Canada law, the stay of proceedings is equivalent to a dismissal. See Canada Crim. Code §579.[508]. The BIA provided no reason for its unwillingness to accept that the charges were dismissed, there is no evidence that they were still pending, and the government concedes that the evidence indicates the charges were dismissed.

Pending charges, without more, do not lead to disqualification under Mr. Burgoon's policy. If Mr. Burgoon had known about the charges, he would have held issuance of the visas in abeyance; he would not have denied them. The government has not suggested that there is any other disqualifying fact that an investigation would have uncovered, so the visas would have been issued after the charges were dropped.

The government contends that because we must examine the circumstances as they existed at the time the visas were issued, the relevant fact is that the Consul would not have issued the visas on September 1, 1977 had it been aware of the pending charges. This argument misses the point. The relevant fact is that the government has presented no evidence "that a statutory disqualifying fact actually existed" on September 1, 1977. Kungys, 485 U.S. at 783. Indeed, the government did not even produce evidence showing that the INS would have conducted an investigation as a result of the pending charges. The BIA therefore erred in concluding that the misrepresentation was material.

We draw support for our holding from the Tenth Circuit's decision in *United States v. Sheshtawy,* 714 F.2d 1038 (10th Cir. 1983). The facts in Sheshtawy are almost identical to the circumstances in the instant case. Sheshtawy was arrested and charged with concealing stolen property shortly before his naturalization hearing. He subsequently filled out an INS form in connection with his application and answered no to a question asking whether he had ever been arrested. Sheshtawy was naturalized, and the charges were later dismissed. Id. at 1039. Evidence in the record indicated that if the INS had known of the arrest, it would have delayed its decision and conducted an investigation. Id. at 1040. The court held that the misrepresentation was not material since the government did not "attempt to show that an investigation would have turned up other facts warranting a denial of citizenship." Id. at 1040. Although Sheshtawy involved an application for naturalization rather than permanent residence, its holding coincides with the Kungys requirement that the government must produce evidence raising an inference that a disqualify fact existed.

The misrepresentation on Dr. Forbes' application was not material. The BIA therefore erred in finding petitioners excludable.

PETITION GRANTED.

EXERCISES

1. A client of the law office where you work is a major U.S. corporation that wants to transfer one of its South American managers to the U.S. to work in the corporation's headquarters for three years. Indicate the procedures and forms you would follow and complete to assist the client.
2. The foreign fiancée of an American citizen comes to the U.S. on a K visa in order to marry. The wedding is set for 60 days after her arrival, but one week before the ceremony the mother of the groom becomes seriously ill. The wedding is postponed for three months. The fiancée stays in the U.S. to help nurse her future mother-in-law. After the wedding, the bride attempts to have her status adjusted, but the INS officer determines that she does not qualify because she was unlawfully in the United States once her K visa expired. Argue on the bride's behalf.
3. What is your opinion of using private legislation to admit aliens to the United States who would otherwise not qualify for admission? Explain.
4. An alien obtains a nonimmigrant visa in the hope of being able to adjust his status once he is in the United States. Do you believe he should be entitled to adjust his status? Was his nonimmigrant visa valid? How would you prove his intent? Explain your answer.
5. In order to understand U.S. laws better, choose a foreign country and contact its consular office to find out what you would have to do to obtain an immigrant or nonimmigrant visa to enter that country. Determine which categories you might qualify for, and any restrictions on your stay. Compare these requirements to the U.S. counterpart.

Chapter Six

REMOVAL PRIOR TO ENTRY INTO THE UNITED STATES

CHAPTER PREVIEW

Prior to the enactment of the Illegal Immigration Reform and Immigrant Responsibility Act of 1996 (1996 Act) (see Chapter One), **exclusion** was the term used to describe the denial of entry, or admission, to an alien attempting to enter the United States. Since 1996, exclusion and deportation (see Chapter Seven) have been merged into one term, **removal**. Consequently, in order to distinguish between those aliens who have been denied admission and those who have been admitted but are being expelled, the concepts are being called **removal prior to entry** and **removal subsequent to entry**. This chapter will focus on the grounds for denying an alien entry into the United States and the procedures incident to that determination. The following chapter will discuss removal subsequent to entry.

Removal prior to entry takes place either at the U.S. border when the alien attempts to enter, or at the U.S. consular office overseas when the alien applies for a visa. Currently, three broad grounds are most commonly used as the basis for denying entry: the health of the alien, the alien's prior criminal activity, and any threat to national security that could occur by permitting the alien to come to the United States. Many of these grounds have existed since the beginning of federal regulation of immigration (see Chapter One), but they have been broadened because of changing health and security issues. Each of these grounds will be examined in turn.

Pursuant to the 1996 Act, a **visa waiver pilot program** was created that permits citizens and nationals of 24 specified countries to enter the United States without first obtaining a visa, but these persons may be summarily turned away at any U.S. border. All other aliens seeking entry are entitled to challenge the denial of entry at a **removal proceeding** (formerly known as an **exclusion hearing**).

This chapter will discuss the grounds for denying entry into the United States and the procedures the alien may institute in order to seek a reversal of that denial.

GROUNDS FOR REMOVAL PRIOR TO ENTRY

The three most common grounds used as the basis to deny an alien entry into the United States are

1. health (INA §212(a)(1))
2. criminal activity (INA §212(a)(2))
3. security risks (NA §212(a)(3))

Removal Based on Health

Since the Chinese Exclusion Act of 1882 (Chapter One), U.S. immigration policy has been predicated on the concept that entry to the country should be barred for persons who are deemed to be "undesirable." Current law specifies that an alien who has a communicable disease of public health significance will be denied entry. The diseases that are considered to provide a threat to the public health, thereby providing the basis for denying entry, are

- tuberculosis
- HIV and AIDS
- syphilis (in its infectious state)
- gonorrhea
- leprosy
- other communicable diseases.

Evidence of having one of these diseases that appears on the alien's visa application gives rise to denying the petition.

Example: An alien is HIV-positive and wishes to emigrate to the United States to be with his only family, adult brothers and a sister, who are lawful permanent residents of the United States. On his application for a visa the alien indicates his HIV status. His application could be rejected based on his health.

The rationale behind excluding aliens with communicable diseases is to protect the health and welfare of U.S. citizens and lawful permanent residents. As stated in the 1952 Immigration and Nationality Act as amended by the 1990 Immigration Act (INA), any alien who suffers from a physical or mental disease and/or demonstrates behavior associated with that disease who may pose a threat to the property, safety, or welfare of the alien or others, must be excluded from entry into the United States.

Despite the foregoing, for humanitarian reasons the attorney general may waive removal of families of U.S. citizens or lawful permanent residents and may also waive the health-related grounds to enable the alien to attend conferences, receive medical treatment, or to pay a short visit to the United States as a nonimmigrant.

Example: In the preceding example, because the alien infected with HIV is a family member of lawful permanent residents, the attorney general may waive his removal on humanitarian grounds.

Example: An alien who is HIV-positive wishes to come to the United States as an immigrant under a work-related visa. The alien is not related to anyone residing in the United Sates. In this instance it is most likely that his application will be denied based on public health grounds.

Example: An alien who is HIV-positive wishes to come to the United States to attend a conference on HIV and AIDS. Because this person is seeking a nonimmigrant visa to attend a conference, it is most likely that the attorney general will waive the health requirement.

Removal Based on Criminal Activity

Since 1875, aliens who have been engaged in certain criminal activities have been denied entry into the United States. Currently, the United States will deny entry to aliens who have been convicted of felonies and criminal activity involving moral turpitude. The term "crimes of moral turpitude" is a fairly loose one, and includes such activities as prostitution, criminal breaches of fiduciary obligations, embezzlement, and so forth. Additionally, the alien will be denied entry if the alien had been convicted of violating a law relating to controlled substances (drugs).

Example: A Colombian who has been convicted of engaging in criminal activity involving drug smuggling wants to emigrate to the United States. Under current law, this alien's application will be denied.

Example: A woman worked as a prostitute ever since she was orphaned at age 13. She has several prostitution convictions, but now wants to start a new life in the United States. Her application for a visa would probably be denied because of her convictions for crimes involving moral turpitude (prostitution).

The law does provide for exceptions for minor crimes and juvenile offenses, but for the most part, if the alien was convicted of engaging in serious criminal activity or if the U.S. consular office "reasonably believes" that the alien has engaged in drug trafficking (even if the alien has no conviction or arrest record), the application for entry will be denied.

Example: The U.S. consular officer in Bangkok believes that a Thai citizen who wishes to emigrate to the United States has been involved in drug trafficking. The Thai citizen has had no arrests or convictions, but is known to be a close family member and friend of convicted drug traffickers, and has been supported by these family members. In this instance the U.S. consular officer may have a "reasonable belief" that this alien is engaged in drug trafficking and may deny the application for a visa.

Removal Based on National Security

Aliens who are believed to be seeking entry "solely, principally, or in order" to engage in activities that violate U.S. espionage laws, or whose purpose is the overthrow of the U.S. government by unlawful means, may be denied entry based on a national security concern. Also, aliens who have engaged in terrorist activities, or who are believed likely to do so in the future, are to be denied admission to the United States. In order to deny the application, the INS officer must base the decision on the likelihood of the alien engaging in such activities in the United States, and that such activities are harmful to the public order, welfare and safety. This ground for removal has generated greater activity and scrutiny since September 11, 2001.

Example: An alien belongs to a known terrorist organization that has declared its intention of bombing major buildings in "imperialist" countries. The organization has stated that the United States is one such imperialist nation. The alien's application for entry should be denied.

Example: A member of a European socialist party wishes to emigrate to the United States in order to bring about a socialist government in the U.S. The party to which the alien belongs believes in grass roots movements to bring about socialist change by lawful means. This alien does not appear to meet the criteria of posing a security threat to the United States.

Two specific organizations have been singled out by statute as automatically being a threat to national security: the Communist Party and the Nazi Party. Any person who belongs to a Communist or totalitarian organization may be excluded from entry into the United States, unless the alien can demonstrate that such membership was mandatory or that the membership was disavowed at least two years prior to applying for admission to the United States.

Example: The former manager of a factory in Russia wants to emigrate to the United States. In order to manage a factory under the Soviet regime, the Russian was required to belong to the Communist Party. The alien can demonstrate that this membership was involuntary and was primarily related to working as a factory manager. In this instance, the Russian's application may be approved.

Any person who participated or was affiliated with the Nazis is also excludable as a national security concern. At first blush this may appear to be anachronistic, but there has been a rise in Nazism in Europe over the past two decades, and the law, dating from World War II, may still have application.

Example: A 20-year-old German youth wants to live in the United States. He has been an active member of the Nazi Party since he was 17 years old. His application for admission should be denied under current law.

Other Grounds for Removal Prior to Entry

In addition to the three main grounds for removal discussed above, current law also indicates ten other grounds that may be used as the basis for denying entry to an alien. These grounds are

1. Public Charge (INA §212(a)(4)). As discussed in Chapter One, since 1891 the United States has denied entry to persons who are paupers or who are likely to become public charges simply as a matter of public policy.

2. No Labor Certificate (INA §212(a)(5)). If an alien is attempting to enter the United States under one of the employment-related categories that requires a labor certificate, and none has been issued, the alien's application should be denied. (See Chapter Three for a discussion of the employment-related categories.)

3. An alien will be denied entry to the United States if:

   a) the alien was removed after entry within the preceding five years (INA §212(a)(6))
   b) the alien was denied entry within one year of the current application (INA §212(a)(6))
   c) the alien was removed after entry because of having committed an aggravated felony in the United States within the past 20 years (INA §212(a)(6)).

Also note that there are greater penalties with respect to the ability to reenter the country for persons who are removed pursuant to the 1996 Act who were unlawfully resident in the United States. For a discussion of this particular class of alien, see the next chapter.

Example: An alien residing in the United States was convicted of aggravated assault and felony murder 19 years ago. The alien was removed and now seeks reentry. Because the conviction was for an aggravated felony 19 years ago, the alien's application should be denied.

4. Making a Material Misrepresentation of Fact on the Application (INA §212(a)(6)). Provided that the misrepresentation was knowingly made, an alien cannot be granted entry based on false information.

Example: An alien states on her application that she is the illegitimate daughter of a U.S. citizen, and provides a birth certificate as proof. The certificate is forged. The alien should be denied entry.

5. Stowaways (INA §2121(a)(6)). Aliens who attempt to enter the United States by stowing away on a vessel are denied entry.

6. Persons Who Have Aided or Abetted the Illegal Entry of Other Aliens (INA §2121(a)(6)). These persons are also barred from entering the United States if the assistance is rendered outside the country.

Example: A Mexican citizen has been operating a bus "service" to take migrant Mexican workers across the U.S. border illegally. This Mexican now wishes to emigrate to the U.S. Because of the alien's activities in aiding other Mexicans to enter the country without documentation, this application for entry should be denied.

7. The Unexcused Failure to Provide Travel Documents (INA §212(a)(7)). This is primarily a technical violation that may be cured by obtaining the appropriate documentation. The travel documents that an alien is supposed to possess to enter the United States are

   a) a valid visa
   b) a reentry permit if the alien was already legally in the United States
   c) a valid ID card for Canadians and Mexicans
   d) other entry documents, such as a valid passport.

8. Persons Who are Permanently Ineligible for Citizenship (INA §212(a)(8))

9. Aliens Who Have Previously Been in the United States But Who Left to Avoid U.S. Military Service (INA §212(a)(9))

10. Aliens Who Enter the United States in Order to Practice Polygamy (INA §212(a)(9))

REMOVAL PROCEEDINGS

Removal proceedings, formerly known as **exclusion hearings**, apply to aliens who are not yet in the territory of the United States. Therefore, these proceedings are held either at the U.S. consular office abroad or at the U.S. border. The "border" includes any international airport in the United States. If the alien is stopped at the border, he or she may be able to travel away from the border until the hearing date, pending investigation of the alien's case. This provision of permitting the alien limited entry into the United States is called **parole**. However, even though the alien may be physically present in the country, the alien is still not legally within U.S. territory.

Example: An alien buys a plane ticket from her homeland in Africa to Chicago's O'Hare airport. At customs she is stopped because she has no valid visa. She claims that she is seeking asylum in the United States from political persecution in her homeland. Until the claim can be investigated, the INS officer grants her parole, letting her stay in the U.S. until her hearing. At this time she is physically but not legally in the United States. Legally she is considered to still be at the border.

The Proceedings

The burden rests with the alien to prove that he or she has the right to enter the United States. The proceedings for persons who are subject to removal prior to entry commence with a Notice to Applicant for Admission Detained for Hearing, **Form I-222**. The Notice does not make specific allegations with respect to why admission was denied. The proceeding is closed to the public unless the alien wishes to have it open. If the proceeding results in the affirmation of the denial of entry, the alien is returned to the border where he or she attempted to enter. The alien still has the right to challenge the conclusions of the proceedings by a **writ of habeas corpus** (writ demanding the production of a person who is being detained) filed with the federal court. It is important to note that aliens seeking admission to the United States are not afforded any constitutional protections because they are not yet legally within the United States, even if the proceedings take place at a U.S. border. The only legal safeguard afforded aliens in these situations are the procedures specified in the immigration statutes.

At the time of this writing, the procedures for removal proceedings are undergoing revisions pursuant to the 1996 Act. The 1996 Act mandates that the procedures for these proceedings be streamlined, but no procedures have been finalized. Also, many of the procedures are similar to those for removal subsequent to entry. These will be discussed in the next chapter.

A special procedure exists for people fleeing Haiti. If ships carrying Haitians are intercepted by the U.S. Coast Guard, and the Haitians seeking entry to the United States can demonstrate that they qualify for refugee status (see Chapter Eight), they will be permitted to enter the United States; otherwise, they will be forcibly returned to Haiti. This procedure is known as **interdiction**, and the only country with which the United States has such a policy is Haiti.

ETHICAL CONSIDERATIONS

Many of the determinations made with respect to denying entry to the United States at the discretion of the INS officer. This discretionary power can be abused. For example, it is the INS officer who determines whether there is a "reasonable belief" that an alien is involved in drug trafficking if no actual arrest or conviction of the alien can be discovered. These same officials decide whether or not an alien poses a threat to the security of the United States, or that a person's mental or physical state may pose a threat to the alien or others. In all of these instances, this INS officer is given little guidance or direct instructions to use in arriving at a conclusion, and the officer may be influenced by personal prejudices. In a recent incident, a Swiss national who suffers with AIDS was turned back at New York's airport because of his health when his medication was discovered in his suitcase. This alien was coming to the United States on a nonimmigrant visa to participate in an AIDS conference at the request of the United States government. The INS officer simply did not want an AIDS-infected alien to enter the country.

It is these same officials who can permit aliens to enter the United States under parole, and many aliens have "disappeared" once in U.S. territory. Many news programs have indicated that aliens often use the provisions of parole, which basically permits the INS officer to let the alien enter pending investigation of the alien's claims of refuge, to enter the United States unlawfully. These aliens do not necessarily have a valid basis for being granted parole, and so violate the laws.

Because the statute cannot anticipate every situation, human discretion is necessary for a fair interpretation of policy. This is especially true after the events of September 11, 2001. It would be an abuse of discretion if the INS officer began to profile members of certain religions.

CHAPTER REVIEW

Aliens seeking entry to the United States may be subject to removal proceedings if they do not meet the requirements for entry. Since the beginning of U.S. immigration law, the federal government has established standards to keep out persons who are considered "undesirable." Under current regulations, the three most commonly used grounds for denying admission are the health status of the alien, the alien's past criminal activities, and the threat the alien may pose to national security. In addition to these three major grounds for removal prior to entry, ten other categories exist, all based on American policy to keep out paupers and those persons who are guilty of some fraudulent activity with respect to the immigration statutes.

An alien who is denied entry may seek an administrative review by means of a removal proceeding. During the proceeding, the alien is not subject to general constitutional safeguards, but is only afforded the protections specified in the statutes. If admission is still denied at the conclusion of the proceeding, the alien's only recourse is a writ of habeas corpus to a federal court.

Many of the decisions with respect to granting or denying entry to the United States are based on the INS officer's opinions and beliefs with respect to the alien. Because of the discretionary nature of these decisions, it is possible that there may be instances in which the U.S. official abuses his or her discretion. The alien's only recourse, as stated above, is to seek judicial review of the denial of entry.

CHAPTER VOCABULARY

Exclusion — Process of denying an alien the right to enter the U.S. (now termed "removal").

Exclusion hearing — Administrative hearing to determine an alien's right to enter the United States; now called removal proceedings.

Interdiction — Special procedure for Haitians attempting to enter the U.S.

Moral turpitude — Behavior considered reprehensible by society's norms.

Parole — Procedure for allowing aliens limited entry into the United States pending investigation prior to a removal proceeding.

Removal — The process of denying entry to aliens and removing undocumented aliens from the country.

Removal prior to entry — Term under the 1996 act for what used to be called exclusion.

Removal proceeding — Term under the 1996 act for what used to be called exclusion or deportation hearing.

Removal subsequent to entry — Term under the 1996 act for what used to be called deportation.

Visa waiver pilot program — Special provision for persons from 24 specified countries to come to the U.S. without first obtaining a visa.

Writ of habeas corpus — Writ demanding the production of a person who is being detained.

EDITED JUDICIAL DECISIONS

The two decisions included in this section are designed to highlight the material discussed in the text of the chapter. The first case, *Leng May Ma v. Barber*, underscores the problem of parole, and the second case, *Solis-Muela v. INS*, concerns an alien who was convicted of an act of moral turpitude and misrepresented a material fact in his visa application.

LENG MAY MA v. BARBER
357 U.S. 185 (1958).

This is a habeas corpus case involving §243 (h) of the Immigration and Nationality Act, which authorizes the Attorney General "to withhold deportation of any alien within the United States to any country in which in his opinion the alien would be subject to physical persecution. . . ." Claiming to be an alien "within the United States" by reason of her parole in this country while her admissibility was being determined, petitioner contends that she is eligible to receive the benefactions of §243 (h). The Attorney General contends that the section is applicable only to aliens who, in contemplation of law, have entered the United States. He argues that petitioner has never enjoyed that status because she eventually was found ineligible for entry and ordered excluded. The District Court denied a writ of habeas corpus, and the Court of Appeals affirmed. 241 F.2d 85. We granted certiorari. 353 U.S. 981 (1957). We conclude that petitioner's parole did not alter her status as an excluded alien or otherwise bring her "within the United States" in the meaning of §243 (h).

Petitioner is a native of China who arrived in this country in May 1951 claiming United States citizenship on the ground that her father was a United States citizen. Pending determination of her claim, she at first was held in custody, but later, in August 1952, was released on parole. Some three months thereafter, having failed to establish her claim of citizenship, she was ordered excluded, and the Board of Immigration Appeals affirmed. She surrendered for deportation in January 1954, and thereafter applied for a stay of deportation under §243 (h) in which she alleged that her pending deportation to China would subject her to physical persecution and probable death at the hands of the existing government. Her petition for writ of habeas corpus followed administrative notification of her ineligibility for relief under that section. Petitioner does not challenge the validity of her exclusion order or the proceedings culminating therein. She merely contends that by virtue of her physical presence as a parolee she is "within the United States," and hence covered by §243 (h). The question, therefore, is wholly one of statutory construction.

It is important to note at the outset that our immigration laws have long made a distinction between those aliens who have come to our shores seeking admission, such as petitioner, and those who are within the United States after an entry, irrespective of its legality. In the latter instance the Court has recognized additional rights and privileges not extended to those in the former category who are merely "on the threshold of initial entry." *Shaughnessy v. United States ex rel. Mezei*, 345 U.S. 206, 212 (1953). See *Kwong Hai Chew v. Colding*, 344 U.S. 590, 596 (1953). The distinction was carefully preserved in Title II of the Immigration and Nationality Act. (Chapter 4) subjects those seeking admission to "exclusion proceedings" to determine whether they "shall be allowed to enter or shall be excluded and deported." 66 Stat. 200, 8 U. S. C. §1226 (a). On the other hand, Chapter 5 concerns itself with aliens who have already entered the United States and are subject to "expulsion," as distinguished from "exclusion," if they fall within certain "general classes of deportable aliens." 66 Stat. 204, 8 U. S. C. §1251. Proceedings for expulsion under Chapter 5 are commonly referred to as "deportation proceedings." Parenthetically, the word "deportation" appears also in Chapter 4 to refer to the return of excluded aliens from the country, but its use there reflects none of the technical gloss accompanying its use as a word of art in Chapter 5.

For over a half century this Court has held that the detention of an alien in custody pending determination of his admissibility does not legally constitute an entry though the alien is physically within the United States. *Shaughnessy v. United States ex rel. Mezei*, 345 U.S. 206, 215 (1953); *United States v. Ju Toy*, 198 U.S. 253, 263 (1905); *Ekiu v. United States*, 142 U.S. 651, 661 (1892). It seems quite clear that an alien so confined would not be "within the United States" for purposes of §243 (h). This, in fact, was conceded by respondents in the companion case, *Rogers v. Quan*, post, p. 193. Our question is whether the granting of temporary parole somehow effects a change in the alien's legal status. In §212 (d)(5) of the Act, generally a codification of the administrative practice pursuant to which petitioner was paroled, the Congress specifically provided that parole "shall not be regarded as an admission of the alien," and that after the return to custody the alien's case "shall continue to be dealt with in the same manner as that of any other applicant for admission to the United States." (Emphasis added.) Petitioner's concept of the effect of parole certainly finds no support in this statutory language.

This Court previously has had occasion to define the legal status of excluded aliens on parole. In *Kaplan v. Tod*, 267 U.S. 228 (1925), an excluded alien was paroled to a private Immigrant Aid Society pending deportation. The questions posed were whether the alien was "dwelling in the United States" within the meaning of a naturalization statute, and whether she had "entered or [was] found in the United States" for purpose of limitations. Mr. Justice Holmes disposed of the problem by explicitly equating parole with detention:

"The appellant could not lawfully have landed in the United States . . . , and until she legally landed 'could not have dwelt within the United States.' *Zartarian v. Billings*, 204 U.S. 170, 175. Moreover while she was at Ellis Island she was to be regarded as stopped at the boundary line and kept there unless and until her right to enter should be declared. *United States v. Ju Toy*, 198 U.S.253, 263. When her prison bounds were enlarged by committing her to the custody of the Hebrew Society, the nature of her stay within the territory was not changed. She was still in theory of law at the boundary line and had gained no foothold in the United States." 267 U.S., at 230.

We find no evidence that the Congress, in enacting §243 (h) in 1952, intended to depart from this interpretation.

The context in which §243 (h) appears in the Act persuasively indicates the scope of its provisions. As we have observed, Title II of the Act preserves the distinction between exclusion proceedings and deportation (expulsion) proceedings, Chapter 4 dealing with the former and Chapter 5 with the latter. Within the two chapters are enumerated separate administrative procedures for exclusion and expulsion, separate provisions for removal and transportation, and – most significantly – separate provisions for stays of deportation. Section 243 (h), under which petitioner claims relief, was inserted by the Congress not among Chapter 4's "Provisions Relating to Entry and Exclusion," but squarely within Chapter 5 – a strikingly inappropriate place if, as petitioner claims, it was intended to apply to excluded aliens.

The parole of aliens seeking admission is simply a device through which needless confinement is avoided while administrative proceedings are conducted. It was never intended to affect an alien's status, and to hold that petitioner's parole placed her legally "within the United States" is inconsistent with the congressional mandate, the administrative concept of parole, and the decisions of this Court. Physical detention of aliens is now the exception, not the rule, and is generally employed only as to security risks or those likely to abscond. See Annual Reports, Immigration and Naturalization Service, 1955, pp. 5-6; 1956, pp. 5-6. Certainly this policy reflects the humane qualities of an enlightened civilization. The acceptance of petitioner's position in this case, however, with its inherent suggestion of an altered parole status, would be quite likely to prompt some curtailment of current parole policy – an intention we are reluctant to impute to the Congress.

Affirmed.

SOLIS-MUELA v. IMMIGRATION & NATURALIZATION SERVICE

13 F.3d 372(10th Cir, 1993)

Raul Solis-Muela petitions for review of a decision of the Board of Immigration Appeals ("BIA") determining that Solis-Muela was deportable under section 241(a)(1) of the Immigration and Nationality Act ("Act"), 8 U.S.C. 1251(a)(1). We deny the petition for review and affirm the decision of the BIA.

BACKGROUND

Solis-Muela, a native and citizen of Mexico, was admitted to the United States in 1987. In 1988, the Immigration and Naturalization Service ("INS") issued an Order to Show Cause ("OSC") charging him with deportability under section 241(a)(1) of the Act on the ground that he was an alien: (1) excludable at the time of entry under section 212(a)(9) of the Act because he had been convicted of a crime involving moral turpitude; and (2) excludable under section 212(a)(19) of the Act because he had procured a visa or other documentation by fraud or misrepresentation of a material fact.

These charges were based on the fact that in 1986, Solis-Muela had been arrested and convicted by a Wyoming state court of disposing of stolen property in violation of Wyo. Stat. 6-3-403(a). The Wyoming state court imposed the following sentence on Solis-Muela:

IT IS THE SENTENCE OF THE COURT that the defendant, Raul Solis, be incarcerated in the Wyoming State Penitentiary ... for a period of not less than 1 year nor more than 5 years.... IT IS FURTHER ORDERED that all but 365 days of said sentence are hereby suspended. The defendant shall be incarcerated in the Campbell County Detention Center for a period of 365 days with credit to be given for 107 days already served....

IT IS FURTHER ORDERED that if the defendant voluntarily submits to deportation the defendant may be released from the Campbell County Detention Center immediately.

IT IS FURTHER ORDERED that if the defendant is deported the defendant may not return illegally to the United States. *State v. Solis*, Crim. No. 2191 (Dist. Ct. Wyo.), Admin. R. at 93. Solis-Muela elected to voluntarily submit to deportation, and he was immediately released from the county jail after serving 107 days, from where he returned to Mexico.

In March 1987, Solis-Muela applied for admission to the United States as an immigrant and received his immigrant visa. In so doing, he filled out an application for immigrant visa and alien registration, without the assistance of an attorney, in which he indicated he did not belong to any of the classes of aliens who are not admissible into the United States, including those convicted of a crime involving moral turpitude. He testified at his deportation hearing that he did not understand the meaning of the phrase "crime involving moral turpitude." Tr. of Hr'g, Admin. R. at 58. He further testified that when the consular officer asked him if he had been in jail, he stated that he had served 107 days in the county jail, that he did not have a court document with him, but that he did have a police certificate. Id. at 58-59. The police certificate which he showed to the officer states:

There is no record in this department that Raul Solis has ever been handled by reason for any violation or infraction of the law or ordinances of this city or county nor is any civil or criminal action pending against him at this time.

Police Clearance Letter, Admin. R. at 98. However, the following was typed in the lower left corner, beneath the notarization seal: "This person does have an arrest record through our department." Id.

Solis-Muela was thereafter issued a "green card" and entered the United States as a lawful resident alien until the OSC was issued in June 1988.

At his deportation hearing, Solis-Muela argued that he was not deportable under either charge. As to the first charge – having been convicted of a crime involving moral turpitude – he argued that his prior conviction for receiving stolen property fell within the so-called "petty offense" exception to deportability contained in section 212(a)(9). As to the second charge, he argued he did not obtain his visa by fraud or misrepresentation because he told the consular officer that he had been arrested and served 107 days in the county jail and he never attempted to hide the fact of his prior conviction.

After a hearing stretching over several days, an Immigration Judge ("IJ") found him deportable under both sections, and concluded he was ineligible for voluntary departure. The BIA affirmed the decision of the IJ and Solis-Muela filed this petition for review.

DISCUSSION

I. "Petty Offense" Exception

Solis-Muela argues the BIA erred in finding him deportable under section 241(a)(1), because his offense fell within the "petty offense" exception to excludability contained in section 212(a)(9), 8 U.S.C. 1182(a)(9). Under section 212(a) as it was written at the time of Solis-Muela's hearing in July, 1988:

(a) Except as otherwise provided in this Act, the following classes of aliens shall be ineligible to receive visas and shall be excluded from admission into the United States:

(9) Aliens who have been convicted of a crime involving moral turpitude .... An alien who would be excludable because of the conviction of an offense for which the sentence actually imposed did not exceed a term of imprisonment in excess of six months ... may be granted a visa and admitted to the United States if otherwise admissible ....

8 U.S.C. 1182(a)(9). Solis-Muela argues that the "sentence actually imposed" for purposes of the statute was the 107 days he served on the condition that he voluntarily depart the United States, and he therefore qualifies for exception to deportation because that sentence did not exceed six months.

The IJ and the BIA rejected that argument. The BIA held that "where the criminal court suspends the imposition of a sentence, no sentence has been actually imposed .... However, where the criminal court imposes a sentence and then suspends the execution of that sentence, the inquiry must focus on the length of the suspended sentence." In re: Solis-Muela, In Deportation Proceedings at 5 (citing Matter of Castro, 1988 BIA LEXIS 32, 19 I. & N. Dec. 692 (BIA 1988)). In this case, the BIA concluded that the Wyoming court "convicted the respondent of a crime involving moral turpitude, namely disposing of stolen property, and sentenced him to between one and five years imprisonment but suspended execution of all but one year of his sentence." In re: Solis-Muela, In Deportation Proceedings at 6. Thus, the BIA concluded that the "'sentence actually imposed' in [Solis-Muela's] case was between one and five years imprisonment so that the respondent does not qualify for relief under the exception in section 212(a)(9) of the Act." Id. We agree with the BIA.

The government in deportation proceedings must establish its allegations by "clear, unequivocal, and convincing evidence." *Woodby v. INS*, 385 U.S. 276, 285, 17 L. Ed. 2d 362, 87 S. Ct. 483 (1966). We review the BIA's legal conclusions de novo. *Kapcia v. INS*, 944 F.2d 702, 705 (10th Cir. 1991). Factual findings must be supported by substantial evidence. *Rivera-Zurita v. INS*, 946 F.2d 118, 120 (10th Cir. 1991). Here, our task is to determine if the BIA correctly determined that Solis-Muela was deportable under a particular statutory provision.

As the First Circuit has recently observed:

If the statutory language makes the intent of Congress clear and unambiguous, we give full effect to that intent; if the statute is "silent or ambiguous with respect to the specific issue," however, we do not simply impose our own construction on the statute, but give due deference to the BIA's interpretation of the INA [Immigration and Nationality Act] unless it is arbitrary, capricious, or manifestly contrary to the statute.

Mosquera-Perez v. INS, 3 F.3d 553, 555 (1st Cir. 1993) (citing *Chevron, U.S.A., Inc. v. Natural Resources Defense Council, Inc.*, 467 U.S. 837, 842-45, 81 L. Ed. 2d 694, 104 S. Ct. 2778 (1984)). Since the exact meaning of the phrase "sentence actually imposed" – i.e., whether it means, as Solis-Muela urges, the time actually served or whether it means, as the BIA found, the sentence imposed, regardless of whether the execution of the sentence is suspended and regardless of actual time served – is ambiguous, we must defer to the BIA's interpretation unless it is "arbitrary, capricious, or manifestly contrary to the statute." Mosquera-Perez, 3 F.3d at 555.

We cannot say that the BIA's interpretation is anything other than sensible and reasonable. It followed its earlier decision, Matter of Castro, 1988 BIA LEXIS 32, 19 I. & N. Dec. 692 (BIA 1988), in which the BIA reasoned that "when imposition of the sentence is suspended, no sentence has been actually imposed," whereas "where the execution of the sentence is suspended, a sentence has actually been imposed, even though probation may also be granted." 1988 BIA LEXIS 32 at * 6-7 (emphasis added). It gave two reasons for that conclusion. First, to hold otherwise would "ignore the plain meaning" of the term "sentence actually imposed." Id. at * 8. Second, the BIA observed that the previous version of the statute defined the "petty offense" exception by reference to the "punishment actually imposed" instead of the "sentence actually imposed." Cases interpreting that previous version had held that no "punishment" was imposed where execution of the sentence was suspended. "By changing the statutory language from 'punishment actually imposed' to 'sentence actually imposed,' Congress must have intended a different result." Id. at * 8-9. Thus, the BIA in Matter of Castro held that the defendant did not qualify for the petty offense exception because the sentence imposed was two years, even though "he spent only 23 days in jail." Id. at * 9.

Similarly, in this case the BIA concluded that the transcript of the sentencing proceeding indicated that the court imposed a sentence "for a period of not less than 1 year nor more than 5 years." In so doing, the BIA noted that the Wyoming court employed the split sentencing provision permitted by Wyoming statute, under which a court may impose a sentence and then suspend its execution. We agree that the Wyoming court did so, and under the BIA's Matter of Castro interpretation of the "petty offense" exception, the sentence actually imposed on Solis-Muela was one to five years. We cannot say that the BIA's interpretation in Matter of Castro, which it followed in this case, is arbitrary, capricious, or clearly contrary to the statute. We therefore affirm its conclusion that Solis-Muela is deportable under section 241(a)(1) because he was excludable at the time of entry under section 212(a)(9) for having been convicted of a crime involving moral turpitude.

II. Fraud or Misrepresentation

The BIA also affirmed the IJ's conclusion that Solis-Muela was deportable for violating section 212(a)(19) of the Act because he had procured a visa by fraud or misrepresentation of a material fact. Section 212(a)(19) at the time provided for exclusion of:

Any alien who, by fraud or willfully misrepresenting a material fact, seeks to procure, or has sought to procure or has procured, a visa, other documentation, or entry into the United States ....

8 U.S.C. 1182(a)(19). Thus, there must have been a misrepresentation and it must have related to a material fact. The BIA held that Solis-Muela's responses on his visa application and to questioning by the consular officer constituted a misrepresentation concerning his prior conviction. We hold that substantial evidence supports that finding. As the BIA found:

We, like the immigration judge, find the respondent's answer when asked whether he had ever been "arrested, convicted, or confined in a prison" to be problematic. The respondent answered this question in the affirmative; however, in the space provided for an explanation concerning why he had answered in the affirmative, he merely indicated that he had been arrested. At the deportation hearing, he clarified his interchange with the consular officer by explaining that he had also informed the officer that he had been in prison for 107 days. The respondent, on appeal, emphasizes the fact that he made no effort to hide his conviction. We find, however, that while the respondent may have acknowledged his arrest and imprisonment, his failure to disclose his conviction and the nature of that conviction resulted in a material misrepresentation.

In re: Solis Muela, In Deportation Proceedings at 7.

With respect to materiality, the BIA held that the "materiality standard of section 212(a)(19) is satisfied if either (1) the alien is excludable on the true facts or (2) the misrepresentation tends to shut off a line of inquiry which is relevant to the alien's eligibility and which might well have resulted in a proper determination that he be excluded." Id. (citing *Kassab v. INS*, 364 F.2d 806 (6th Cir. 1966); Matter of Ng, 17 I. & N. Dec. 536 (BIA 1980); Matter of Bosuego, 17 I. & N. Dec. 125 (BIA 1980)). The Supreme Court has held that, in the context of denaturalization proceedings, the test for materiality is "whether they [the concealment of a material fact or the willful misrepresentation] had a natural tendency to influence the decision of the [INS*]. " Kungys v. United States*, 485 U.S. 759, 772, 99 L. Ed. 2d 839, 108 S. Ct. 1537 (1988). At least one circuit court has applied the Kungys materiality standard to the procurement of a visa by fraud or willful misrepresentation of a material fact. *Kalejs v. INS*, No. 92-2198, 10 F.3d 441, 1993 U.S. App. LEXIS 29865, at * 15-16 (7th Cir. Nov. 17, 1993). Regardless of the standard employed, Solis-Muela's misrepresentation as to the facts of his prior conviction was material. Had the consular officer known of Solis-Muela's conviction and sentence, he would have found him excludable under section 212(a)(9). The materiality test is therefore met.

For the foregoing reasons, we DENY the petition for review and

AFFIRM the decision of the BIA.

EXERCISES

1. Ever since World War II, being a member of the Nazi Party has been an automatic ground for removal, both prior and subsequent to entry. Do you believe this is a valid exclusionary category? Why or why not? If being a member of the Communist Party does not automatically exclude an alien from entry, why should membership in the Nazi Party be different? Explain.
2. Several of the physical conditions that give rise to removal are only communicated by sexual activity, not causal contact, yet the alien is still not permitted to enter the United States. Do you believe this is a valid ground for removal? Isn't the alien being discriminated against because of a status rather than because of conduct? Do you believe this law should be changed? Explain.
3. What is your opinion of the fact that aliens subject to removal proceedings prior to entry are not afforded any constitutional guarantees? Explain your answer. Which, if any, constitutional guarantees do you think the alien should have?
4. What is your opinion of the provision for parole? Do you feel it is warranted, or should it be eliminated? Is your answer affected by the events of September 11, 2001? Explain.
5. Should the laws regarding polygamy be applied to practicing Moslems or Mormons, whose religious beliefs mandate multiple wives? If a Moslem wishes to enter the country with his three wives, all legally married in their homeland, should they be entitled to enter? Or do you believe this is an act of moral turpitude? Explain.

Chapter Seven

REMOVAL SUBSEQUENT TO ENTRY

CHAPTER PREVIEW

Pursuant to the Illegal Immigrant and Immigration Reform Act of 1996 (1996 Act), the procedure for compelling an alien to leave the United States is now referred to as **removal**. Prior to the 1996 Act such procedures were referred to as **deportation**.

Removal only applies to persons who are not citizens of the United States but who are residing in the United States either without documentation or under the color of law (a presumptively valid visa). Currently, the procedures for removal are being revised to streamline the process, once again pursuant to the provisions of the 1996 Act. However, it is important to note that removal procedures are not criminal in nature; their purpose is to expel from the United States persons who are considered to be undesirable.

Removal procedures do not apply to diplomatic personnel such as ambassadors, public ministers, consuls, career diplomats, officers of international organizations, and their families. Because of various treaties and general international law, if these persons commit acts that make them "undesirable," the United States government will ask their home nation to recall the official, which, in consideration of international comity, is usually acceded to by the foreign state.

> **Example:** The son of the Madagascan consul to the United States is living in New York pursuant to a diplomatic visa. The son is involved in several robberies, but as the son of a diplomat is immune from arrest. The State Department requests that the Madagascar government recall the son home, which it does, because the diplomat's son is not subject to removal procedures.

This chapter will concentrate on the grounds for removal of an alien, the procedures involved in determining that the alien should be removed, and the relief that may be available to the alien once a determination has been made that the alien should be removed.

GROUNDS FOR REMOVAL

The grounds for removing an alien fall into two broad categories: first, for acts committed by the alien prior to entry into the United Sates; and second, for acts committed by the alien subsequent to entry. Broadly speaking, in the first category fall such offenses as falsifying documents to gain entry, being determined to be a security risk, or any other factor that would have made the alien excludable prior to entry to the United States.

Example: A man from the Middle East stated on his visa that he was a member of an organization that is known to be a terrorist organization, but the immigration officer mistakenly granted him a visa. Once in the United States, the alien bombs a major building in New York. This man, in addition to other charges, is subject to removal because he was a security risk and should not have been granted entry. His entry was based on the error of the immigration officer.

The second category includes such grounds as committing a criminal offense in the United States, failing to register as an alien, falsifying documents once in the United States, becoming a public charge, or being deemed a security risk.

Example: In the example above, the alien would be subject to removal proceedings both for the criminal actions he committed while in the United States and for being a security risk. This situation would fall under both categories.

The constitutional guarantees against *ex post facto* laws **do not apply** to immigration matters. This means that an alien may be found to have committed an illegal act even though the act, when committed, was legal. The most frequently cited example of this type of circumstance concerns persons who were members of the Communist or Nazi Parties in their homelands. Consequently, many of the provisions of the immigration laws depend upon the time at which the person entered the United States.

Acts Prior to Entry

Under the 1996 Act, Congress mandated expedited removal procedures for aliens who are found guilty of fraud, misrepresentation, or who entered the United States without valid entry documents. The main purpose of these expedited procedures is to rid the country of persons who have entered the country illegally. Under the Act there are exceptions for persons who fall into the following categories:

- aliens who have a credible fear of persecution in their homelands (see Chapter Eight)
- aliens who intend to apply for asylum (see Chapter Eight)
- returning asylees (see Chapter Eight)
- returning lawful residents.

Example: A lawful permanent resident in the United States returns to her homeland for a period exceeding the statutory provisions regarding length of absence from the country. On return, she falsifies the documents in order to reenter. When the misrepresentation is discovered, she would be subject to expedited removal proceedings, but for the fact that she falls into one of the statutory exceptions.

Other acts prior to entry that would give rise to removal are entering into a fraudulent marriage or being a member of the Nazi Party.

Example: An Algerian persuades an American tourist to marry him so that he can come to the United States. After entry, once the marriage fraud is discovered, the Algerian is subject to removal proceedings.

Acts Subsequent to Entry

There is no statute of limitations with respect to the immigration laws, meaning that an alien may be removed from the United States regardless of how long ago the alleged act was committed. Under this category there are generally five situations that would give rise to removal proceedings:

1. The alien violates U.S. espionage laws.

Example: Once validly in the United States on an employment-related visa, the alien is recruited by his native government to pass information to it regarding the alien's employer, who is involved in several U.S. government contracts. If the alien obliges, the alien has violated U.S. espionage law and is subject to removal.

2. The alien engages in criminal activity that endangers public safety or national security, or engages in any activity that is designed to overthrow the U.S. government by illegal means. Terrorist activity falls into this category.

Example: In the earlier situation in which the alien bombed a U.S. building, the alien engaged in criminal terrorist activity that endangered public safety and so is removable.

3. The alien commits a criminal offense that involves moral turpitude. To fall within this category, the crime must be committed within five years of entry and be subject to a sentence of confinement for a year or longer. This category also applies if at any time after entry, the alien is convicted of two offenses involving moral turpitude, regardless of the sentence. The alien must actually be found guilty; removal cannot be based on convictions resulting from the alien's admission of guilt. Furthermore, the sentence imposed must be confinement, not rehabilitation.

Example: An alien legally in the United States is convicted of two counts of prostitution and is sentenced to two three-month sentences. These crimes involve moral turpitude. Even though they are misdemeanors, because they constitute two offenses the alien is subject to removal.

Example: An alien is found guilty of drug possession, but at trial it is determined that the alien is a drug addict and possessed the drugs solely for personal use, not for sale. The judge sentences the alien to a mandatory rehabilitation program. Because the sentence is not confinement but rehabilitation because the crime was based on the alien's status as a drug addict, the alien is not subject to removal.

4. The alien is convicted of an aggravated felony. The crimes which are deemed to be **aggravated felonies** are
    a) murder

b) drug trafficking
c) firearm trafficking
d) money laundering
e) crimes of violence for which the sentence is a minimum of five years' imprisonment
f) arson.

5. A general grouping of offenses including
   a) becoming a public charge within five years of entry
   b) abusing or becoming addicted to drugs
   c) convictions of firearm possession
   d) violating the Selective Service Act.

Example: An alien who is a lawful permanent resident turns 18 years of age but refuses to register with the Selective Service. This is a violation of the Selective Service Act and may make the alien subject to removal.

In addition to the foregoing, a nonimmigrant may be removed for any violation of his or her visa condition, such as accepting employment under a visa in which employment is prohibited, or violating the Immigration Marriage Fraud Act.

Example: A nonimmigrant student wants to remain in the United States at the expiration of his visa. He persuades a fellow student to marry him so he can remain in the country. This is a violation of the Immigration Marriage Fraud Act and makes the foreign student subject to removal proceedings.

REMOVAL PROCEEDINGS

Under the immigration law, the Immigration and Naturalization Service (INS) has the power to arrest persons suspected of violating the immigration laws. These powers extend to arrests without a warrant for persons attempting to enter the country illegally, interrogating aliens without a warrant, and searching vehicles or within one hundred miles of the border. If the INS determines, at the border, that the alien should not be admitted to the country, the alien may be detained for further inquiry. This detention and inquiry is referred to as **secondary inspection** (the first inspection being a preboarding screening by an INS officer at the alien's port of embarkation). The alien is not entitled to a Miranda warning unless and until the proceeding becomes custodial. The detention of the alien for inspection is not deemed to be custodial.

Example: An alien lands at JFK International Airport. The INS officer believes that there is misrepresented information on the alien's papers and stops the alien for a secondary inspection. At this point, because the alien is not yet in custody, the alien is not entitled to a Miranda warning. The INS officer, after inspection, believes that the alien should be removed and places the alien in custody. At this point the alien is entitled to a Miranda warning.

The INS officer makes these decisions regarding the alien's entry based on "reasonable suspicions." The factors that the officer may use in reaching his or her conclusion are

- the proximity to the border
- normal traffic patterns
- the officer's previous experience with alien traffic
- the behavior of the driver of the vehicle
- the appearance of the vehicle
- the general experience of the officer.

Example: An INS officer has worked at the U.S.-Mexican border at Juarez for 10 years. One night a truck tries to cross the border at 3:00 a.m. In the officer's experience this is totally unusual – most trucks cross the border during normal work hours. Also, the driver of the truck appears nervous. Based on these factors the officer may detain the driver for questioning and search the vehicle; reasonable suspicion of the vehicle and the driver can be demonstrated.

Away from the border, INS officers have the authority to search businesses and buildings where they have a reasonable suspicion that undocumented aliens may be found.

Example: The INS has been given a tip by a reliable source that undocumented aliens are employed at a particular factory. Without a warrant, and without notice, the INS may send officers to inspect the factory for undocumented aliens based on its reasonable suspicions.

If a warrant is issued, INS powers are even broader. However, the warrant must be properly issued (see below), and can only cover persons, not property.

Arrests Without Warrants

An INS officer has inherent power to arrest any alien in the United States if the officer has reason to believe that the alien is in the United States in violation of any immigration law or regulation *and* is likely to escape before a warrant can be issued.

Example: An INS officer, on reasonable suspicion, searches a factory on the U.S.-Canadian border where the officer finds four undocumented aliens are working. Because of the proximity to the border, the INS officer may arrest these aliens without a warrant because they could escape the country before a warrant could be issued.

Arrests with a Warrant

The INS itself has the authority to issue warrants for the arrest of aliens illegally in the United States and those who are subject to removal. Prior to the 1996 Act the warrant could only be issued along with an **Order to Show Cause** why the alien is not removable. The 1996 Act removed the necessity of issuing an Order to Show Cause. The warrant may be issued by:

- an INS district director
- an INS deputy district director
- an INS assistant director
- the chief or assistant patrol agent

- the director of the Organized Crime Drug Enforcement Task Force (only if it is necessary to have the alien in custody)

Once the alien has been arrested, the alien must be informed of his or her rights and the reasons for the arrest. INS provides **Form I-214** to inform the alien of the rights the alien has pursuant to an arrest. The alien may be released on bond or on personal recognizance if the alien poses no national security or bail risk (also review the discussion of parole in the previous chapter). A hearing date is set, and the attorney general has the power to authorize expedited proceedings for persons found to be aggravated felons.

Example: An alien is arrested pursuant to a valid arrest warrant. The alien is in the United States without proper documentation, but has lived here for several years with his two small children. The alien is employed and supports his family. The alien is given Form I-214 to inform him of his rights, and is released on his personal recognizance. It is felt that he poses no risk to national security, nor is he likely to escape before the hearing.

REMOVAL HEARING

The proceedings for removal commence before an **immigration judge**. An immigration judge is an administrative official who performs functions similar to a judge in a judicial proceeding. Under the statute, the alien must be informed of the following information (8 C.F.R. §243.1):

- a statement regarding the nature of the proceeding
- the legal authority that is the basis for the proceeding
- a statement of the factual allegations upon which the proceeding is founded
- a description of the charges against the alien
- the time and place of the hearing.

Service of notice is by "routine service," i.e., any manner of service permitted under law, such as personal service, or mailed service if personal service is not applicable or appropriate.

At the hearing the alien may be represented by counsel, and an interpreter may be present if the alien so desires. The proceeding is presided over by the immigration judge, and a trial attorney represents the government's interests. Except in very limited circumstances, unless the requirements of due process demand otherwise, the alien is responsible for all counsel fees. If the alien were indigent or fundamental fairness would mandate appointed counsel, counsel would be appointed. Note that in proceedings for removal of aliens who are already in the country certain constitutional safeguards, such as the right of due process, do apply. In the removal proceeding prior to entry, the alien is not considered to be legally within the United States.

Example: An alien is not indigent, but has very little money and a family to support. If the alien had to pay for his own counsel, the alien's family would suffer. In these circumstances fundamental fairness would require that counsel be provided for the alien.

The alien may be represented by anyone falling into one of the following categories (8 C.F.R. §216(a)):

1. licensed attorney
2. a law student under special circumstances, such as part of a law school clinical program in which the student is supervised by an attorney
3. a representative of an organization recognized by the Board of Immigration Appeals
4. officials of the government to which the alien owes allegiance, such as a consul or consular official or employee
5. persons who meet certain statutory criteria as reputable representatives for the alien
6. attorneys licensed outside of the United States who receive permission to represent the alien
7. any person to whom the Board of Immigration Appeals gives permission

At the hearing, pursuant to the requirements of due process, the alien has the right to examine government evidence and material, and has the right either to participate or to remain silent. Pursuant to the 1996 Act, the burden is on the alien to prove that he or she should be permitted to enter or remain in the United States. Under this Act, the burden for persons seeking admission is "beyond doubt," and for status questions the burden is "clear and convincing," and the alien must show a lawful presence in the United States under a prior admission. The government's burden is only "clear and convincing."

Example: The government seeks to remove an alien who claims immigrant status as the spouse of an American citizen. The government claims that the marriage is a sham. The alien has the burden to show that it is indeed a valid marriage by clear and convincing evidence, and must further show that she was lawfully admitted to the United States (for instance, as a student). The government's burden is to show, by clear and convincing evidence, that the marriage was fraudulently entered into solely to help the alien remain in the United States.

The general rules of evidence that apply in criminal proceedings do not apply to removal hearings because such proceedings are not considered criminal in nature. All evidence, including hearsay, is admissible if it is material and relevant to the proceedings. 8 C.F.R. §242.14.

Example: In the preceding example, the government calls as a witness a friend of the American spouse's cousin, who testifies that the cousin told him that the spouse only married the alien to let her stay in the country, but they have never lived together as man and wife. In a regular court such evidence would be excludable as hearsay, but it is admissible in a removal hearing.

The removal hearing is open to the public unless the immigration judge determines that it would be in the best interests of fairness to keep the public out. Once the hearing commences, additional charges may be added against the alien, if they are made in writing.

If the judge finds for the alien, the alien may remain in the United States. If the judge finds against the alien, the alien may choose the country to which he or she will be removed. The decision of the judge, regardless of whether it is oral or written, must discuss the evidence, findings and law upon which the ultimate decision was based. After the decision is rendered, the decision may be administratively and/or judicially reviewed.

REVIEW OF REMOVAL HEARING DECISIONS

Once the immigration judge has rendered a decision in the removal hearing, there are three avenues of review that may be sought:

1. **Motion to Reopen or Reconsider**. (8 C.F.R. §242.22) The judge's decision may be reopened by either the alien or the judge. An alien who seeks a reconsideration must complete **Form I-328**. The judge may also seek a reconsideration on his or her own motion. In either case, the same immigration judge who presided at the initial hearing will decide the motion.

2. **Administrative Appeal.** (8 C.F.R. §242.21) The Board of Immigration Appeals, supervised by the Department of Justice, has the authority to review the following matters:

   a) removal proceedings
   b) decisions involving discretionary relief (see below)
   c) imposition of administrative fines
   d) petitions for immigrant status
   e) decisions affecting parole or bond
   f) decisions affecting an alien's adjustment of status
   g) asylum decisions
   h) decisions regarding temporary protected status (see below)

The BIA has the power either to summarily deny the appeal or to remand it, or to reopen the case for decision by the attorney general.

Once the BIA has acted, the alien is considered to have exhausted all administrative remedies and may seek judicial review.

3. **Judicial Review**. (INA §106) Once the BIA has rendered its final decision, the alien may file in federal Court of Appeals for judicial review. The appeal must be filed within six months of the final order of removal. In order to file for review in federal court, the following requirements must be met:

   a) The alien must have received a final removal order, which includes:
      - denial of discretionary relief (see below)
      - denial of a motion to reopen
      - denial of suspension of removal (see below)
      - denial of withholding of removal (see below)
      - denial of voluntary departure (see below)

   b) All administrative remedies have been exhausted.
   c) The alien must still be present in the United States. An alien may not seek judicial review of an order of removal if the alien has already left the country.

The Court of Appeals is limited in its review of the proceedings to a determination of whether all of the requirements of due process have been met and whether or not the administrative decision was not arbitrary, capricious or contrary to law. The federal court does not have the authority to review the fundamental issues or facts presented at the hearing.

> **Example:** The alien from the preceding example has been ordered to leave the United States because the immigration judge determined that her marriage was a sham. This decision was affirmed by the BIA. In the Court of Appeals the alien attempts to prove that the marriage was not a sham. The court will not hear this argument. This is a review of fact, not law, and not within the jurisdiction of the court.

The Supreme Court *may* hear appeals from the appellate courts. If the final judicial decision goes against the alien, the alien will be ordered removed from the United States.

DISCRETIONARY RELIEF FROM AN ORDER OF REMOVAL

An alien who has been removed from the United States may seek certain relief from the removal at the discretion of the immigration judge. There are generally eight types of relief from removal that may be available to the alien, and each one shall be discussed in turn. To qualify for such relief, the alien must prove that he or she is entitled to such relief by a preponderance of the evidence. The types of discretionary relief that may be available are:

1. **Voluntary departure.** (INA §242) Voluntary departure is the most often sought form of relief from removal. Voluntary departure means that the alien has agreed to leave the United States on his or her own volition and not pursuant to an order of removal. Leaving under the terms of voluntary departure leaves no stigma on the alien's record. (See Appendix 7-1.)

An alien may apply for voluntary departure any time during the removal proceedings. In order to qualify, the alien must have been in the United States for at least one year and be able to demonstrate "good moral character" for the five years prior to the application. This relief is not available to aliens who have been convicted of an aggravated felony or who pose a national security risk. If voluntary departure is granted during the removal hearing, the alien must leave the country within 120 days of such grant or, if granted at the conclusion of the hearing, the alien's departure must take place within 60 days of the grant. An alien who fails to leave under the terms of the voluntary departure becomes subject to criminal penalties and is barred from reentering the United States for ten years. Furthermore, the alien must be able to pay for his or her own departure.

Pursuant to the 1996 Act, if the alien is unlawfully present in the United States for a period of 180 days to one year and voluntarily departs, the alien may not reenter the United States for three years. If the alien is unlawfully within the United States for more than one year, the alien is barred from reentry for ten years. The time period for unlawful presence is cumulative, and may be acquired by multiple visits to the United States. There is no statute of limitations with respect to this Act.

> **Example:** An alien illegally entered the United States by running over the U.S. border from Canada. The alien stayed in the United States for 10 months and then left. Two years later the alien again illegally entered the U.S., and three months later the alien's undocumented status was discovered by the INS. If the alien applies for and receives voluntary departure, the alien will be barred from reentering the United States for ten years; the ten months plus three months exceeds a total of one year.

An alien who is permitted to leave voluntarily and whose unlawful presence in the United States has been for less than one year may seek a waiver from the three-year bar to reentry if the alien has a spouse or child who is a U.S. citizen or lawful permanent resident. But, under the 1996 Act, these waivers are not easily granted.

Example: An alien who has been unlawfully in the United States for 11 months applies for and is granted Voluntary Departure. The alien then seeks a waiver of the three-year bar to reentry because the alien's child was born in the United States when the alien was in the country lawfully under a tourist visa, and therefore the child is a U.S. citizen. The alien may be granted a waiver, but such waiver is not guaranteed.

2. **Extended voluntary departure**. (INA §244(a)(1)) Extended voluntary departure permits an alien who qualifies for voluntary departure to remain in the United States for a longer period than is normally permitted because of dangerous conditions in the alien's homeland. Extended voluntary departure merely delays the alien's departure. It does not cancel it.

Example: An alien applies for and is granted voluntary departure. However, the alien's country is undergoing a violent civil war. The alien may be granted extended voluntary departure until the conditions in the alien's homeland settle down.

3. **Cancellation of removal and adjustment of status for certain nonpermanent residents.** (INA §244(a)(2)) Prior to the 1996 Act, this category of relief was known as **suspension of deportation**. To qualify for this relief, the alien must demonstrate:

    a) A physical presence in the United States for ten years, which may be interrupted by
        - service of Form I-862
        - any single absence of 90 days or more
        - aggregate absences of more than 180 days
        - commission of any offense that would give rise to removal proceedings

    b) An exceptional and extremely unusual hardship to a U.S. citizen spouse or child.

This provision of the 1996 Act requires that the physical presence be continuous and a showing that extreme hardship would be created for a U.S. citizen if the alien were removed. These decisions will be based on a case-by-case basis.

Example: An alien unlawfully entered the United States eleven years ago. While in the U.S. he married another alien who was lawfully in the U.S., and they now have three children. When the alien is ordered removed from the United States, he applies for a Cancellation of Removal based on his continuous presence in the U.S. for over ten years, and the fact that his family will be unable to support themselves if he is removed. If the wife and children leave with him, this would cause the involuntary exile of the children, who are American citizens. In this instance, the government might be willing to grant a Cancellation of Removal.

4. **Adjustment of status.** (INA §245(a)) An alien may seek relief from removal if the alien can have his or her visa status adjusted. In order to qualify for an adjustment of status:

    a) the alien must have been inspected and lawfully admitted to the United States

b) the alien must be eligible for a permanent resident visa (no disqualifying characteristics)

c) an immigrant visa must be immediately available.

An adjustment of status is not permitted for persons who are unlawfully in the United States, because such persons would not meet the first requirement of a valid entry. Also, if the immigrant status sought is subject to numerical limitations, a visa must be available in the particular category under which the alien applies. However, pursuant to the Legal Immigration and Family Equity Act, undocumented aliens who meet the previously discussed criteria may adjust their status if they applied for such adjustment between January 1 and April 30, 2001.

> **Example:** An alien entered the United States as a student. The alien overstays the visa, and becomes subject to removal proceedings. The alien seeks to have his status adjusted because he married an American citizen he met while at school. Assuming that the marriage is not a sham, the alien may have his status adjusted because he lawfully entered the United States, and there is no bar to his being an immigrant. Since the spouse of a U.S. citizen is not subject to numerical limitations, an immigrant visa would be immediately available.

5. **Asylum.** An alien may seek asylum from persecution in his or her homeland, and may do so even if he or she is subject to removal proceedings. For a discussion of refugees and asylees, see the next chapter.

6. **Withholding of removal.** (INA §243)) In a fashion similar to asylum, an alien who can prove that his or her life or freedom would be threatened in the homeland because of race, religion, nationality, or membership in a particular social or political group, can seek withholding of removal. If the alien seeks withholding of removal, the application must be made as part of the removal hearing. If the alien seeks asylum, the application may be made at any time, even after the hearing is concluded.

7. **Stay of removal.** (INA §243)) An alien may apply for this relief by filing **Form I-246** (see Appendix 7-2) with the INS district director in the geographic location where the alien is staying. Typically, this relief is afforded aliens pending a reopening of the removal proceedings or while the alien is attempting an adjustment of status. This form of relief is only temporary in nature and does not override the removal order. If the district director denies the application, the decision is not appealable, but it may be reviewed by the BIA.

8. Other Relief. In addition to the foregoing, certain other very limited discretionary relief exists.

   a) The first of these is known as **registry** (INA §249) in which an alien who is unlawfully in the United States is given a "grace period" during which the alien may apply for permanent resident status. The purpose of registry is to avoid the consequences of removal for persons who have lived in the United States for a long period of time; however, the period during which the alien could have registered pursuant to the 1996 Act has passed as of this writing.

   b) The second form of limited relief is known as **deferred removal** or **nonpriority status,** which is granted under INS guidelines for circumstances under which removal would be unconscionable. (Operations Instructions 242(1)(a)(23)) An example might be a very elderly person who had lived for a long period in the United States and who has no family in either the United States or his or her homeland.

c) Persons who qualify under the Legal Immigration and Family Equity Act.

Finally, an alien who can demonstrate that he or she relied on false information provided by a government employee with respect to the immigration law may seek an **estoppel** to prevent removal. In order to qualify, it is generally necessary to demonstrate actual misconduct on the part of the government employee. However, when the matter is reviewed by the courts, the courts generally fail to find "affirmative misconduct." Therefore, this form of relief is rarely viable.

ETHICAL CONSIDERATIONS

Many areas of ethical concern may apply to removal proceedings. First and foremost, the government has determined that certain persons are considered to be "undesirable" and therefore not worthy of entering or remaining in the United States. Several of these categories refer to the health of the individual, thus making removal a status issue. The individual is being penalized because of his or her health status. Also, with respect to crimes that give rise to grounds for removal, it is always an ethical determination that classifies a crime as one of moral turpitude.

Once it has been determined that an alien is subject to removal proceedings, the alien is only afforded limited due process rights. If constitutional guarantees are presumed to be necessary for the fair administration of the laws, how can a group be singled out to be worthy of less than full constitutional protections? It might appear as though the immigration laws qualify as a bill of attainder.

Be aware a lay person may represent an alien before an immigration judge. Such representation is not considered the unauthorized practice of law, provided the lay person has qualified to be a representative pursuant to 8 C.F.R. Sec. 216(a).

Finally, if removal has been ordered, the alien has the right to seek relief from removal, but most of the relief is discretionary with the immigration judge or the INS. Whenever a government employee is granted discretion, there is always the opportunity for the official to abuse that discretion in the administration of the law and few, if any, of these decisions are appealable or reviewable.

CHAPTER REVIEW

Since passage of the Illegal Immigration Reform and Immigrant Responsibility Act of 1996, the terms "exclusion" and "deportation" have been merged into the single word "removal." An alien may be removed either for acts committed by the alien prior to the alien's entry to the United States or for acts committed by the alien after entering the country.

An alien may be denied entry if found guilty of fraud or misrepresentation on an immigration document or in falsifying documents. An alien may be removed after entry if it can be proved that the alien was incorrectly permitted to enter the country, poses a security risk, has become a public charge, has violated any terms of his or her visa, or has been convicted of various types of crimes involving moral turpitude or aggravated felony.

The INS has the power to detain an alien with or without a warrant. Once the alien has been arrested by INS, the alien is entitled to a hearing on the matter of his or her status. Counsel may be appointed for certain indigent aliens, and certain limited constitutional safeguards are permitted to the alien under the concept of due process. However, the general rules of evidence for criminal proceedings are inapplicable to removal hearings.

If the immigration judge determines that the alien should be removed, the alien has the right to an administrative appeal to the Board of Immigration Appeals. An alien who has exhausted all administrative procedures may seek review in the federal court of appeals.

In addition to administrative and judicial review of the matter, the alien may also apply directly to the immigration judge for certain discretionary relief from removal, such as voluntary departure, extended voluntary departure, cancellation of removal, adjustment of status, asylum, withholding of removal, and other limited discretionary methods of relief.

CHAPTER VOCABULARY

Adjustment of status — Changing an alien's classification from one category to another.

Aggravated felony — Grounds for removal.

Asylum — Status granted to qualifying refugees who apply for status as asylees either within the U.S. or at its borders.

Board of Immigration Appeals — The Department of Justice board created to hear appeals from the Immigration Court.

Cancellation of Removal — A form of discretionary relief from removal.

Deferred removal — Discretionary relief from removal granted on humanitarian grounds.

Deportation — The process of removing aliens from the United States (now termed "removal").

Estoppel — Form of relief from removal for an alien who has relied on the representations of a government official with respect to immigration matters.

Ex post facto — Latin for "after the fact."

Extended voluntary departure — Special category that permits aliens to remain in the United States after issuance of a removal order because of problems in the alien's homeland.

Immigration law judge — Administrative law judge presiding over removal hearings.

Judicial review — The ability of a court of law to review decisions of an administrative agency.

Nonpriority status — Same as "deferred removal."

Order to show cause — Document served on the alien as part of the removal proceedings prior to the 1996 Act.

Parole — Procedure for allowing aliens limited entry into the United States pending investigation prior to a removal proceeding.

Registry — Permitted for a limited time under the 1996 Act to permit aliens who had resided in the United States for a long time to adjust their status and remain in the country.

Removal — The process of denying entry to aliens and removing undocumented aliens from the country.

Secondary inspection — INS inspection of aliens when they attempt to enter the U.S.

Stay of removal — Discretionary relief permitting an alien to stay in the U.S. pending a reopening of his or her case or while the alien attempts to obtain a status adjustment.

Suspension of removal — Permitting the alien to remain in the U.S. for a period longer than that specified in the removal order.

Voluntary departure — Permitting the alien to leave the country on his or her own volition without the stigma of removal.

Withholding of removal — Similar to seeking asylum; must be requested at the commencement of the removal proceedings.

EDITED JUDICIAL DECISIONS

The first case, *Ramsay v. U.S. Immigration and Naturalization Service*, discusses the procedures involved in a removal proceeding, and the second case, *Iredia v. Immigration and Naturalization Service*, concerns the removal of an alien who was convicted of two crimes of moral turpitude.

RAMSAY v. U.S. IMMIGRATION & NATURALIZATION SERVICE

14 F.3d 206(4th Cir. 1994)

I

The facts of this appeal are not disputed by either party. Ramsay is a native and citizen of Great Britain. He originally entered the United States in February 1987 on a J-1 exchange visa as a post-doctoral research associate in the Department of Chemistry at the University of New Orleans. His visa was valid through January 31, 1989, but, upon expiration of his visa, Ramsay failed to leave the United States or file a request for an extension of his visa.

On June 23, 1989, Ramsay married Cheryl Caine, a United States citizen. The next day, the couple traveled to Canada. When the couple attempted to reenter the United States on the same day at Niagara Falls, New York, the United States Immigration Inspector refused entry to Ramsay because his J-1 visa had expired. The Inspector told Ramsay that he was ineligible for an automatic visa revalidation and suggested that he attempt to obtain a new J-1 visa from the United States Consulate in Toronto, Canada. Instead of going to Toronto, Ramsay, his wife and a third individual traveled to a second inspection point. There, a second Inspector asked the three occupants of the vehicle "where are you from," to which Ramsay and the other two vehicle occupants each responded: "U.S." (A.R. 176). Ramsay concedes that he offered his response "intending to enter the U.S. by misrepresentation." (Brief of Petitioner 13). Thereafter, the Inspector permitted the three vehicle occupants to enter the United States without further questioning or delay.

On July 21, 1989, in an attempt to remain legally in the United States, Ramsay, along with his wife, filed an Immigrant Visa Petition for an Alien Relative (Form I-130), an Application for Adjustment of Status to Permanent Resident (Form I-485), and an Application for Waiver of Grounds of Excludability (Form I-601) with the Immigration and Naturalization Service (INS) district office in New Orleans, Louisiana. Along with the submission of these forms, Ramsay voluntarily submitted an affidavit fully disclosing the circumstances of his last entry into the United States. The couple hoped the Application for Waiver would allow Ramsay to avoid any adverse consequences resulting from the misrepresentations used to enter the United States.

The INS subsequently denied the Adjustment of Status application, reasoning that Ramsay had not been "inspected" as an alien upon his last entry into the United States. In its denial, the INS failed specifically to address whether Ramsay was excludable, but the INS examiner noted on Ramsay's Form I-130, which was forwarded to the United States Embassy in London, that she believed Ramsay was excludable from the United States.

Subsequently, Ramsay requested the INS to reconsider its decision and also requested advance parole which would allow him to remain in the United States while his Application for Waiver of Grounds of Excludability was adjudicated. On December 7, 1989, the INS denied the request for reconsideration and advance parole. On January 23, 1990, the INS District Director in New Orleans issued a formal decision denying Ramsay's Application for Adjustment of Status on the basis that he was statutorily ineligible for adjustment of status because he had entered the United States without "inspection." (A.R. 198-99). However, the District Director granted Ramsay voluntary departure until February 22, 1990.

On February 22, 1990, in an attempt to challenge the INS's decision, Ramsay filed suit in the United States District Court for the Eastern District of Louisiana. In his complaint, Ramsay sought a declaratory judgment that he was eligible for adjustment of status and advance parole. Thereafter, both Ramsay and the INS filed motions for summary judgment. On March 19, 1990, pending resolution of the summary judgment motions, the INS issued an Order to Show Cause, charging Ramsay with deportability because he entered the United States without inspection.

On January 14, 1991, the district court granted the INS's motion for summary judgment in the declaratory judgment action. The district court concluded that Ramsay did not qualify for adjustment of status pursuant to §245(a) of the Act, 8 U.S.C. §1255(a), finding that "by his explicit and overt actions, Ramsay intentionally avoided the inspection process by alleging he was a United States citizen when re-entering the United States from Canada in June 1989." (A.R. 143). Ramsay then filed a notice of appeal with the United States Court of Appeals for the Fifth Circuit, intending to challenge the district court's grant of summary judgment. However, Ramsay subsequently dismissed the appeal on his own motion.

On August 14, 1991, the Immigration Judge (IJ) acted on the pending deportation charges against Ramsay, finding Ramsay deportable as an alien who had entered the United States without inspection pursuant to §241(a)(2)(B) of the Act, 8 U.S.C.§1251(a)(2)(B). The IJ reasoned in part:

There is no way on earth I would go beyond or over or through [the prior judgment of the district court] and gainsay any of the findings that were made by the judge in that case. And I think the judge clearly found that Dr. Ramsay was not inspected.

(A.R. 59). However, the IJ exercised its discretion by granting Ramsay a six-month voluntary departure, lasting until February 14, 1992. (A.R. 61).

On August 23, 1991, Ramsay filed his notice of appeal to the BIA. n5 (A.R. 42). On February 8, 1993, the BIA dismissed the appeals. (A.R. 2-8). The BIA concluded that Ramsay entered the United States without inspection, reasoning that Ramsay's response to the Immigration Inspector was "tantamount to a claim of United States citizenship," and, therefore, "had the effect of significantly frustrating or circumventing the inspection process to which he would have been subjected had he properly identified himself." (A.R. 6). In the alternative, the BIA found that collateral estoppel barred Ramsay's challenge to the issue of inspection. The BIA reasoned that the prior judgment by the district court in favor of the INS served "as res judicata as to its finding that [Dr. Ramsay] evaded inspection upon his reentry into this country." (A.R. 7).

Finally, the BIA held that the IJ "was justified in allowing [Ramsay] the minimal deportation relief of voluntary departure." (A.R. 8). Thus, the BIA ordered that Ramsay was "permitted to depart from the United States voluntarily within 30 days from the date of this order . . . ." Id.

On March 9, 1993, Ramsay filed his petition for review of the BIA's order with this court.

II

In his petition for review, Ramsay claims that the IJ and the BIA erred in concluding that he evaded inspection upon entering the United States on June 24, 1989. In response, the INS contends the doctrine of collateral estoppel bars Ramsay from asserting this claim. Specifically, the INS reasons that the United States District Court for the Eastern District of Louisiana previously adjudicated the issue of inspection when it found that Ramsay was not entitled to adjustment of status. Because Ramsay's challenge to the deportation order in the present case raises the identical inspection issue, the INS concludes that Ramsay should be collaterally estopped from rearguing the inspection issue. We agree.

Collateral estoppel or issue preclusion forecloses "the relitigation of issues of fact or law that are identical to issues which have been actually determined and necessarily decided in prior litigation in which the party against whom [issue preclusion] is asserted had a full and fair opportunity to litigate." *Virginia Hosp. Ass'n. v. Baliles*, 830 F.2d 1308, 1311 (4th Cir. 1987) (citation omitted). For this doctrine to apply, the party asserting it must establish five elements:

(1) the issue precluded must be identical to one previously litigated;

(2) the issue must have been actually determined in the prior proceeding;

(3) determination of the issue must have been a critical and necessary part of the decision in the prior proceeding;

(4) the prior judgment must be final and valid; and

(5) the party against whom estoppel is asserted must have had a full and fair opportunity to litigate the issue in the previous forum.

Coffey v. Dean Witter Reynolds, Inc., 961 F.2d 922, 925 (10th Cir. 1992); *Central Transport, Inc. v. Four Phase Systems, Inc.*, 936 F.2d 256, 259 (6th Cir. 1990).

In the present case, Ramsay does not question whether the first four elements exist and we believe these elements are clearly established. However, Ramsay does contest whether he had a full and fair opportunity to litigate the issue of inspection in the prior proceeding. Ramsay reasons that in the prior proceedings the district court merely reviewed the INS's denial of his adjustment of status application to determine whether the INS acted arbitrarily or capriciously. Because the district court in the prior proceeding did not conduct a full *de novo* review of the inspection issue, Ramsay contends that the prior proceeding did not afford him a full and fair opportunity to litigate the inspection issue. We disagree.

Our review of the prior proceedings indicates that the analysis by the district court was tantamount to a de novo review of the INS's denial of Ramsay's Adjustment of Status application. Specifically, the district court began its analysis by recognizing that, pursuant to 8 U.S.C. §1255(a), an alien may only receive an adjustment of status if he is "inspected." Then, after considering the undisputed facts – which are identical to the ones before us – and the relevant BIA precedent, the district court "found[ ] that by his explicit and overt actions,

Dr. Ramsay intentionally avoided the inspection process by alleging he was a United States citizen when re-entering the United States from Canada in June 1989." (A.R. 143). Thus, instead of merely determining whether sufficient evidence justified the INS's decision, the district court made a de novo finding that Ramsay avoided inspection upon entering the United States. Under such circumstances, we cannot say that the proceedings before the district court deprived Ramsay of a full and fair opportunity to litigate the inspection issue.

Accordingly, we hold that collateral estoppel precluded Ramsay from relitigating the inspection issue before the IJ, the BIA or this court. Because Ramsay was not inspected upon his entry into the United States, the BIA did not err in finding Ramsay subject to deportation under §241(a)(2)(B) of the Act, 8 U.S.C. §1251(a)(2)(B).

III

Ramsay next argues that, if we determine Ramsay is subject to deportation, we should also reinstate the BIA's grant of a thirty-day voluntary departure. In response, the INS claims that only the District Director for the INS has the discretion to grant voluntary departures. Because a decision to grant or extend voluntary departure requires several factual findings which a court of appeals is not suited to make, the INS argues that, in the present case, we should refrain from reinstating Ramsay's voluntary departure. For the reasons that follow, we find Ramsay's argument more persuasive.

Section 244(e)(1) of the Act, 8 U.S.C. §1254(e)(1), authorizes the grant of voluntary departure. That statute provides, in pertinent part:

> The Attorney General may, in his discretion, permit any alien under deportation proceedings . . . to depart voluntarily from the United States at his own expense in lieu of deportation . . . .

Id. Although a voluntary departure may be initially granted by an Immigration Judge or the BIA, the decision to extend the voluntary departure period is within the sole discretion of the INS District Director. 8 C.F.R. §§244.1, 244.2. Determining an alien's eligibility for voluntary departure or an extension thereof requires the following factual findings: (a) the alien "is, and has been a person of good moral character for at least five years immediately preceding [the] application for voluntary departure"; (b) the alien has not been convicted of an aggravated felony; and (c) the alien "is willing and has the immediate means with which to depart promptly from the United States." 8 U.S.C. §1254(e)(1), 8 C.F.R. §244.1.

The authorities are apparently divided on whether a court of appeals should automatically reinstate a voluntary departure when it affirms a deportation order. For example, in Contreras-Aragon, 852 F.2d at 1092-93, the Ninth Circuit held that if the BIA's deportation order included a grant of voluntary departure, affirming the deportation order necessarily encompassed the reinstatement of the voluntary departure. The court reasoned:

> The result of the deportation hearing, including the discretionary determinations, is one final order of deportation reviewable by the courts of appeals . . . . It is clear that a determination concerning voluntary departure is one of those determinations made during the deportation hearing that form a part of the final order of deportation.

Id. at 1092 (citation omitted). In other words, the Ninth Circuit viewed the grant of voluntary departure as an inseverable component of the deportation order such that affirming the deportation order necessarily required reinstatement of the voluntary departure.

Other courts, while not expressly rejecting Contreras-Aragon, have reached a contrary conclusion. For example, in *Kaczmarczyk v. INS*, 933 F.2d 588, 598 (7th Cir.), cert. denied, 116 L. Ed. 2d 608, 112 S. Ct. 583 (1991), the Seventh Circuit declined to reinstate the voluntary departure granted by the BIA even though it affirmed the BIA's deportation order. In reaching this conclusion, the court emphasized that 8 C.F.R. §244.2 vests the District Director with the "sole discretion" to reinstate voluntary departures and, so long as the INS refrains from "wielding its discretion to withhold voluntary departure to deter applicants from seeking judicial review of BIA decisions," aliens should seek to extend the period for voluntary departure "by filing a motion with the district director to reinstate voluntary departure." Kaczmarczyk, 933 F.2d at 598.

The First Circuit adopted a similar approach to the one created by the Seventh Circuit, with one important addition. Specifically, in *Umanzor-Alvarado v. INS*, 896 F.2d 14, 16 (1st Cir. 1990), the court held that it had the authority to reinstate voluntary departure when the INS offered no evidence suggesting that, in the interim period between the BIA's and its decisions, the alien had become ineligible for voluntary departure. The court opined:

We note that the government does not suggest it will present the district director with any other reason for refusing the reinstatement. Under these circumstances, to require the petitioner to apply to the district director to pass upon the matter would be pointless, for the director could not lawfully refuse the reinstatement. We see nothing in the law that requires us to waste time and resources or that deprives us of the legal power to order the legally appropriate remedy – a remedy already granted by the Board.

Id.

We find the approach utilized by the Seventh Circuit, as modified by the First Circuit, to be the most principled. As mentioned, a decision to extend the period for voluntary departure requires consideration of several facts, including whether the alien is of good moral character and has the present means with which to depart the United States. A court of appeals is not suited to undertake such a factual analysis. The approach adopted by the Seventh Circuit, as modified by the First Circuit, addresses these concerns in that it leaves the discretion to extend the period for voluntary departures with the District Director except where the INS is "wielding its discretion to withhold voluntary departure to deter applicants from seeking judicial review of BIA decisions," Kaczmarczyk, 933 F.2d at 598, or when "the [INS] does not suggest it will present the district director with any other reason for refusing the reinstatement." Umanzor-Alvarado, 896 F.2d at 16.

In contrast, the Ninth Circuit's approach creates a potentially undesirable result. Specifically, under the Contreras-Aragon rule, a court might reinstate voluntary departure even though, in the interim period between the BIA's and court of appeals' decisions, the alien may have committed acts which would preclude him from eligibility for voluntary departure, e.g., an armed bank robbery.

Thus, we hold that the decision to reinstate or extend voluntary departures should usually be left to the discretion of the District Director, who is better suited to consider the factual prerequisites which determine an alien's eligibility for voluntary departure. A court of appeals should reinstate a voluntary departure granted by the BIA only when: (1) the INS is "wielding its discretion to withhold voluntary departure to deter applicants from seeking judicial review of BIA decisions," Kaczmarczyk, 933 F.2d at 598, or (2) "the [INS] does not suggest it will present the district director with any other reason for refusing the reinstatement." Umanzor-Alvarado, 896 F.2d at 16.

Applying these principles to the present case indicates that we should reinstate Ramsay's thirty-day period for voluntary departure. Specifically, the record contains no evidence that circumstances which originally entitled Ramsay to voluntary departure have changed. Nor has the INS "suggested [that] it will present the district director with any other reason for refusing the reinstatement" for Ramsay. Umanzor-Alvarado, 896 F.2d at 16. Thus, "the director could not lawfully refuse [Ramsay's] reinstatement." Id. Accordingly, we hereby reinstate the thirty-day period for Ramsay's voluntary departure.

IV

For the reasons stated herein, we deny Ramsay's petition for review and direct the government to treat the voluntary departure period as beginning to run on the date this court's mandate becomes effective.

SO ORDERED

IREDIA v. IMMIGRATION AND NATURALIZATION SERVICE

981 F.2d 847(5th Cir. 1993)

Minister David Iredia, a Nigerian citizen, appeals his deportation pursuant to section 241(a)(4) of the Immigration and Nationality Act (INA), 8 U.S.C. §1251(a)(4), as an alien who, after entering the United States, was convicted of two crimes involving moral turpitude not arising out of a single scheme of criminal misconduct. Iredia was determined deportable under this provision by an immigration judge whose findings were upheld by the Board of Immigration Appeals. Iredia contends that his criminal misconduct involved only a "single scheme". Further, he argues that the immigration judge denied him due process by not allowing him to testify on this point. We find Iredia's arguments concerning the interpretation of the statute incorrect in light of the deference we owe to the INS's interpretation of the immigration laws and, on the record presented, the immigration judge did not abuse his discretion in truncating Iredia's testimony. The decision of the Board of Immigration Appeals is affirmed.

FACTS

Iredia entered the United States as a non-immigrant visitor in 1982. His status was later changed to that of a lawful permanent resident. Using addresses and social security numbers of six different individuals, Iredia applied for 13 credit cards in their names without their consent. Once the credit card applications were approved they were mailed to post office boxes petitioner had rented under false names. In 1987, he created a fictitious business from which purchases of non-existent equipment were made with the illegal credit cards. Iredia deposited the fraudulent credit card vouchers in the Alief Alamo Bank.

On February 22, 1988, Iredia was convicted in federal court in Houston, Texas, on 13 counts of unauthorized use of credit cards. On seven of these counts, he received concurrent sentences of six years imprisonment; on the remaining six counts, he also received concurrent sentences of six years imprisonment running consecutively to the first sentences. The latter sentences were suspended, however, and five years probation imposed. Iredia was also fined $91,000 as a special condition of probation, $45,059.28 as restitution and $650 as a special monetary assessment.

The immigration judge and, subsequently, the Board of Immigration Appeals found that Iredia's conduct involved more than one single scheme of criminal misconduct because he committed separate and distinct crimes each time he made unauthorized use of a different credit card for more than $1,000. Iredia argues that since all of his crimes were executed in accordance with a single, pre-arranged plan they were part of a single scheme of criminal misconduct.

STANDARD OF REVIEW

A two-prong standard of review applies to cases such as these. Interpretations of ambiguous law by an executive agency are accorded considerable weight and deference. *Chevron, U.S.A., Inc. v. National Resources Defense Counsel, Inc.*, 467 U.S. 837, 844-45, 104 S. Ct. 2778, 2782-83, 81 L. Ed. 2d 694 (1984). This court has accepted the Chevron standard and upheld reasonable agency interpretations of governing law when that law did not speak clearly to the question at hand. See, e.g., *National Grain and Feed Ass'n v. Occupational Safety and Health Administration*, 866 F.2d 717, 733 (5th Cir.1988); *Amberg v. Federal Deposit Insurance Corporation*, 934 F.2d 681, 687-88 (5th Cir.1991); *Corrosion Proof Fittings v. Environmental Protection Agency*, 947 F.2d 1201, 1210 (5th Cir.1991).

After considering the legal standard under which the INS should operate, we review the Board's findings under the substantial evidence test. 8 U.S.C. §1105a(a)(4); *Rojas v. INS*, 937 F.2d 186, 189 (5th Cir.1991); *Zamora-Morel v. INS*, 905 F.2d 833, 837 (5th Cir.1990).

DISCUSSION

Although there is an obvious conflict between INS's long-standing interpretation of the pertinent provision of the statute and that of the circuit courts upon which Minister Iredia relies, we do not find INS's interpretation unreasonable under Chevron. The cases cited by both sides agree that there is no clear Congressional intent on the definition of a "single scheme" of criminal misconduct. Wood, 266 F.2d at 828; Pacheco, 546 F.2d at 449; Nason, 394 F.2d at 227. Since the legislature has not spoken, Chevron directs us to accept the interpretation of the statute by the administrative agency so long as it is reasonable.

None of the cases cited by Iredia takes into account the Chevron presumption. The only case decided after Chevron, Gonzalez-Sandoval, 910 F.2d 614, does not address the issue. The INS in this case gives a convincing account of the reasonableness of its interpretation of the word "scheme" in explaining that "a focus on the pre-planning aspect of criminal activity can lead to theoretical absurdities." As INS states, under Iredia's theory, "an alien who is convicted of ten bank robberies cannot be deported under the part of 8 U.S.C. §1251(a)(4) requiring that the crime does not arise out of a single scheme of criminal misconduct if he establishes the robberies were all carried out pursuant to a plan that he devised prior to executing them." The INS's position that a scheme exists based upon the execution of all the elements of a crime and that another scheme comprises the execution of another set of elements is more reasonable than Iredia's interpretation. Under Chevron, however, this does not have to be the case to compel judicial deference to INS's interpretation. The INS merely has to show that its construction is reasonable, not that it is the more reasonable among alternatives. INS clearly meets this burden.

Applying INS's standard, there is no doubt that substantial evidence exists, including multiple convictions, to demonstrate Iredia's participation in multiple criminal schemes. Iredia further asserts that since he was not allowed to testify orally regarding facts that would support his interpretation of "a single scheme," he was denied due process. Because the legal standard that Minister Iredia was attempting to evidence was the wrong one, and because the nature of the scheme was thoroughly presented to the immigration judge in other ways, the error, if any, was harmless.

For the foregoing reasons, the deportation of Minister Iredia is AFFIRMED.

EXERCISES

1. An alien who legally entered the country but who subsequently became a public charge may be removed. Do you believe that this is fair? Why or why not? Is this a form of "status" penalty? Explain.
2. Discuss some of the circumstances that you believe may give rise to a showing of "extreme hardship to a U.S. citizen spouse or child," entitling an alien to a waiver of the removal order.
3. The 1996 Act increased the period during which a removed alien may be barred from reentering the United States. What is your opinion of this provision? Are such penalties justified in all circumstances? If not, when?
4. Registry was initially introduced many years ago in order to prevent persons who had unlawfully entered the United States but who had been in the country for a substantial number of years to remain legally in the U.S. It is a form of amnesty. Do you believe that such provisions are appropriate? Why or why not? Explain your answer in detail.
5. What is your opinion of the INS's power to arrest without a warrant? Do you believe that it is a good idea to permit the INS to issue a warrant without a judge's authorization? How is your answer affected by the events of September 11, 2001? Explain.

Chapter Eight

REFUGEES AND ASYLUM

CHAPTER PREVIEW

Throughout history people have been forced to leave their homes because of persecution, invasion, famine, earthquake, flood, and other man-made and natural upheavals. When these people seek a safe haven in a place other than their homelands, they become subject to the laws of the countries granting them sanctuary. Seeking solace, these people are usually granted entry based on humanitarian concepts embodied in natural law and international convention.

In the United States the law with respect to granting refuge or asylum is contained in the **Refugee Act of 1980**, the **Immigration and Nationality Act (INA)**, and the regulations accompanying those statutes. Being granted status as a refugee or asylee is a method whereby a foreign national may gain admission into the United States if he or she could not enter one of the immigrant or nonimmigrant categories.

A person will only be granted entry as a refugee or asylee if he or she meets the definition of "refugee" as set forth in Section 101(a)(42) of the INA:

- any person who is outside any country of such person's nationality, or in the case of a person having no nationality, is outside any country in which such person last habitually resided and who is unable or unwilling to return to, and is unable or unwilling to avail him or herself of the protection of that country because of persecution or a well-founded fear of persecution on account of race, religion, nationality, membership in a particular social group, or political opinion, or
- in such special circumstances as the president...may specify.

A person is considered for refugee status if he or she applies for such status outside of the United States. Status as an **asylee** may be granted to an applicant who is already in the United States or at its borders and who meets the criteria of being a refugee as defined above. The classification as refugee or asylee depends upon the location of the place in which the application is made.

> **Example:** An alien is being persecuted because of her religion in her homeland. While on a trip to a country bordering her homeland, she applies at the U.S. consular office for status as a refugee in order to enter the United States.
>
> **Example:** An alien is being persecuted because of her religion in her homeland. On arrival at O'Hare airport in Chicago on a tourist visa she applies for status as an asylee in order to be able to remain in the United States.

To be a refugee or asylee, the applicant must prove that he or she has a **well-founded fear** of persecution in his or her home country because of belonging to one of the categories enumerated in Section 101(a)(42) of the INA. A well-founded fear is not specifically defined by the statute. Some courts have interpreted "well-founded fear" to require a showing of a **clear probability** or **credible fear** of being persecuted. A credible fear means that it is more likely than not that the applicant or his or her family will be persecuted. This necessitates a showing of clear evidence of specific threats either to the applicant or the applicant's family. A standard of showing a clear probability is not as generous as merely proving a well-founded fear. In 1987, the U.S. Supreme Court in *INS v. Cardozo-Fonseca* held that the burden of demonstrating a clear probability of persecution does not apply to asylum applicants (but may still apply to persons applying as refugees).

Under the 1990 regulations, an applicant can meet this burden of proof if a pattern or practice of persecution exists in his or her homeland on account of race, religion, nationality or political opinion, and the applicant has been clearly identified with one of these groups.

Example: An applicant for status as an asylee brings with him newspaper accounts of government-sponsored executions of persons who belong to the same political group as the applicant. The newspapers indicate that the government of the applicant's homeland has enunciated a policy of retribution against this political group because of its supposed revolutionary ideology. In this instance, the applicant may be considered to have met the requirement of documenting a well-founded fear of persecution in his homeland because of his political beliefs.

Take careful note of the fact that a person will be denied status as a refugee if it can be shown that the applicant participated in persecuting other persons who fall into one of the specified categories indicated above, regardless of the persecution the applicant may have actually suffered.

Example: In the preceding example there is a change of government, and a high-ranking member of the erstwhile ruling party now seeks asylum in the United States because she is afraid of retributions against her. This applicant will probably be denied entry because she participated in persecuting other people because of their political beliefs.

Status as a refugee or asylee is not granted lightly. This chapter focuses on the procedures for being granted or denied status as a refugee or asylee, special quasi-asylee status that may be granted for humanitarian reasons, and the ethical considerations that go into these decisions.

REFUGEES

General Requirements

Pursuant to the Immigration and Nationality Act, the president has the power to admit refugees into the country and may establish a ceiling on refugees from any one country in a single year. These ceilings may be adjusted upon a showing of an unforeseen emergency situation.

Example: The United States has established a ceiling of no more than 50,000 refugees from one particular country in any given year. Suddenly there is a *coup d'etat* in that country and the new leaders are far more reactionary than their predecessors. The new government begins a policy of persecution of a racial minority within its borders. Under these circumstances the president may raise the ceiling due to unforeseen circumstances.

Refugees who enter the country under the general ceiling are called **normal flow refugees**; those who enter because of special emergency circumstances are considered **refugees on special humanitarian grounds**.

The definition of "refugee" under the INA appears in the previous section. In order to be considered for refugee status, the applicant must show that he or she belongs to a group that falls into one of the categories specified by the statute and that this group has been subject to persecution in his or her homeland.

Example: An applicant can prove that she belongs to the Church of Scientology, but cannot produce any evidence of persecution or threats of persecution against this group in her homeland. She has not met the burden imposed by the statute.

Example: An applicant can prove that members of the Church of Scientology are being persecuted in her homeland, but she cannot prove that she is a member of that Church. She has not met the burden of proof imposed by the statute.

It is not necessary that the applicant prove that the persecution of the specified group is constant, current or perpetual. Even sporadic or previous persecution of the group may be sufficient, provided that the applicant can demonstrate that he or she belongs to the group and that a well-founded fear exists that persecution of the group may recur.

Example: An applicant can prove that throughout history whenever a natural disaster occurs in his homeland, the government uses the members of a particular minority living in the country as scapegoats. In order to appease the general populace, these people are denied basic human rights. Once the country recovers, the persecution stops. The country has not suffered a disaster in 30 years, but the applicant, a member of this minority race, fears that any new disaster will result in further persecutions. The applicant may be considered to meet the statutory requirements.

Once these primary statutory requirements have been met, the applicant must meet three further requirements before refugee status may be granted:

1. The applicant must be generally admissible to the United States and not subject to grounds for removal as discussed in Chapter Six.

2. The applicant must not be permanently settled in another country (other than his or her homeland) when seeking entry. If the applicant is permanently resettled somewhere other than the country of persecution, the need for refuge would appear to be diminished. The burden of proof is on the applicant to show that he or she has not permanently resettled. The determination of this resettlement is based on the facts and circumstances of each individual situation, but the government tends to look at such factors as family attachments, work, length of time in the country, government assistance, immigrant status in that country, and so forth.

Example: In an actual situation, an applicant left Russia for Israel because that was the only exit visa he could receive from the Soviet government. As a member of the Jewish religion, he was automatically granted entry into Israel under Israeli law. After two years the applicant applied to be considered a refugee by the U.S. in order to come to America. It was shown that during his residence in Israel he never sought permanent residence status, avoided all but minimal government assistance, and indicated a constant desire to enter the United States. Under these circumstances the court found that he had not permanently settled in Israel but was in Israel merely on a transitory basis.

3. The grounds for the applicant's entry must be shown to be of particular humanitarian concerns to the United States. This means that the applicant's category group must not profess a policy inimical to American standards, and the group must be defined under Section 101(a)(42) of the INA or part of a special category created by the president.

Example: The applicant belongs to a group that advocates the violent overthrow of democratic governments and the extermination of all members of a particular ethnic group. Members of this group would not be granted entry into the U.S. as refugees.

If the foregoing requirements are met, the applicant does not need to meet the other general immigration requirements for entry, such as having a labor certificate, proof of self-sufficiency, a valid entry document or visa, or meet the general literacy standards. However, under regulations appearing in the Code of Federal Regulations, the applicant must be sponsored by a responsible person or organization who will guarantee the applicant's transportation costs.

Example: Because of a three-year drought in Africa, many children are dying of malnutrition and starvation. The president has created a special category of refugee to admit these children, and a church group in Alabama decides to sponsor as many children as possible for entry into the United States. This church group is guaranteeing the transportation cost of these children so that the regulation can be satisfied.

Application Procedure

If the applicant believes that he or she meets the requirements detailed above, he or she must follow the application procedures found in Section 207.2 of Title 8 of the Code of Federal Regulations. The regulations specify that the applicant complete **Form I-590**, Request for Classification as Refugee (see Appendix 8-1), with an immigration officer at a U.S. embassy or consulate. If the applicant is under 14 years of age, **Form G-325A** and biographic information, must be filed. All supplemental statements and documents required by the forms must be supplied by the applicant.

The applicant must be interviewed by an immigration officer and must submit to a medical examination. There is a waiting list for approving applications, but the attorney general may adopt procedures for assigning priorities among applicants. If the application is approved, the applicant must enter the United States within four months of the approval (8 C.F.R. §207.4), and the applicant may be accompanied by a spouse and children. (8 C.F.R. §207.1(e))

Once in the United States, the applicant retains refugee status for one year, at which point he or she becomes eligible for a status readjustment as a permanent resident pursuant to Sections 207 and 209 of the INA. The refugee must apply for the readjustment of status with the Immigration and Naturalization Service (INS.) There the applicant will be inspected and examined to determine his or her admissibility as an immigrant. If permanent resident status is approved, the readjustment will be granted and made effective from the date of the refugee's entry into the country. There is no numerical limitation on status readjustments for refugees.

Example: One year after entering the United States as a refugee, the applicant files with INS for a status readjustment as a permanent resident. After examination, the refugee is found admissible, and his status is readjusted to reflect an entry as an immigrant from the date of his original entry. The timing detail affects the date on which the person may apply for naturalization as an American citizen. See Chapter Two.

If an alien has entered the United States as a refugee and the INS subsequently determines that he or she did not meet the requirements of Section 101(a)(42), the alien becomes subject to **removal** proceedings in order to be removed from the United States. See below.

Example: When the refugee applies for status readjustment with the INS after being in the U.S. for one year, the Service discovers that the person, rather than being persecuted in his homeland, was guilty of persecuting persons belonging to the categories enumerated in Section 101 (a)(42) of the INA Because this person should never have been admitted to the country as a refugee, the INS institutes removal proceedings against him.

GRANTING ASYLUM

Unlike quotas that exist for persons applying for refugee status, there is no numerical limitation imposed on persons who are seeking asylum in the United States. In order to be eligible to apply for status as an asylee, the alien must

- be present in the United States or at a U.S. border; and
- qualify as a refugee.

The same restrictions that apply to refugees apply to asylees as well, and the burden of proving that the alien meets the definition of "refugee" under Section 101(a)(42) of the INA is on the alien.

Example: While on a holiday in Mexico, an alien from Africa goes to Tijuana, the Mexican-American border town, and seeks entry into the United States as a refugee, claiming that she is being persecuted for her religious beliefs in her homeland. Because application is made at a U.S. border, the alien applies for status as an asylee. She may have a better chance of being admitted to the U.S. because there are no numerical limitations on her application.

The government officials who have jurisdiction over asylum applications are the **asylum officers** in the **Central Office of Refugees, Asylum, Parole (CORAP)** in the Immigration and Naturalization Service. The basis for this jurisdiction arises from Title 8 of the Code of Federal Regulations Section

208.2. The asylum officers have jurisdiction over all applications except those filed by aliens who are subject to removal proceedings; such applications fall under the jurisdiction of **immigration judges**.

> **Example:** An alien has entered the United States as an immigrant, but because he lied on his application about his criminal record, the government is seeking to remove him. At his hearing he claims that he is entitled to status as a refugee Because this claim for refugee status is made at a deportation hearing, the application comes within the jurisdiction of the immigration judge

In order to apply for asylum, the applicant must submit **Form I-589**, Application for Asylum (see Appendix 8-2), **Form G-325A**, Biographic Information (see Appendix 2-3), and **Form FD-258**, Fingerprint Chart (see Appendix 8-3). The applicant must be examined by the asylum officer in a nonpublic setting, and the applicant has the right to be represented by counsel at the interview and to submit pertinent affidavits in support of the application. There is a question as to whether the applicant must be informed of this right to counsel; at the present time there is a split in the judicial decisions on this matter.

Pursuant to the regulations, if the applicant leaves the United States or fails to appear at the interview for any unexcused reason, it is assumed that the alien has withdrawn his or her application for asylum, and the asylum officer will terminate the application process.

> **Example:** The day before her interview, an applicant for asylum has an appendicitis attack and is rushed to the hospital for emergency surgery. Because she is in the hospital, she does not attend her interview; however, because she has a valid reason for not attending, her application will not be terminated and the interview will be rescheduled.

At the hearing, under the auspices of the **Alien Prescreening Office**, a parole program for asylum applicants, the applicant must show that he or she has a well-founded fear of persecution in his or her homeland, must not be removable as a refugee under Section 101 of the INA, must not have resettled in another country, and must comply with all INS requirements. A "well-founded fear" can be proven by a showing of past persecution or that a pattern of persecution exists in the applicant's home country.

If asylum is granted, it is granted for an indefinite period. If the situation in the asylee's homeland changes, the asylee's status may be revoked, a situation that does not apply to refugees. After one year as an asylee, the asylee may apply for status reclassification, provided he or she meets all of the normal requirements for such reclassification as previously discussed in the text. Before the status will be readjusted, there must be slots left in the quotas for such reclassification to immigrant status. If reclassification is granted, the date of reclassification is recorded as of the year prior to the application approval under Section 209(b) of the INA.

DENYING ASYLUM

The preceding section discussed the forms and formalities required for an alien to apply for asylum to the United States; however, not every applicant is approved by the asylum officers. Under Sections 208 (d) and 243 (h)(2) of the Immigration and Nationality Act, there are six specified grounds for denying asylum. These enumerated grounds are

1. The applicant fails to qualify as a refugee. In order to be granted asylum, the alien must show that he or she comes within the definition of "refugee" under Section 101(a)(42) of the INA. An alien who cannot prove such refugee qualification will be denied asylum.

Example: An alien claims to have a fear of persecution in his home country because of his ethnic nationality but cannot demonstrate any such persecution. He does not meet the definition of "refugee" and consequently his application for asylum will be denied.

2. The applicant has permanently resettled in another country. If the applicant has left the home country where there was a well-founded fear of persecution but has already resettled in a second country, he or she cannot be classified as an asylee because he or she has already permanently escaped the country of persecution.

Example: A woman, fearing persecution in her home country of Iran, moved to France five years ago. Once in France she married a French national and has given birth to two children in France. She now wishes to divorce her husband, and on a pleasure trip to the United States applies for asylum. In this instance it would appear that she has already resettled in France because she has established significant ties to France: therefore, she would not qualify as an asylee.

3. The applicant has participated in the persecution of persons in his or her home country. If the applicant was the persecutor rather than the persecuted, asylum will be denied.

Example: An applicant for asylum was a high-ranking official of the former government in his homeland. This former government persecuted members of minority religions. The government was overthrown, and the new government is prosecuting former government officials. The applicant escaped, eventually arriving at the U.S. border. Because the applicant participated in the persecution of a protected category of persons, he will be denied asylum.

4. The applicant was convicted of a felony. The United States has a policy of refusing entry to convicted felons or persons who have committed crimes of violence.

Example: The applicant for asylum was convicted of drug dealing and money laundering in his home country. These are felony convictions and asylum will be denied.

5. There is a reason to believe that the applicant committed a serious nonpolitical crime outside the United States. The determination as to what is serious and what is nonpolitical is determined on a case-by-case basis.

Example: The applicant for asylum is shown to have participated in a *coup d'etat* in his home country. Depending upon the circumstances, this may be considered a political act and therefore not a bar to entry into the United States as an asylee.

6. The applicant presents a security risk to the United States. This ground is very subjective and must be determined on a case-by-case basis, typically with instructions from the State Department.

Example: An applicant for asylum belongs to a group in his home country that advocates a totalitarian state. The U.S. government believes that membership in this organization may present a security risk, and the applicant will be denied entry.

In addition to these grounds, both asylum officers and immigration judges are given a certain degree of discretion to deny asylum if it can be shown that the applicant has fraudulently bypassed U.S. laws in an attempt to apply for asylum.

If the application is denied, the applicant will be subject to exclusion or deportation proceedings. If the application was made at a U.S. border, the proceeding is one for removal prior to entry, similar to the rejection of a refugee application. If the application was made by an alien already in the United States, the applicant is subject to removal proceedings or may be granted voluntary departure as discussed in earlier chapters under Section 208.8(f) of the regulations.

The decision of the asylum officer is reviewed by the assistant commissioner of CORAP and the deputy attorney general, although there is no right to such review. Also, asylum status may be revoked by the assistant commissioner for:

- changed country conditions: the asylee's home country has indicated a changed policy, thereby negating the asylee's fear of persecution;
- fraud: a finding that the applicant participated in a fraud in order to be granted asylum; or
- commission of an Act that is Grounds for Denying Asylum: the applicant is found to have committed any act that prohibits granting asylum as discussed above.

If an asylum officer denies an application for asylum, an immigration judge will review the application. If the applicant disagrees with the decision denying his or her application, the applicant may avail pursue one of three courses of action:

1. The applicant may make a motion to reopen the file for a rehearing;
2. The applicant may appeal to the Board of Immigration Appeals (BIA); or
3. The applicant may seek judicial review of the matter by filing in one of the United States appellate courts.

In addition to all the foregoing, any alien in the United States under a nonrefugee or nonasylee status who is subject to removal proceedings may, at that time, apply for asylum; however, the application may be denied if the alien cannot reasonably explain why such application was not made before. An alien may not use the procedures for seeking asylum as a delaying tactic to his or her deportation from the country.

SPECIAL ASYLUM CATEGORIES

Since 1990 the United States has permitted aliens to stay or enter the country under special categories that ideologically fall under the concepts of refuge and asylum but which are not specified as such. These categories are extended voluntary departure, temporary protected status, and the ABC settlement cases.

Extended Voluntary Departure

This status is granted to persons pursuant to 8 C.F.R. §274.12(a)(11). Extended voluntary departure applies to persons who cannot return to their own country because of a civil war or some other such crisis. One example of this category was the Chinese Detained Departure Program, which ended on July 1, 1994. This program permitted Chinese students to remain in the United States after their visas expired because of political turmoil in the People's Republic.

Temporary Protected Status

Under Section 244A of the INA, temporary protected status may be granted to nationals of countries that the attorney general has determined to be undergoing unstable or unsafe conditions. The conditions that may give rise to this classification are

- an ongoing war or armed conflict
- earthquake, flood, drought, or other environmental problem
- the alien's safe return is precluded by extraordinary and temporary conditions.

Temporary protected status may be granted to aliens for periods ranging from six to eighteen months, and these periods may be extended until such time as the emergency situation in the alien's homeland no longer exists. To date, citizens of the following countries have been granted temporary protected status: Bosnia-Herzegovina, El Salvador, Kuwait, Lebanon, Liberia, Rwanda, Somalia, and Yugoslavia.

In order to qualify under this category, the alien must file **Form I-821**, Application for Temporary Protected Status (see Appendix 8-4), **Form I-765**, Application for Employment Authorization (see Appendix 8-5), and **Form FD-258** (see Appendix 8-3), a Fingerprint Chart, and be interviewed by an asylum officer.

ABC Settlements

In 1991 the United States District Court for the Northern District of California in *American Baptist Church v. Thornburgh* found that the INS had been denying certain asylum cases in a discriminatory manner and, consequently, all Salvadorans who were in the United States as of September 19, 1990, and all Guatemalans who were in the United States as of October 1, 1990, and who were denied asylum could have their cases reopened unless they had been convicted of a felony. This reopening suspends all removal proceedings against them and, in redetermining asylum, the government is estopped from considering the following factors:

- U.S. foreign policy with respect to El Salvador or Guatemala
- border enforcement conditions
- the applicant's political beliefs
- the U.S. government's support of the applicant's homeland.

This judicial settlement may be considered as a subset of the temporary protected status discussed above.

It is important to note that these three categories exist for persons in the United States who had not originally entered as refugees or asylees but under some other temporary nonimmigrant status.

ETHICAL CONSIDERATIONS

Persons seeking refuge have always been granted special standing under the general principles of international law. These principles have been enunciated in the 1951 Convention relating to the Status of Refugees and the 1967 Protocol in which "refugee" was defined in the same fashion as was adopted by the United States in Section 101 of the Immigration and Nationality Act. Generally and subject to national imperatives, nations are willing to accept foreigners who meet the definition of "refugee" and to grant them asylum within their borders. However, the determination of rights of the refugee or asylee involve questions of morals and ethics.

In most instances the request for refuge is made under traumatic circumstances, and yet little guidance may be given to the asylum officer to make the appropriate determination of status. Because many questions are left up to individual discretion or determination, the prejudices of a particular officer may cloud his or her judgment with respect to the application. For example, assume the officer is prejudiced against a particular race or nationality and a member of the group is seeking asylum in the U.S. because of persecution at home. It is possible that the officer would deny the application if proof of persecution is not clear-cut and the decision could be made either way. In this instance, the officer's own dislike of the category of refugee could have severe and/or life-threatening consequences for the applicant. Note the ABC settlements discussed above.

How far should the United States government go in advising and/or permitting counsel for aliens who are seeking refuge or asylum? Should free counsel be provided if the alien is unable to pay legal fees? Should the alien be given appropriate interpreters to interview with the government and the attorneys?

If an attorney is representing an alien in seeking refuge or asylum in the United States, should the attorney obfuscate or confuse the facts in order to have the alien admitted, or is there a greater need to assure that the laws are strictly and appropriately enforced? There is always the ethical concern that providing effective counsel may conflict with the attorney's role as an officer of the court. Also, should an attorney advise an alien client who is subject to removal proceedings to apply for asylum status merely to prolong the alien's stay in the country?

Many problems have arisen with respect to aliens being permitted to work in the United States. Many Americans feel that these foreigners are taking jobs away from American citizens, and they resent the laws that permit refugees to work while their final status is still in question. However, because the United States was founded by aliens who were, for the most part, seeking refuge from persecution at home and who were hoping for a place to work in order to make better lives for themselves and their families, these criticisms would seem to fly in the face of American history.

CHAPTER REVIEW

Foreign nationals may enter the United States even if they do not fall within the quotas or general limitations of an immigrant or nonimmigrant status if they can demonstrate that they are "refugees" within the meaning of the INA. Generally, an alien who can prove that he or she has a well-founded fear of being persecuted in his or her homeland because of race, religion, national origin, political affiliation, or other category specified in Section 101(a)(42 may seek refuge or asylum in the United States.

The difference between applying for refuge or asylum is dependent upon the location at which such application is made. If the alien applies outside of the United States, he or she applies for status as a refugee. If the application is made by someone already within the country or at a U.S. border, the application is one for asylum. In both instances, the application can only be granted if the applicant meets the definition of "refugee" discussed above.

Once the applicant is granted status as a refugee or asylee, he or she may obtain permission to work in the country, and after one year may apply for status readjustment to be classified as a permanent resident. There is no limitation on status readjustment for refugees, but asylees must still come within the appropriate quota restrictions in order to have their status changed. The status readjustment is dated from the date of the alien's entry into the U.S.

An application for refuge may be denied because the applicant does not meet the statutory standards enumerated in the INA, or he or she has already resettled in a country other than his or her homeland. Asylum may be denied for the same reasons, or because the applicant had been convicted of various offenses specified in Sections 208(d) and 243(h)(2) of the INA. The decision denying the application may be reviewed by the assistant commissioner of CORAP and the deputy attorney general, and the applicant has the right either to move to reopen the file for a new hearing, appeal to the Board of Immigration Appeals, or to appeal to the federal court system.

In addition to being granted entry as a refugee or asylee, an alien already in the United States under some other visa category may be permitted to remain in the country under the provisions of extended voluntary departure if his or her home country is in a state of civil war or turmoil, or may be granted temporary protected status if his or her homeland is suffering under a special extraordinary and temporary disaster situation.

The forms that an applicant for refuge or asylum may be required to complete are:

- Form I-590, Registration for Classification as Refugee (Appendix 8-1)
- Form G-325A, Biographic Information (Appendix 2-3)
- Form FD-258, Fingerprint Chart (Appendix 8-3)
- Form I-765, Application for Employment Authorization (Appendix 8-5)
- Form I-589, Application for Asylum and for Withholding of Removal (Appendix 8-2)
- Form I-821, Application for Temporary Protected Status (Appendix 8-4)

CHAPTER VOCABULARY

ABC settlement — Court case that permits rehearing of denials of application for asylum for Salvadorans and Guatemalans because of U.S. discrimination.

Alien Prescreening Office — Government office that interviews prospective refugees.

Asylee — Person granted asylum.

Asylum — Status granted to qualifying refugees who apply for status as asylees either within the U.S. or at its borders.

Asylum officer — Government official who decides on applications for refuge or asylum for persons not subject to removal proceedings.

Central Office of Refugees, Asylum, Parole (CORAP) — INS office with jurisdiction over refugees and asylees.

Clear probability (credible fear) — Standard of documenting a likelihood of persecution in the applicant's home country; a more severe standard than well-founded fear.

Extended voluntary departure — Special category that permits aliens to remain in the United States after issuance of a removal order because of problems in their homelands.

Immigration & Nationality Act of 1952 (INA) — Federal law governing immigration and naturalization of foreigners to the U.S.

Immigration judge — Government official with jurisdiction over refugees and asylees subject to removal proceedings.

Normal flow refugee — A refugee who enters under the normal refugee ceilings.

Refugee — Alien seeking entry into the U.S. because he or she is persecuted in his or her homeland because of race, religion, sex, national origin or political beliefs.

Refugee Act of 1980 — Federal statute covering the entry into the country of refugees.

Refugee on special humanitarian grounds — Category of refugees who enter under special circumstances not limited to the typical refugee ceilings.

Temporary protected status — Status granted to aliens in the United States so that they may remain in the U.S. while their homelands are in turmoil.

Well-founded fear — The statutory standard that must be met with respect to the applicant's worry about being persecuted in his or her homeland.

EDITED JUDICIAL DECISIONS

The following decisions are included in order to underscore the concepts discussed in the body of the text. *Orantes-Hernandez v. Thornburgh* concerns abuse of discretion by an INS officer, and *Shirazi-Parsa v. INS* discusses a denial of asylum.

ORANTES-HERNANDEZ v. THORNBURGH

919 F.2d 549 (9th Cir. 1990)

This is an appeal from the entry of a permanent injunction in favor of the plaintiffs in a class action against United States government immigration officials. The plaintiff class is composed of Salvadoran nationals who are eligible to apply for political asylum, and who have been or will be taken into custody by the Immigration and Naturalization Service (INS). The district court's injunction, together with its extensive supporting findings of fact and conclusions of law, is reported in *Orantes-Hernandez v. Meese*, 685 F. Supp. 1488 (C.D. Cal. 1988) (Orantes II).

The complaint alleged that INS officials and Border Patrol Agents prevented members of the class from exercising their statutory right to apply for asylum under the provisions of 8 U.S.C. §1158(a) (1988). The complaint also alleged INS interference with plaintiffs' ability to obtain counsel, a right guaranteed by 8 U.S.C. Sec, 1362 and the due process clause. See *United States v. Villa-Fabela*, 882 F.2d 434, 438 (9th Cir. 1989).

The injunction appealed from requires the INS to notify Salvadoran detainees both of their right to apply for political asylum and of their right to be represented by counsel, though not at government expense. Orantes II, 685 F. Supp. at 1512. It enjoins the INS from coercing Salvadoran detainees into signing voluntary departure agreements and from interfering with detainees' ability to obtain counsel at their own expense. Id. at 1511-1513.

This injunction makes permanent a preliminary injunction imposing similar requirements. See *Orantes-Hernandez v. Smith*, 541 F. Supp. 351 (C.D. Cal. 1982) (Orantes I). The preliminary injunction, entered in 1982, was not stayed and the government did not pursue an appeal. The preliminary injunction remained in effect for the six years preceding the entry of the permanent injunction in 1988.

Although the government has raised some legal questions on appeal, the main issue we must decide is factual in nature: whether certain findings of the district court regarding government interference with plaintiffs' rights to apply for asylum and to seek the assistance of counsel at non-government expense are clearly erroneous.

II. Legal Background

A. Asylum

Plaintiffs' action arises under the Refugee Act of 1980 in which Congress sought to bring United States refugee law into conformity with the 1967 United Nations Protocol Relating to the Status of Refugees (UN Protocol). The UN Protocol, to which the United States acceded in 1968, binds parties to comply with the substantive provisions of Articles 2 through 34 of the United Nations Convention Relating to the Status of Refugees (1951 Convention) with respect to "refugees" as defined in *Article 1.2 of the UN Protocol. INS v. Stevic*, 467 U.S. 407, 416, 81 L. Ed. 2d 321, 104 S. Ct. 2489 (1984).

The Refugee Act was passed with the intention of codifying existing practices. It "place[d] into law what we do for refugees now by custom, and on an ad hoc basis. . . ." S. Rep. No. 256, 96th Cong., 2d Sess. 1, reprinted in 1980 U.S. Code Cong. & Admin. News 141, 141. The Act expressly declared that its purpose was to enforce the "historic policy of the United States to respond to the urgent needs of the persons subject to persecution in their homelands," n6 and to provide "statutory meaning to our national commitment to human rights and humanitarian concerns."

Prior to passage of the Refugee Act, there was no specific statutory basis for United States asylum policy with respect to aliens already in this country. See *INS v. Cardoza-Fonseca*, 480 U.S. 421, 433, 94 L. Ed. 2d 434, 107 S. Ct. 1207 (1987); *Carvajal-Munoz v. INS*, 743 F.2d 562, 564 (7th Cir. 1984). n8 Congress, therefore, established for the first time a provision in federal law specifically relating to requests for asylum. Carvajal-Munoz, 743 F.2d at 564. Section 201(b) of the Refugee Act created section 208 of the Immigration and Naturalization Act (INA) directing the Attorney General to establish a procedure for an alien physically present in the United States or at a land border or port of entry, irrespective of such alien's status, to apply for asylum, and the alien may be granted asylum in the discretion of the Attorney General if the Attorney General determines that such alien is a refugee within the meaning of section 101(a)(42)(A) of this title.

INA §208(a), 8 U.S.C. §1158(a) (1988); Cardoza-Fonseca, 480 U.S. at 427. Congressional intent was to create a "uniform procedure" for consideration of asylum claims which would include an opportunity for aliens to have asylum applications "considered outside a deportation and/or exclusion hearing setting." See S. Rep. No. 256, 96th Cong., 2d Sess. 1, 9, reprinted in 1980 U.S. Code Cong. & Admin. News 141, 149.

Congress added a new statutory definition of "refugee" to the INA in order to eliminate the geographical and ideological restrictions then applicable under the INA. See S. Rep. No. 256, 96th Cong., 2d Sess. 1, 4, reprinted in 1980 U.S. Code Cong. & Admin. News 141, 144. In formulating this definition, Congress noted its intent to bring the definition of "refugee" under United States immigration law into conformity with the UN Protocol. See id. The definition adopted by Congress is virtually identical to the definition of "refugee" in the 1951 Convention, see Cardoza-Fonseca, 480 U.S. at 437, and is an expanded version of the UN Protocol definition of "refugee", see Stevic, 467 U.S. at 422.

Section 101(a)(42)(A) of the INA defines a refugee as any person who is outside any country of such person's nationality or, in the case of a person having no nationality, is outside any country in which such person last habitually resided, and who is unable or unwilling to return to, and is unable or unwilling to avail himself or herself of the protection of, that country because of persecution or a well-founded fear of persecution on account of race, religion, nationality, membership in a particular social group, or political opinion.

8 U.S.C. §1101(a)(42)(A) (1988). This litigation focuses on those provisions of the Refugee Act establishing the right of aliens to apply for asylum. It is undisputed that all aliens possess such a right under the Act. See 8 U.S.C. § 1158(a) (1988); *Jean v. Nelson*, 727 F.2d 957, 982 (11th Cir. 1984) (en banc) (section 1158 confers upon all aliens the right to apply for asylum), aff'd as modified, 472 U.S. 846, 105 S. Ct. 2992, 86 L. Ed. 2d 664 (1985); *Haitian Refugee Center v. Smith*, 676 F.2d 1023, 1038-39 (5th Cir. 1982) (same). One of the major concerns of the plaintiffs-appellees has been to ensure their ability to apply for asylum pursuant to the provisions of the Act. Much of this litigation has centered around plaintiffs' contentions that the INS was forcing them to apply for "voluntary departure" and preventing them from making an application for refugee status. It is therefore necessary to have some understanding of "voluntary departure."

An alien who is in the United States illegally may be apprehended and taken into custody by INS officials. INA §242, 8 U.S.C. §1252(a) (1988). After an alien is apprehended, the alien is presented with a Notice and Request for Disposition Form I-274 which allows the alien to choose to depart voluntarily from the United States at the alien's own expense before deportation proceedings are instituted, or to request a deportation hearing. *United States v. Doe*, 862 F.2d 776, 778 (9th Cir. 1988). Section 242(b) of the INA vests the Attorney General with discretion to award voluntary departure in lieu of initiating deportation proceedings. 8 U.S.C. §1252(b) (1988); *Contreras-Aragon v. INS*, 852 F.2d 1088, 1094 (9th Cir. 1988). This voluntary departure procedure has been called a "rough immigration equivalent of a guilty plea," allowing an alien knowingly to waive his right to a hearing in exchange for being able to depart

An advantage of voluntary departure over deportation is that it "permits the alien to select his or her own destination." Id. at 1090. In addition, it "facilitates the possibility of return to the United States" because an alien who leaves under a grant of voluntary departure, unlike a deported alien, does not need special permission to reenter the United States and does not face criminal penalties for failure to obtain that permission. Id.; see also INA §§212(a)(17) and 276, 8 U.S.C. §1182(a)(17) and 1326 (1988).

There are disadvantages to voluntary departure as well. Aliens who voluntarily depart this country lose the right to apply for asylum before deportation proceedings are initiated. They also give up their right to a deportation hearing at which they may also apply for and have their asylum claim considered before an Immigration Judge. Not only do aliens who accept voluntary departure lose these rights, they may leave the United States without even knowing of these rights and options.

An application for voluntary departure under section 242(b) of the INA must be made prior to the commencement of a deportation hearing and no appeal lies from the denial of the application. Contreras-Aragon, 852 F.2d at 1094. If an alien chooses not to depart voluntarily, a proceeding to determine the deportability of the alien is commenced by an immigration official who issues and files an order to show cause with the Office of the Immigration Judge.

n11 8 C.F.R. §242.1(a) (1990). INS regulations give exclusive jurisdiction to the Immigration Judge to consider asylum applications once an alien is in custody, the characteristic that defines the plaintiff class in this case. See generally 2 Gordon & Gordon, Immigration Law and Procedure § 18.04[1](a) (rev. ed. 1990).

B. Counsel

The INA also provides aliens with the right to be represented by counsel in deportation proceedings at no expense to the government. See (INA §292), 8 U.S.C. §1362 (1988). The Act specifically requires the Attorney General to adopt regulations to assure the right of counsel of one's choice. See(INA §242(b)(2)), 8 U.S.C. §1252(b)(2) (1988). The INS has done so in a regulation requiring that upon personal service of an order to show cause why an alien should not be deported, the alien "shall . . . be advised of his right to representation by counsel of his own choice at no expense to the Government." 8 C.F.R. §242.1(c) (1990). The regulations go on to describe persons and groups entitled to represent aliens in deportation proceedings, and make it possible for persons who are not attorneys to represent aliens in such proceedings. See id. §292.1.

This court has held that aliens have a due process right to obtain counsel of their choice at their own expense. *Rios-Berrios v. INS*, 776 F.2d 859, 862 (9th Cir. 1985). We have "consistently emphasized the critical role of counsel in deportation proceedings. We have characterized an alien's right to counsel as 'Fundamental' and have warned the INS not to treat it casually. . . . That right must be respected in substance as well as in name." *Baires v. INS*, 856 F.2d 89, 91 (9th Cir. 1988) (citations omitted). Other circuits agree that counsel may play a critical role in deportation proceedings. See *Lozada v. INS*, 857 F.2d 10, 13 (1st Cir. 1988); *United States v. Saucedo-Velasquez*, 843 F.2d 832, 834-35 (5th Cir. 1988); *Cobourne v. INS*, 779 F.2d 1564, 1566 (11th Cir. 1986); *Casteneda-Delgado v. INS*, 525 F.2d 1295, 1300 (7th Cir. 1975).

III. The History of This Litigation (Deleted)

IV. Legal Analysis

The district court's injunction is designed to ensure the ability of the plaintiff class members to exercise their rights to apply for political asylum and to seek the assistance of counsel. The existence of those rights is not seriously in issue. Hence, what is disputed is not rights but remedies.

With respect to asylum, the key remedy contained in the district court's injunction is the "Orantes advisal," the provision requiring the government to give members of the plaintiff class actual written notice of their right to apply for asylum. This remedy rests upon three alternative and independent legal bases. One is that notice is required as a matter of due process. See Orantes II, 685 F. Supp. at 1506-07, conclusions 24-25. The second is that notice is required in order to fully effectuate the intent of the Refugee Act. See id. At 1506, conclusions 19-23. The third is that such notice is required in this case as a remedial measure to counteract the pattern of interference by the INS with the plaintiff class members' ability to exercise their rights. See id. At 1507-08, conclusions 26-43.

The government's threshold attack on the injunction is focused on the first two bases for the injunction, namely that as a matter of law the INS is required to give notice of the right to apply for asylum to all aliens it processes. This court has not considered this issue, but other courts have. See Jean, 727 F.2d 957; *Ramirez-Osorio v. INS*, 745 F.2d 937 (5th Cir. 1984). The decisions in those cases stop short of holding that aliens have a statutory or constitutional right to blanket notice of the right to apply for asylum. The decisions agree, however, that notice should be given to those aliens who indicate that they fear persecution if they were to be returned home. See Jean, 727 F.2d at 983 n.35; Ramirez-Osorio, 745 F.2d at 943-44.

The issue of notice was discussed at some length in Jean. The Eleventh Circuit held that there is no notice requirement in the statute itself and further, that aliens have no due process right to notice of the right to apply for asylum. See 727 F.2d at 981-83. The court recognized, however, that the Act would be violated if aliens who indicated they feared persecution if returned home were not advised of the right to seek asylum. See id. at 983 The court said that "if INS officials were refusing to inform aliens of their right to seek asylum even if they did indicate that they feared persecution if returned to their home countries . . . this would constitute a clear violation of the Refugee Act, and remedial action would be justified. . . ." Id.

The Eleventh Circuit in Jean concluded, however, that no remedial action was necessary in that case. It reached this conclusion based on the testimony of the Acting Commissioner of the INS who represented during congressional hearings that it is INS policy for agents to provide notification of the right to apply for asylum to those aliens who indicate they have a fear of persecution if returned home. See id. (citing Caribbean Migration: Oversight Hearings Before the Subcomm. on Immigration, Refugees and International Law of the House Comm. on the Judiciary, 96th Cong., 2d Sess. 225 (1980) (statement of David Crosland, Acting Commissioner, INS) (hereinafter "Oversight Hearings"). Other courts have relied upon this testimony as an accurate description of INS policy when those courts declined to impose a remedial notice requirement. See *Duran v. INS*, 756 F.2d 1338, 1341 (9th Cir. 1985); Ramirez-Osorio, 745 F.2d at 941, 943-44 (court refused to require INS to provide aliens with blanket notice of the right to apply for asylum but found it "significant" that INS gives notice to aliens who express a fear of persecution). Cf. Haitian Refugee Center, 676 F.2d at 1041 (agency deviation from its own regulations and policies may justify judicial relief).

In this case, the government has not gone so far as to acknowledge that aliens who have a good faith fear of persecution should be advised of their right to apply for asylum. Such acknowledgment would, in the context of this case, amount to a concession that the Orantes advisal is required as a matter of law to many members of the plaintiff class. The government has, however, appropriately conceded in oral argument that if the evidence in this case supports the district court's findings of a pattern of coercion and interference with the plaintiff class members' right to apply for asylum, then the INS would be violating the Act and remedial action would be justified.

Accordingly, it is not necessary for us to reach any constitutional or even statutory interpretation issues with regard to the notice requirement if the record in this case supports the district court's findings with regard to the INS's conduct and reflects the appropriateness of the injunctive relief ordered. Such an approach is consistent with the general principle that we should not reach constitutional issues if the case can be decided on another basis. A fundamental rule of judicial restraint requires courts to consider nonconstitutional grounds for decisions before reaching any constitutional questions. Jean, 472 U.S. at 854; *Gulf Oil Co. v. Bernard*, 452 U.S. 89, 99, 68 L. Ed. 2d 693, 101 S. Ct. 2193 (1981). We therefore direct our focus to the district court's alternative grounds for ordering the INS to advise the plaintiff class members of the possibility of applying for refugee status.

Before turning to the district court's findings, we review the legal standards under which we weigh the appropriateness of injunctive relief against an agency of the federal government. We agree with the government that to obtain injunctive relief against government actions which allegedly violate the law, "the injury or threat of injury must be both 'real and immediate,' not 'conjectural' or 'hypothetical.'" *Los Angeles v. Lyons*, 461

U.S. 95, 101-02, 75 L. Ed. 2d 675, 103 S. Ct. 1660 (1983) (citations omitted). Thus, a "showing at trial of relatively few instances of violations by [defendants], without any showing of a deliberate policy on behalf of the named defendants, [does] not provide a basis for equitable relief." Id. at 104 (discussing *Rizzo v. Goode*, 423 U.S. 362, 46 L. Ed. 2d 561, 96 S. Ct. 598 (1976)). Injunctive relief, however, is available to combat a persistent pattern of misconduct violative of plaintiff's rights. See *Allee v. Medrano*, 416 U.S. 802, 815, 40 L. Ed. 2d 566, 94 S. Ct. 2191 (1974); *Hague v. CIO*, 307 U.S. 496, 83 L. Ed. 1423, 59 S. Ct. 954 (1939); *LaDuke v. Nelson*, 762 F.2d 1318, 1324 (9th Cir. 1985), modified on other grounds, 796 F.2d 309 (9th Cir. 1986). See also Rizzo, 423 U.S. at 375 (distinguishing Allee and Hague as involving patterns of misbehavior, not isolated incidents).

Plaintiffs must demonstrate "'the likelihood of substantial and immediate irreparable injury and the inadequacy of remedies at law.'" LaDuke, 762 F.2d at 1330 (quoting *O'Shea v. Littleton*, 414 U.S. 488, 502, 38 L. Ed. 2d 674, 94 S. Ct. 669 (1974)). To satisfy this standard, plaintiffs must establish actual success on the merits, and that the balance of equities favors injunctive relief. Id. That is, the plaintiff seeking an injunction must prove the plaintiff's own case and adduce the requisite proof, by a preponderance of the evidence, of the conditions and circumstances upon which the plaintiff bases the right to and necessity for injunctive relief. *Citizens Concerned for Separation of Church & State v. Denver*, 628 F.2d 1289, 1299 (10th Cir. 1980), cert. denied, 452 U.S. 963, 101 S. Ct. 3114, 69 L. Ed. 2d 975 (1981).

Once plaintiffs establish they are entitled to injunctive relief, the district court has broad discretion in fashioning a remedy. *Lemon v. Kurtzman*, 411 U.S. 192, 200, 36 L. Ed. 2d 151, 93 S. Ct. 1463 (1973) ("In shaping equity decrees, the trial court is vested with broad discretionary power; appellate review is correspondingly narrow"); *Coca-Cola Co. v. Overland, Inc.*, 692 F.2d 1250, 1256 n. 16 (9th Cir. 1982). See also *Toussaint v. McCarthy*, 801 F.2d 1080, 1087 (9th Cir. 1986), cert. denied, 481 U.S. 1069, 95 L. Ed. 2d 871, 107 S. Ct. 2462 (1987) (scope of injunctive relief is reviewed for an abuse of discretion). There are limitations on this discretion; an injunction must be narrowly tailored to give only the relief to which plaintiffs are entitled. See *Califano v. Yamasaki*, 442 U.S. 682, 702, 61 L. Ed. 2d 176, 99 S. Ct. 2545 (1979).

In other cases involving INS actions, this court has upheld injunctive relief based on findings that the INS engaged in a persistent pattern of misconduct violating aliens' rights. See *International Molders' and Allied Workers' Local U. v. Nelson*, 799 F.2d 547, 551 (9th Cir. 1986) (findings of "extensive evidence of INS agents exceeding official policy" could hardly be characterized as isolated incidents); *Nicacio v. INS*, 797 F.2d 700, 702 (9th Cir. 1985) (INS officers' conduct "recurrent and in violation of plaintiffs' constitutional rights"); LaDuke, 762 F.2d at 1324 (INS officers "engaged in a standard pattern" of misconduct); *Zepeda v. INS*, 753 F.2d 719, 726 (9th Cir. 1983) (pattern of INS violations of the fourth amendment).

The decisions of this court involving injunctions against the INS have focused additionally upon the important role of the federal courts in constraining misconduct by federal agents. We have observed that the "prudential limitations circumscribing federal court intervention in state law enforcement matters" involved in Lyons and Rizzo were inapplicable. See LaDuke, 762 F.2d at 1324; Nicacio, 797 F.2d at 702; International Molders', 799 F.2d at 551-52.

In this case, the equities favor issuance of the injunction if the findings of the district court with respect to INS practices are supported by the evidence. The government has not pointed to any evidence in the record to show that the issuance of the preliminary injunction caused any additional burden to it or that compliance with the permanent injunction would result in any appreciable burden. The government has asserted that informing all aliens of the right to apply for asylum is "potentially" burdensome because it will foster frivolous claims. However, the government does not provide support for this supposition.

Our decision in this case therefore must focus on whether the court's factual findings concerning the conduct of INS agents are clearly erroneous. We thus must turn to the nature of the district court's findings and a more comprehensive description of the evidence in the case.

V. The District Court's Findings and Evidence Concerning INS Interference With the Right to Apply for Asylum

The injunction on appeal to this court made permanent a preliminary injunction based mainly upon the district court's findings of a pattern and practice of interference and coercion on the part of INS agents which prevented Salvadoran aliens who feared return to their country from exercising their right to apply for asylum. One of the government's major contentions on appeal is that the entry of the permanent injunction was unwarranted because there were significant changes in circumstances after the entry of the preliminary injunction which made a permanent injunction unnecessary. In order to analyze this contention, it is necessary to have some familiarity with the voluminous record in this case concerning conditions as they existed both before and after the preliminary injunction.

A. The Record Supporting the Preliminary Injunction (Deleted)

We agree with the government that injunctive relief is designed to deter future misdeeds, not to punish past misconduct. See *United States v. W.T. Grant Co.*, 345 U.S. 629, 633, 97 L. Ed. 1303, 73 S. Ct. 894 (1953); *Loya v. INS*, 583 F.2d 1110, 1114 (9th Cir. 1978). However, a district court has "broad power to restrain acts which are of the same type or class as unlawful acts which the court has found to have been committed or whose commission in the future, unless enjoined, may be fairly anticipated from the defendant's conduct in the past." *N.L.R.B. v. Express Publishing Co.*, 312 U.S. 426, 435, 85 L. Ed. 930, 61 S. Ct. 693 (1941). Permanent injunctive relief is warranted where, as here, defendant's past and present misconduct indicates a strong likelihood of future violations. See *Green v. McCall*, 822 F.2d 284, 293 (2nd Cir. 1987) (permanent injunctive relief appropriate in light of U.S. Parole Commission's repeated failure to comply with preliminary injunction and with its own procedures in past); *United States v. An Article of Drug*, 661 F.2d 742, 747 (9th Cir. 1981) (permanent injunction proper because appellant continued to distribute drug despite jury's finding that it had no "safe and effective use"). The record does not support the government's contentions that there were material changes in circumstances making the entry of the permanent injunction unnecessary.

VI. The District Court's Findings With Respect to INS Interference With the Right to Counsel

The permanent injunction dealt not only with the right to apply for asylum, but also with the related right to consult with counsel. The INA provides aliens a right to be represented by counsel at no expense to the government. See (INA §292), 8 U.S.C.§1362 (1988). Regulations adopted to effectuate this section require INS officials to notify aliens of their right to counsel and the availability of free legal services programs, 8 C.F.R. §242.1(c) (1990), and to maintain a current list of such programs and provide the list to aliens, id. §§292a.1, 292a.2. The regulations also expressly require that juvenile detainees must be given access to a telephone and cannot be presented with a voluntary departure form until they have communicated with a parent, adult relative, friend, or organization on the free legal services list. Id. §242.24(g). See *Perez-Funez v. INS*, 619 F. Supp. 656, 670 (C.D. Cal. 1985). an attorney....

VII. The Government's Other Challenges

The government makes a number of other contentions, apart from the claims that the district court's findings were clearly erroneous.

The government faults the district court for adopting many of the plaintiffs' findings "essentially word for word." However, there is no legal infirmity in the district court's so doing. As the government concedes, even when the trial judge adopts proposed findings of facts verbatim, those findings may be reversed only if clearly erroneous. See Fed. R. Civ. P. 52. See also *Anderson v. City of Bessemer*, 470 U.S. 564, 571-73, 84 L. Ed. 2d 518, 105 S. Ct. 1504 (1985); *L.K. Comstock & Co., Inc. v. United Eng. & Constructors, Inc.*, 880 F.2d 219, 222 (9th Cir. 1989). As shown above, the findings here are not clearly erroneous.

Moreover, the district court did not accept the findings verbatim, but made material changes in the findings. Of the court's 118 factual findings, 10 were not proposed by the plaintiffs in any form and an additional 37 were modified, some substantially. The district court also materially reorganized the findings as presented by plaintiffs. These deviations indicate the district court did not uncritically accept plaintiffs' proposals. See Anderson, 470 U.S. at 572-73; L.K. Comstock & Co., 880 F.2d at 222. There is no basis for reversing the court's decision due to the form of the factual findings.

The government also contends that the district court improperly relied upon testimony of a psychologist on the distinctive personality traits of Salvadorans. Such testimony was relevant and material only to the extent that it tended to show that a substantial number of Salvadorans feared return and did not understand asylum principles. The findings of the district court to that effect are more than adequately supported by other evidence in the record discussed in Part V(B) of this opinion.

The government also challenges the injunction on the ground that it is "country specific" in that it is directed to the INS's treatment of aliens from El Salvador. This limitation on the scope of the injunction results from the identity of the plaintiff class and not from any improperly restrictive interpretation of the INA.

A final government contention concerns testimony from lawyers of their experiences in attempting to assist Salvadoran aliens in applying for asylum. The government challenges some of this evidence as hearsay, particularly the evidence of statements by the aliens to their attorneys of what the aliens had in turn been told by INS agents. Such evidence would be hearsay if admitted for the truth of the statements and relied upon by the district court for that purpose. The record reflects, however, that the district court was well aware that the testimony would be inadmissible for that purpose, and its findings give no indication that it relied upon this evidence for the truth of the matter asserted. Indeed, the testimony was not needed to show INS coercion, since the record is replete with non-hearsay evidence that supports the district court's findings as to the conduct of the agents, including their own testimony. See Part V(A) & (B). Most of the attorneys' testimony related to their own experiences in attempting to contact, interview and represent their clients in the face of conduct amounting to obstruction on the part of the INS. This testimony was not hearsay and there was certainly no abuse of discretion in admitting it.

VIII. Conclusion

After careful study of the record in this case based upon the government's challenges to the district court's findings of fact, we conclude the challenged findings are not clearly erroneous. The district court's entry of this injunction, which makes permanent the preliminary injunction entered in 1982, was not an abuse of discretion.

AFFIRMED.

SHIRAZI-PARSA v. IMMIGRATION & NATURALIZATION SERVICE
14 F.3d 1424(9th Cir. 1994)

Petitioner, Masood Shirazi-Parsa, and his wife, Georgina Shirazi-Parsa, petition this court for review of a final order of the Board of Immigration Appeals ("BIA" or "Board") that denied their request for asylum pursuant to 8 U.S.C. §1158(a) but granted them voluntary departure under 8 U.S.C. §1254(e). We reverse the decision of the Board and remand for further proceedings.

I. Factual and Procedural Background

Masood Shirazi-Parsa is a native and citizen of Iran. His wife, Georgina, is a native and citizen of Mexico. They met while students in the United States, and, in 1982, moved to Iran and married. Georgina Shirazi-Parsa made three trips to the United States during the course of their marriage. The first, in 1983, was to give birth to their daughter; the second occurred in 1985 when her husband was drafted into the Iranian army. The third and final trip, Petitioner contends, was occasioned by a series of events that occurred about August 1988. The couple was invited to dinner at an army officer's home. During the course of the evening, Georgina became very upset when the officer's wife made insulting remarks about Georgina' s Mormon religion. Petitioner and his wife testified that the following night the Revolutionary Guard came to their home, seized Masood, beat him, questioned him concerning his wife's employment at the Argentine Embassy, their contacts with Argentine soldiers attached to the United Nations, and his wife's religion, and accused him of being a spy. Petitioner and his wife further testified that, prior to these incidents, he had been interrogated weekly on each of these subjects while in the army. After this incident, Georgina left Iran for Mexico, later entering the United States about January 1989 with a tourist visa. Masood remained in Iran; he fled after receiving a letter from a prosecutor that ordered him to appear at the appropriate office but did not specify any charges. After traveling through Turkey to Mexico (where he was denied asylum because of his inability to meet the Mexican government's requirement that he be able to start a business capitalized at $200,000), Masood entered the United States without inspection in January 1989.

Petitioner applied for asylum and withholding of deportation under 8 U.S.C. §§1158(a) & 1253(h)(1) in March 1989, asserting that he would be "imprisoned by the regime, and perhaps, tortured and killed" because of his and his wife's political and religious beliefs. Petitioners conceded deportability. On April 11, 1991, after a hearing, the Immigration Judge (IJ) denied Petitioner's requests, but granted him and his wife voluntary departure under 8 U.S.C. §1254(e). The IJ found that Petitioner had failed to satisfy his burden of demonstrating a "well-founded" fear of political or religious persecution. The IJ concluded that although Petitioner relied heavily on his receipt of a summons from the Iranian authorities to explain his sudden departure from Iran, he had failed to advance a plausible reason for failing to produce it. Petitioner also testified that he feared reprisals because of his father's membership in the SAVAK, the Shah's intelligence service, his own connections with the SAVAK while a student in the United States, and his brother's troubles with the regime. However, because Petitioner's father had lived unmolested in Iran for a number of years and because there was no evidence that the authorities had ever interrogated Petitioner concerning any of these subjects, the IJ found any fear of persecution based on them implausible.

Petitioner appealed to the BIA, which denied his petition and affirmed the IJ in an opinion dated April 22, 1992....

II. Applicable Provisions and Standard of Review

Under 8 U.S.C. §1158(a), the Attorney General has discretion to grant an alien asylum if the alien is determined to be a "refugee." See 8 U.S.C.A. §1158 (a) (West 1993). A refugee is defined as any person who is unable or unwilling to return to his or her country of origin "because of persecution or a well-founded fear of persecution on account of . . . religion . . . or political opinion." Id. §1101(a)(42)(A). As both the IJ and the BIA correctly noted, the "well-founded fear" standard has both objective and subjective components. The subjective component may be satisfied by "an applicant's credible testimony that he genuinely fears persecution." *Acewicz v. INS*, 984 F.2d 1056, 1061 (9th Cir. 1993) (citing *Berroteran-Melendez v. INS*, 955 F.2d 1251 (9th Cir. 1992)). The objective component "requires a showing by 'credible, direct, and specific evidence' of facts supporting a reasonable fear of persecution" on the relevant ground. Id. (quoting *Rodriguez-Rivera v. INS*, 848 F.2d 998, 1002 (9th Cir. 1988) (per curiam)). The burden is on the applicant to meet this standard. See id.; 8 C.F.R. §208.5 (1990).....

III. Analysis

A. Inability to Produce the Summons

Petitioner asserts that the IJ placed undue emphasis on his inability to produce the summons. However, the BIA expressly denied that "the absence of the actual summons itself should preclude the respondent from [obtaining] relief." Admin. Rec. at 7 n.2 (citing Matter of Mogharrabi, 19 I. & N. Dec. 439, 445 (BIA 1987)). Indeed, the Board conducted its de novo analysis based on the assumption that the summons contained precisely that which Petitioner contended: his name, the date and location of his appearance, but no specific charges. As this court only reviews the BIA's decision, and not that of the IJ, see, e.g., Charlesworth, 966 F.2d at 1325, the IJ's reliance on Shirazi-Parsa's nonproduction of the summons is irrelevant. Therefore, Petitioner' s first argument is without merit.

B. The Board's Failure to Take Administrative Notice

Petitioner's second contention is that the BIA should have taken administrative notice of certain State Department reports that detail the nature and frequency of random political arrests and brutal treatment of detainees by government authorities in Iran. Failure to take administrative notice is reviewed under the abuse of discretion standard. See *Paul v. INS*, 521 F.2d 194, 199 (5th Cir. 1975).

We find it unnecessary to rule on this matter. First, it is unclear that the Board refused to consider the reports. Although they are not mentioned in the opinion, the Board considered and rejected the broad argument in which they were discussed - that all the incidents when considered together evinced political persecution. Thus, it is most reasonable to conclude that the Board took notice of the reports, but found them unpersuasive. Second, whether or not the Board took administrative notice of the reports, or erred in failing to do so, we choose to exercise our discretion and take judicial notice of them. See *Lazo-Majano v. INS*, 813 F.2d 1432, 1434 (9th Cir. 1987). As discussed below, we believe that the reports provide the vital context in which Petitioner's claim of political persecution must be evaluated.

C. The Board's Conclusions Were Not Supported By Substantial Evidence

The Board's central conclusion was that Petitioner did not have a well-founded fear of persecution on account of political or religious persecution. The Board reasoned that the incidents of interrogation, both those that occurred while Petitioner was in the army and that which followed the dinner dispute, did not evince a political motive on the part of the regime, but rather a legitimate concern with espionage. Similarly, although Petitioner's wife's status as a Mormon was mentioned during these incidents, the Board concluded that "any mention of the Mormon religion during these interrogations appears to be tangential to the main purpose of the interrogations, and not the result of religious persecution by the government." Admin. Rec. at 7. Finally, the Board concluded that because the summons contained no charges "there [was] no evidence indicating why the Revolutionary Guard wanted to speak to [Petitioner], and we note the possibility that it could be for any reason, including those completely unrelated to the respondent's religious status, or the incident at the dinner party." Id. Thus, the Board concluded that the summons "even [when] taken in conjunction with the prior inquiries and the [dinner incident could not] provide a reasonable basis for persecution on account of religion or any of the other enumerated grounds." Id.

We believe the Board erred in taking this last step: first, by concluding that the summons was unrelated to the prior incidents, and second, by concluding that the cumulative effect of the incidents did not give rise to a well-founded fear of persecution on account of political opinion. Specifically with respect to this second point, by failing to consider the totality of the circumstances, the Board erred in concluding that "any mention of [politics or] religion during [Petitioner's] interrogations appeared tangential" to legitimate espionage-related concerns. Admin. Rec. at 7.

The Board concluded that Petitioner's immediate release after his abduction and interrogation by the revolutionary guard indicates that the event was merely an "isolated" "incident of violence" and that the regime's "interest in him was limited." Id. From this, and from the lack of any specific charges in the summons, the Board concluded that the summons was unrelated to the prior incidents. However, as the State Department Country Reports cited by the Petitioner aptly demonstrate, it was common in Iran to experience a brief detention and then have it followed by a more formal arrest by the Revolutionary Guard:

Political arrests are made by members of the Revolutionary Guard or, less commonly, by members of the *komiteths*, local neighborhood groups which have assumed a quasi-official role. No judicial determination of the legality of detention exists in Iranian law . . . . Suspects are held for questioning at local Revolutionary Guard offices or in jails [and] it is unclear whether this questioning constitutes a trial by a Revolutionary court or whether it is part of the investigation process. Sometimes defendants are released after several hours or days, but the process may be repeated two or three times before the authorities decide the detainee is innocent or that he is guilty and should be jailed.

Department of State, Country Reports on Human Rights Practices for 1987, at 1161(1988) [hereinafter Country Reports] (emphasis added).

Undoubtedly, Petitioner's experience fits this pattern. Although Petitioner had been questioned on numerous prior occasions, he was seized and beaten only immediately following the dinner-party incident during which his wife and an officer's wife got into a fight concerning his wife's religion. His detention was occasioned by this incident, and it is clear that the incident at the dinner had resparked the authorities' interest in him. Thus, in light of the pattern described in the Country Reports, the receipt of a summons several weeks later can only be viewed as related to this incident. While the Board emphasized Petitioner's testimony that the summons contained no charges, the Country Reports indicate that arbitrary detentions are the norm. Moreover, unlike the Board, we do not perceive the time-lag between the time of the abduction and beating and receipt of the summons to indicate that the two incidents were unrelated. As the Country Reports indicate, informal detentions often conclude with the victim's release, only to be followed again later by more formal incarcerations.

Once it is recognized that the summons fit into an overall pattern of political arrests and detentions on the part of the Iranian regime, we have little trouble concluding that the evidence compels the conclusion that a reasonable person in Petitioner's position would possess, upon receipt of the summons, a well-founded fear of persecution on account of political opinion. While in the army, Petitioner was subjected to weekly interrogations. He testifies that the subject of these interrogations included the purpose of the time he spent in the United States, the fact that he was married to a Mormon, his wife's employment at the Argentine Embassy, and their fraternization with two Argentine United Nations soldiers. According to Petitioner, it was on the basis of this friendship with the Argentine soldiers that he was "suspected of . . . being a spy; working against the regime."

Similarly, he was questioned by the Revolutionary Guard concerning possible espionage that might have been accomplished through his wife's employment with the Argentine Embassy. However, despite this similarity in substance, it is clear that the tenor of the interrogations after the dinner party incident was different than those Petitioner experienced earlier. Petitioner was abducted by the Revolutionary Guard; as the Country Reports indicate, this in itself provides a political overtone to the interrogations that was absent during those conducted by the army. It is also clear that there was a greater emphasis placed on Petitioner's connections with America. As Petitioner testified:

Different people started interrogating me, and I stayed overnight and . . . I was beaten and kicked and punched and [they called me "] you American.["] They looked at me as an American person coming from the United States[. They said] ["] you spy,["] you know.

This additional emphasis on Petitioner's American connections was also testified to by his wife. Although she did not believe that the regime abducted her husband because of her specific religious beliefs, she asserted that the fact she was a Mormon led the regime to view her husband as a political enemy:

What [the Revolutionary Guard said was] that if I was a Mormon, okay, I could be a spy because the Mormon[s were] a CIA [front] - and it was just a name for a religion to be able to control people to enter [into] another country, just to control another spy.

We believe that the nature and circumstances of the post-dinner incident interrogations indicate that, as the Petitioner puts it, the regime had come to the conclusion that Petitioner did not hold "politically correct" views. First, as recounted above, the Revolutionary Guard placed a much greater emphasis on the Petitioner's connections with the West than had the prior army interrogations. While Petitioner's past connections with America and his wife's Mormon religion were discussed in prior interrogations, he was only accused of espionage because of their specific contacts with Argentine soldiers. The interrogations that took place after the abduction, however, demonstrate that Petitioner's and his wife's connections with the West branded them in the eyes of the Revolutionary Guard as suspected political enemies of the regime.

Second, while it is true that the regime indicated that they suspected that he and his wife were spies, the authorities knew of all the relevant information – their connections with the Argentines and past travels in the West – years before the dinner incident. Thus, assuming arguendo that the regime might have been within its rights to interrogate Petitioner for espionage, the timing of his abduction by the Revolutionary Guard indicates that the motive for the interrogations stemmed from the dinner incident and a suspicion of political disloyalty.

This conclusion is supported by Petitioner's testimony that, after the abduction incident, he tried to obtain a passport, but could not because he was "blacklisted," and shortly afterwards received the summons from the Revolutionary Guard. The receipt of the summons, in addition to bringing home to Petitioner on a subjective level that he was in danger, indicates to us that the regime was not interested in him merely for suspected espionage. If Petitioner was still suspected of conveying his country's secrets to the West following his interrogation, there would have been little point in waiting for a month before taking action. However, as described in the Country Reports, political arrests are made on a much more haphazard basis and might involve repeated detentions over a period of time.

Thus, the cumulative effect of the incidents when considered in light of the general pattern by which political arrests are carried out in Iran, compels the conclusion that the regime's interest in Petitioner was political in nature. Whether or not Petitioner actually held the beliefs that the regime attributed to him, it is enough that the regime "falsely attributes an opinion to the victim, and then persecutes the victim because of that mistaken belief about the victim's views." *Canas-Segovia v. INS*, 970 F.2d 599, 602 (9th Cir. 1992). Moreover, Petitioner's receipt of the summons demonstrates that the regime is likely to persecute him on that basis in the future. Persecution is all the more probable because Petitioner fled Iran through Turkey without a passport. Consequently, we conclude that the evidence compels the conclusion that Petitioner has a well-founded fear that, if he is returned to Iran, he will be persecuted by the regime because it regards him as a political enemy; accordingly, the Board's decision must be reversed.

IV. Conclusion

For the above reasons, the Petition is granted, and the decision of the BIA with respect to Petitioner's eligibility for asylum is reversed, and the case remanded to the Board to consider whether, in its discretion, see *INS v. Cardoza-Fonseca*, 480 U.S. 421, 428 n.5, 94 L. Ed. 2d 434, 107 S. Ct. 1207(1987), Petitioner and his wife should be granted asylum.

Reversed and Remanded.

EXERCISES

1. Your office represents an alien who is seeking asylum in the United States. Three years ago he left his homeland and has been living in Canada since that time. The INS claims that he has already resettled in Canada. What factors would need to be considered to show that the client has not in fact resettled?
2. The law states that an alien who is subject to removal proceedings may apply for asylum, but that asylum will be denied if he cannot reasonably explain why he did not apply prior to the removal proceedings. Discuss some of the reasons that might be considered "reasonable" for his failure to apply before.
3. Your office is asked to represent, at a prescreening interview, an alien who is seeking asylum. You are convinced that the alien is merely making the request in order to be let into the country, after which she will disappear. What are the ethical responsibilities of the lawyer? What are your ethical responsibilities as a legal assistant?
4. What evidence may be given to demonstrate that an alien has a well-founded fear of persecution? Are these the same factors that would prove a credible fear? Discuss.
5. Compare the similarities and differences of Forms I-589 (Appendix 8-2) and I-590 (Appendix 8-1).

APPENDIX 2-1
Form N-400, Application for Naturalization

U.S. Department of Justice

Immigration and Naturalization Service

OMB # 1115-0009

Application for Naturalization

INSTRUCTIONS

Purpose of This Form.
This form is for use to apply to become a naturalized citizen of the United States.

Who May File.
You may apply for naturalization if:

- you have been a lawful permanent resident for five years;
- you have been a lawful permanent resident for three years, have been married to a United States citizen for those three years, and continue to be married to that U.S. citizen;
- you are the lawful permanent resident child of United States citizen parents; or
- you have qualifying military service.

Children under 18 may automatically become citizens when their parents naturalize. You may inquire at your local Service office for further information. If you do not meet the qualifications listed above but believe that you are eligible for naturalization, you may inquire at your local Service office for additional information.

General Instructions.
Please answer all questions by typing or clearly printing in black ink. Indicate that an item is not applicable with "N/A". If an answer is "none," write "none". If you need extra space to answer any item, attach a sheet of paper with your name and your alien registration number (A#), if any, and indicate the number of the item.

Every application must be properly signed and filed with the correct fee. If you are under 18 years of age, your parent or guardian must sign the application.

If you wish to be called for your examination at the same time as another person who is also applying for naturalization, make your request on a separate cover sheet. Be sure to give the name and alien registration number of that person.

Initial Evidence Requirements.
You must file your application with the following evidence:

A copy of your alien registration card.

Photographs. You must submit two color photographs of yourself taken within 30 days of this application. These photos must be glossy, unretouched and unmounted, and have a white background. Dimension of the face should be about 1 inch from chin to top of hair. Face should be 3/4 frontal view of right side with right ear visible. Using pencil or felt pen, lightly print name and A#, if any, on the back of each photo. This requirement may be waived by the Service if you can establish that you are confined because of age or physical infirmity.

Fingerprints. If you are between the ages of 14 and 75, you must submit your fingerprints on Form FD-258. Fill out the form and write your Alien Registration Number in the space marked "Your No. OCA" or "Miscellaneous No. MNU". Take the chart and these instructions to a police station, sheriff's office or an office of this Service, or other reputable person or organization for fingerprinting. (You should contact the police or sheriff's office before going there since some of these offices do not take fingerprints for other government agencies.) You must sign the chart in the presence of the person taking your fingerprints and have that person sign his/her name, title, and the date in the space provided. Do not bend, fold, or crease the fingerprint chart.

U.S. Military Service. If you have ever served in the Armed Forces of the United States at any time, you must submit a completed Form G-325B. If your application is based on your military service you must also submit Form N-426, "Request for Certification of Military or Naval Service."

Application for Child. If this application is for a permanent resident child of U.S. citizen parents, you must also submit copies of the child's birth certificate, the parents' marriage certificate, and evidence of the parents' U.S. citizenship. If the parents are divorced, you must also submit the divorce decree and evidence that the citizen parent has legal custody of the child.

Where to File.
File this application at the local Service office having jurisdiction over your place of residence.

Fee.
The fee for this application is **$95.00.** The fee must be submitted in the exact amount. It cannot be refunded. **DO NOT MAIL CASH.**

All checks and money orders must be drawn on a bank or other institution located in the United States and must be payable in United States currency. The check or money order should be made payable to the Immigration and Naturalization Service, except that:

- If you live in Guam, and are filing this application in Guam, make your check or money order payable to the "Treasurer, Guam."
- If you live in the Virgin Islands, and are filing this application in the Virgin Islands, make your check or money order payable to the "Commissioner of Finance of the Virgin Islands."

Checks are accepted subject to collection. An uncollected check will render the application and any document issued invalid. A charge of $5.00 will be imposed if a check in payment of a fee is not honored by the bank on which it is drawn.

Processing Information.
Rejection. Any application that is not signed or is not accompanied by the proper fee will be rejected with a notice that the application is deficient. You may correct the deficiency and resubmit the application. However, an application is not considered properly filed until it is accepted by the Service.

Requests for more information. We may request more information or evidence. We may also request that you submit the originals of any copy. We will return these originals when they are no longer required.

Interview. After you file your application, you will be notified to appear at a Service office to be examined under oath or affirmation. This interview may not be waived. If you are an adult, you must show that you have a knowledge and understanding of the history, principles, and form of government of the United States. There is no exemption from this requirement.

You will also be examined on your ability to read, write, and speak English. If on the date of your examination you are more than 50 years of age and have been a lawful permanent resident for 20 years or more, or you are 55 years of age and have been a lawful permanent resident for at least 15 years, you will be exempt from the English language requirements of the law. If you are exempt, you may take the examination in any language you wish.

Oath of Allegiance. If your application is approved, you will be required to take the following oath of allegiance to the United States in order to become a citizen:

"I hereby declare, on oath, that I absolutely and entirely renounce and abjure all allegiance and fidelity to any foreign prince, potentate, state or sovereignty, of whom or which I have heretofore been a subject or citizen; that I will support and defend the Constitution and laws of the United States of America against all enemies, foreign and domestic; that I will bear true faith and allegiance to the same; that I will bear arms on behalf of the United States when required by the law; that I will perform noncombatant service in the armed forces of the United States when required by the law; that I will perform work of national importance under civilian direction when required by the law; and that I take this obligation freely without any mental reservation or purpose of evasion; so help me God."

If you cannot promise to bear arms or perform noncombatant service because of religious training and belief, you may omit those statements when taking the oath. "Religious training and belief" means a person's belief in relation to a Supreme Being involving duties superior to those arising from any human relation, but does not include essentially political, sociological, or philosophical views or merely a personal moral code.

Oath ceremony. You may choose to have the oath of allegiance administered in a ceremony conducted by the Service or request to be scheduled for an oath ceremony in a court that has jurisdiction over the applicant's place of residence. At the time of your examination you will be asked to elect either form of ceremony. You will become a citizen on the date of the oath ceremony and the Attorney General will issue a Certificate of Naturalization as evidence of United States citizenship.

If you wish to change your name as part of the naturalization process, you will have to take the oath in court.

Penalties.
If you knowingly and willfully falsify or conceal a material fact or submit a false document with this request, we will deny the benefit you are filing for, and may deny any other immigration benefit. In addition, you will face severe penalties provided by law, and may be subject to criminal prosecution.

Privacy Act Notice.
We ask for the information on this form, and associated evidence, to determine if you have established eligibility for the immigration benefit you are filing for. Our legal right to ask for this information is in 8 USC 1439, 1440, 1443, 1445, 1446, and 1452. We may provide this information to other government agencies. Failure to provide this information, and any requested evidence, may delay a final decision or result in denial of your request.

Paperwork Reduction Act Notice.
We try to create forms and instructions that are accurate, can be easily understood, and which impose the least possible burden on you to provide us with information. Often this is difficult because some immigration laws are very complex. Accordingly, the reporting burden for this collection of information is computed as follows: (1) learning about the law and form, 20 minutes; (2) completing the form, 25 minutes; and (3) assembling and filing the application (includes statutory required interview and travel time, after filing of application), 3 hours and 35 minutes, for an estimated average of 4 hours and 20 minutes per response. If you have comments regarding the accuracy of this estimate, or suggestions for making this form simpler, you can write to both the Immigration and Naturalization Service, 425 I Street, N.W., Room 5304, Washington, D.C. 20536; and the Office of Management and Budget, Paperwork Reduction Project, OMB No. 1115-0009, Washington, D.C. 20503.

For sale by the U.S. Government Printing Office
Superintendent of Documents, Mail Stop: SSOP, Washington, DC 20402-9328

U.S. Department of Justice
Immigration and Naturalization Service

OMB #1115-0009
Application for Naturalization

START HERE - Please Type or Print

FOR INS USE ONLY

Returned	Receipt
Resubmitted	
Reloc Sent	
Reloc Rec'd	
☐ Applicant Interviewed	

At interview
☐ request naturalization ceremony at court

Remarks

Action

To Be Completed by *Attorney or Representative*, if any
☐ Fill in box if G-28 is attached to represent the applicant

VOLAG#

ATTY State License #

Part 1. Information about you.

Family Name	Given Name	Middle Initial

U.S. Mailing Address - Care of

Street Number and Name	Apt. #
City	County
State	ZIP Code
Date of Birth (month/day/year)	Country of Birth
Social Security #	A #

Part 2. Basis for Eligibility *(check one)*.

a. ☐ I have been a permanent resident for at least five (5) years

b. ☐ I have been a permanent resident for at least three (3) years and have been married to a United States Citizen for those three years.

c. ☐ I am a permanent resident child of United States citizen parent(s)

d. ☐ I am applying on the basis of qualifying military service in the Armed Forces of the U.S. and have attached completed Forms N-426 and G-325B

e. ☐ Other. (Please specify section of law) ____________________

Part 3. Additional information about you.

Date you became a permanent resident (month/day/year)	Port admitted with an immigrant visa or INS Office where granted adjustment of status.

Citizenship

Name on alien registration card (if different than in Part 1)

Other names used since you became a permanent resident (including maiden name)

Sex ☐ Male ☐ Female	Height	Marital Status: ☐ Single ☐ Married ☐ Divorced ☐ Widowed

Can you speak, read and write English ? ☐No ☐Yes.

Absences from the U.S.:

Have you been absent from the U.S. since becoming a permanent resident? ☐ No ☐Yes

If you answered **"Yes"**, complete the following, Begin with your most recent absence. If you need more room to explain the reason for an absence or to list more trips, continue on separate paper.

Date left U.S.	Date returned	Did absence last 6 months or more?	Destination	Reason for trip
		☐ Yes ☐ No		
		☐ Yes ☐ No		
		☐ Yes ☐ No		
		☐ Yes ☐ No		
		☐ Yes ☐ No		
		☐ Yes ☐ No		

Form N-400 (Rev. 07/17/91)N

Continued on back.

Part 4. Information about your residences and employment.

A. List your addresses during the last five (5) years or since you became a permanent resident, whichever is less. Begin with your current address. If you need more space, continue on separate paper:

Street Number and Name, City, State, Country, and Zip Code	Dates (month/day/year)	
	From	To

B. List your employers during the last five (5) years. List your present or most recent employer first. If none, write "None". If you need more space, continue on separate paper.

Employer's Name	Employer's Address	Dates Employed (month/day/year)		Occupation/position
	Street Name and Number - City, State and ZIP Code	From	To	

Part 5. Information about your marital history.

A. Total number of times you have been married _______ . If you are now married, complete the following regarding your husband or wife.

Family name	Given name	Middle initial
Address		

Date of birth (month/day/year)	Country of birth	Citizenship
Social Security#	A# (if applicable)	Immigration status (If not a U.S. citizen)

Naturalization (If applicable) (month/day/year) Place (City, State)

If you have ever previously been married or if your current spouse has been previously married, please provide the following on separate paper: Name of prior spouse, date of marriage, date marriage ended, how marriage ended and immigration status of prior spouse.

Part 6. Information about your children.

B. Total Number of Children ________ . Complete the following information for each of your children. If the child lives with you, state "with me" in the address column; otherwise give city/state/country of child's current residence. If deceased, write "deceased" in the address column. If you need more space, continue on separate paper.

Full name of child	Date of birth	Country of birth	Citizenship	A - Number	Address

Form N-400 (Rev 07/17/91)N

Continued on next page

Continued on back

Part 7. Additional eligibility factors.

Please answer each of the following questions. If your answer is "**Yes**", explain on a separate paper.

1. Are you now, or have you ever been a member of, or in any way connected or associated with the Communist Party, or ever knowingly aided or supported the Communist Party directly, or indirectly through another organization, group or person, or ever advocated, taught, believed in, or knowingly supported or furthered the interests of communism? ☐ Yes ☐ No
2. During the period March 23, 1933 to May 8, 1945, did you serve in, or were you in any way affiliated with, either directly or indirectly, any military unit, paramilitary unit, police unit, self-defense unit, vigilante unit, citizen unit of the Nazi party or SS, government agency or office, extermination camp, concentration camp, prisoner of war camp, prison, labor camp, detention camp or transit camp, under the control or affiliated with:
   a. The Nazi Government of Germany? ☐ Yes ☐ No
   b. Any government in any area occupied by, allied with, or established with the assistance or cooperation of, the Nazi Government of Germany? ☐ Yes ☐ No
3. Have you at any time, anywhere, ever ordered, incited, assisted, or otherwise participated in the persecution of any person because of race, religion, national origin, or political opinion? ☐ Yes ☐ No
4. Have you ever left the United States to avoid being drafted into the U.S. Armed Forces? ☐ Yes ☐ No
5. Have you ever failed to comply with Selective Service laws? ☐ Yes ☐ No

   If you have registered under the Selective Service laws, complete the following information:

   Selective Service Number:____________________ Date Registered:____________

   If you registered before 1978, also provide the following:

   Local Board Number:____________________ Classification:________________
6. Did you ever apply for exemption from military service because of alienage, conscientious objections or other reasons? ☐ Yes ☐ No
7. Have you ever deserted from the military, air or naval forces of the United States? ☐ Yes ☐ No
8. Since becoming a permanent resident, have you ever failed to file a federal income tax return ? ☐ Yes ☐ No
9. Since becoming a permanent resident, have you filed a federal income tax return as a nonresident or failed to file a federal return because you considered yourself to be a nonresident? ☐ Yes ☐ No
10. Are deportation proceedings pending against you, or have you ever been deported, or ordered deported, or have you ever applied for suspension of deportation? ☐ Yes ☐ No
11. Have you ever claimed in writing, or in any way, to be a United States citizen? ☐ Yes ☐ No
12. Have you ever:
    a. been a habitual drunkard? ☐ Yes ☐ No
    b. advocated or practiced polygamy? ☐ Yes ☐ No
    c. been a prostitute or procured anyone for prostitution? ☐ Yes ☐ No
    d. knowingly and for gain helped any alien to enter the U.S. illegally? ☐ Yes ☐ No
    e. been an illicit trafficker in narcotic drugs or marijuana? ☐ Yes ☐ No
    f. received income from illegal gambling? ☐ Yes ☐ No
    g. given false testimony for the purpose of obtaining any immigration benefit? ☐ Yes ☐ No
13. Have you ever been declared legally incompetent or have you ever been confined as a patient in a mental institution? ☐ Yes ☐ No
14. Were you born with, or have you acquired in same way, any title or order of nobility in any foreign State? ☐ Yes ☐ No
15. Have you ever:
    a. knowingly committed any crime for which you have not been arrested? ☐ Yes ☐ No
    b. been arrested, cited, charged, indicted, convicted, fined or imprisoned for breaking or violating any law or ordinance excluding traffic regulations? ☐ Yes ☐ No

(If you answer yes to 15 , in your explanation give the following information for each incident or occurrence the **city**, **state**, and **country**, where the offense took place, the **date** and **nature** of the offense, and the **outcome** or **disposition** of the case).

Part 8. Allegiance to the U.S.

If your answer to any of the following questions is "**NO**", attach a full explanation:

1. Do you believe in the Constitution and form of government of the U.S.? ☐ Yes ☐ No
2. Are you willing to take the full Oath of Allegiance to the U.S.? (see instructions) ☐ Yes ☐ No
3. If the law requires it, are you willing to bear arms on behalf of the U.S.? ☐ Yes ☐ No
4. If the law requires it, are you willing to perform noncombatant services in the Armed Forces of the U.S.? ☐ Yes ☐ No
5. If the law requires it, are you willing to perform work of national importance under civilian direction? ☐ Yes ☐ No

Continued on back

Part 9. Memberships and organizations.

A. List your present and past membership in or affiliation with every organization, association, fund, foundation, party, club, society, or similar group in the United States or in any other place. Include any military service in this part. If none, write "none". Include the name of organization, location, dates of membership and the nature of the organization. If additional space is needed, use separate paper.

Part 10. Complete only if you checked block " C " in Part 2.

How many of your parents are U.S. citizens? ☐ One ☐ Both (Give the following about one U.S. citizen parent:)

Family Name | Given Name | Middle Name

Address

Basis for citizenship: ☐ Birth ☐ Naturalization Cert. No.

Relationship to you (check one): ☐ natural parent ☐ adoptive parent ☐ parent of child legitimated after birth

If adopted or legitimated after birth, give date of adoption or, legitimation: *(month/day/year)* ____________

Does this parent have legal custody of you? ☐ Yes ☐ No

(Attach a copy of relating evidence to establish that you are the child of this U.S. citizen and evidence of this parent's citizenship.)

Part 11. Signature. *(Read the information on penalties in the instructions before completing this section).*

I certify or, if outside the United States, I swear or affirm, under penalty of perjury under the laws of the United States of America that this application, and the evidence submitted with it, is all true and correct. I authorize the release of any information from my records which the Immigration and Naturalization Service needs to determine eligibility for the benefit I am seeking.

Signature **Date**

Please Note: *If you do not completely fill out this form, or fail to submit required documents listed in the instructions, you may not be found eligible for naturalization and this application may be denied.*

Part 12. Signature of person preparing form if other than above. *(Sign below)*

I declare that I prepared this application at the request of the above person and it is based on all information of which I have knowledge.

Signature **Print Your Name** **Date**

Firm Name and Address

DO NOT COMPLETE THE FOLLOWING UNTIL INSTRUCTED TO DO SO AT THE INTERVIEW

I swear that I know the contents of this application, and supplemental pages 1 through______, that the corrections , numbered 1 through______, were made at my request, and that this amended application, is true to the best of my knowledge and belief.

(Complete and true signature of applicant)

Subscribed and sworn to before me by the applicant.

(Examiner's Signature) *Date*

Form N-400 (Rev. 07/17/91)N

U.S. GOVERNMENT PRINTING OFFICE : 1997 O - 176-348

U. S. IMMIGRATION & NATURALIZATION SERVICE

COLOR PHOTOGRAPH SPECIFICATIONS

IDEAL PHOTOGRAPH ◂

IMAGE MUST FIT INSIDE THIS BOX ▸

THE PICTURE AT LEFT IS IDEAL SIZE, COLOR, BACKGROUND, AND POSE. THE IMAGE SHOULD BE 30MM (1 3/16IN) FROM THE HAIR TO JUST BELOW THE CHIN, AND 26MM (1 IN) FROM LEFT CHEEK TO RIGHT EAR. THE IMAGE MUST FIT IN THE BOX AT RIGHT.

THE PHOTOGRAPH

• THE OVERALL SIZE OF THE PICTURE, INCLUDING THE BACKGROUND, MUST BE AT LEAST 40MM (1 9/16 INCHES) IN HEIGHT BY 35MM (1 3/8IN) IN WIDTH.

• PHOTOS MUST BE FREE OF SHADOWS AND CONTAIN NO MARKS, SPLOTCHES, OR DISCOLORATIONS.

• PHOTOS SHOULD BE HIGH QUALITY, WITH GOOD BACK LIGHTING OR WRAP AROUND LIGHTING, AND MUST HAVE A WHITE OR OFF-WHITE BACKGROUND.

• PHOTOS MUST BE A GLOSSY OR MATTE FINISH AND UN-RETOUCHED.

• POLAROID FILM HYBRID #5 IS ACCEPTABLE; HOWEVER SX-70 TYPE FILM OR ANY OTHER INSTANT PROCESSING TYPE FILM IS UNACCEPTABLE. NON-PEEL APART FILMS ARE EASILY RECOGNIZED BECAUSE THE BACK OF THE FILM IS BLACK. ACCEPTABLE INSTANT COLOR FILM HAS A GRAY-TONED BACKING.

THE IMAGE OF THE PERSON

• THE DIMENSIONS OF THE IMAGE SHOULD BE 30MM (1 3/16 INCHES) FROM THE HAIR TO THE NECK JUST BELOW THE CHIN, AND 26MM (1 INCH) FROM THE RIGHT EAR TO THE LEFT CHEEK. IMAGE CANNOT EXCEED 32MM BY 28MM (1 1/4IN X 1 1/16IN).

• IF THE IMAGE AREA ON THE PHOTOGRAPH IS TOO LARGE OR TOO SMALL, THE PHOTO CANNOT BE USED.

• PHOTOGRAPHS MUST SHOW THE ENTIRE FACE OF THE PERSON IN A 3/4 VIEW SHOWING THE RIGHT EAR AND LEFT EYE.

• FACIAL FEATURES **MUST BE IDENTIFIABLE.**

• CONTRAST BETWEEN THE IMAGE AND BACKGROUND IS ESSENTIAL. PHOTOS FOR VERY LIGHT SKINNED PEOPLE SHOULD BE SLIGHTLY UNDER-EXPOSED. PHOTOS FOR VERY DARK SKINNED PEOPLE SHOULD BE SLIGHTLY OVER-EXPOSED.

SAMPLES OF UNACCEPTABLE PHOTOGRAPHS

INCORRECT POSE

IMAGE TOO LARGE

IMAGE TOO SMALL

IMAGE TOO DARK UNDER-EXPOSED

IMAGE TOO LIGHT

DARK BACKGROUND

OVER-EXPOSED

SHADOWS ON PIC

Form G-325A, Biographic Information

U.S. Department of Justice
Immigration and Naturalization Service

FORM G-325A
BIOGRAPHIC INFORMATION

OMB No. 1115-0066

(Family name) (First name) (Middle name)	☐ MALE ☐ FEMALE	BIRTHDATE (Mo.-Day-Yr.)	NATIONALITY	FILE NUMBER A-
ALL OTHER NAMES USED (Including names by previous marriages)	CITY AND COUNTRY OF BIRTH			SOCIAL SECURITY NO. (If any)

	FAMILY NAME	FIRST NAME	DATE, CITY AND COUNTRY OF BIRTH (If known)	CITY AND COUNTRY OF RESIDENCE
FATHER				
MOTHER (Maiden name)				

HUSBAND (If none, so state) OR WIFE	FAMILY NAME (For wife, give maiden name)	FIRST NAME	BIRTHDATE	CITY & COUNTRY OF BIRTH	DATE OF MARRIAGE	PLACE OF MARRIAGE

FORMER HUSBANDS OR WIVES (if none, so state)

FAMILY NAME (For wife, give maiden name)	FIRST NAME	BIRTHDATE	DATE & PLACE OF MARRIAGE	DATE AND PLACE OF TERMINATION OF MARRIAGE

APPLICANT'S RESIDENCE LAST FIVE YEARS. LIST PRESENT ADDRESS FIRST.

STREET AND NUMBER	CITY	PROVINCE OR STATE	COUNTRY	FROM MONTH	FROM YEAR	TO MONTH	TO YEAR
						PRESENT TIME	

APPLICANT'S LAST ADDRESS OUTSIDE THE UNITED STATES OF MORE THAN ONE YEAR

STREET AND NUMBER	CITY	PROVINCE OR STATE	COUNTRY	FROM MONTH	FROM YEAR	TO MONTH	TO YEAR

APPLICANT'S EMPLOYMENT LAST FIVE YEARS. (IF NONE, SO STATE.) LIST PRESENT EMPLOYMENT FIRST

FULL NAME AND ADDRESS OF EMPLOYER	OCCUPATION (SPECIFY)	FROM MONTH	FROM YEAR	TO MONTH	TO YEAR
				PRESENT TIME	
Show below last occupation abroad if not shown above. (Include all information requested above.)					

THIS FORM IS SUBMITTED IN CONNECTION WITH APPLICATION FOR: ☐ NATURALIZATION ☐ STATUS AS PERMANENT RESIDENT ☐ OTHER (SPECIFY):	SIGNATURE OF APPLICANT	DATE
Are all copies legible? ☐ **Yes**	IF YOUR NATIVE ALPHABET IS IN OTHER THAN ROMAN LETTERS, WRITE YOUR NAME IN YOUR NATIVE ALPHABET IN THIS SPACE	

PENALTIES: SEVERE PENALTIES ARE PROVIDED BY LAW FOR KNOWINGLY AND WILLFULLY FALSIFYING OR CONCEALING A MATERIAL FACT.

APPLICANT: BE SURE TO PUT YOUR NAME AND ALIEN REGISTRATION NUMBER IN THE BOX OUTLINED BY HEAVY BORDER BELOW.

COMPLETE THIS BOX (Family name)	(Given name)	(Middle name)	(Alien registration number)

DEPARTMENT OF JUSTICE
Immigration & Naturalization Service **100 Typical Questions**

1. WHAT ARE THE COLORS OF OUR FLAG?
2. HOW MANY STARS ARE THERE IN OUR FLAG?
3. WHAT COLOR ARE THE STARS ON OUR FLAG?
4. WHAT DO THE STARS ON THE FLAG MEAN?
5. HOW MANY STRIPES ARE THERE IN THE FLAG?
6. WHAT COLOR ARE THE STRIPES?
7. WHAT DO THE STRIPES ON THE FLAG MEAN?
8. HOW MANY STATES ARE THERE IN THE UNION?
9. WHAT IS THE 4TH OF JULY?
10. WHAT IS THE DATE OF INDEPENDENCE DAY?
11. INDEPENDENCE FROM WHOM?
12. WHAT COUNTRY DID WE FIGHT DURING THE REVOLUTIONARY WAR?
13. WHO WAS THE FIRST PRESIDENT OF THE UNITED STATES?
14. WHO IS THE PRESIDENT OF THE UNITED STATES TODAY?
15. WHO IS THE VICE-PRESIDENT OF THE UNITED STATES TODAY?
16. WHO ELECTS THE PRESIDENT OF THE UNITED STATES?
17. WHO BECOMES PRESIDENT OF THE UNITED STATES IF THE PRESIDENT SHOULD DIE?
18. FOR HOW LONG DO WE ELECT THE PRESIDENT?
19. WHAT IS THE CONSTITUTION?
20. CAN THE CONSTITUTION BE CHANGED?
21. WHAT DO WE CALL A CHANGE TO THE CONSTITUTION?
22. HOW MANY CHANGES OR AMENDMENTS ARE THERE TO THE CONSTITUTION?
23. HOW MANY BRANCHES ARE THERE IN OUR GOVERNMENT?
24. WHAT ARE THE THREE BRANCHES OF OUR GOVERNMENT?
25. WHAT IS THE LEGISLATIVE BRANCH OF OUR GOVERNMENT?
26. WHO MAKES THE LAWS IN THE UNITED STATES?
27. WHAT IS CONGRESS?
28. WHAT ARE THE DUTIES OF CONGRESS?
29. WHO ELECTS CONGRESS?
30. HOW MANY SENATORS ARE THERE IN CONGRESS?
31. CAN YOU NAME THE TWO SENATORS FROM YOUR STATE?
32. FOR HOW LONG DO WE ELECT EACH SENATOR?
33. HOW MANY REPRESENTATIVES ARE THERE IN CONGRESS?
34. FOR HOW LONG DO WE ELECT THE REPRESENTATIVES?
35. WHAT IS THE EXECUTIVE BRANCH OF OUR GOVERNMENT?
36. WHAT IS THE JUDICIARY BRANCH OF OUR GOVERNMENT?
37. WHAT ARE THE DUTIES OF THE SUPREME COURT?
38. WHAT IS THE SUPREME LAW OF THE UNITED STATES?
39. WHAT IS THE BILL OF RIGHTS?
40. WHAT IS THE CAPITAL OF YOUR STATE?
41. WHO IS THE CURRENT GOVERNOR OF YOUR STATE?
42. WHO BECOMES PRESIDENT OF THE U.S.A. IF THE PRESIDENT AND THE VICE-PRESIDENT SHOULD DIE?
43. WHO IS THE CHIEF JUSTICE OF THE SUPREME COURT?
44. CAN YOU NAME THE THIRTEEN ORIGINAL STATES?
45. WHO SAID, "GIVE ME LIBERTY OR GIVE ME DEATH"?
46. WHICH COUNTRIES WERE OUR ENEMIES DURING WORLD WAR II?
47. WHAT ARE THE 49TH AND 50TH STATES OF THE UNION?
48. HOW MANY TERMS CAN A PRESIDENT SERVE?
49. WHO WAS MARTIN LUTHER KING, JR.?

WR-709 2211
7/30/93

1

50. WHO IS THE HEAD OF YOUR LOCAL GOVERNMENT?
51. ACCORDING TO THE CONSTITUTION, A PERSON MUST MEET CERTAIN REQUIREMENTS IN ORDER TO BE ELIGIBLE TO BECOME PRESIDENT. NAME ONE OF THESE REQUIREMENTS.
52. WHY ARE THERE 100 SENATORS IN THE SENATE?
53. WHO SELECTS THE SUPREME COURT JUSTICES?
54. HOW MANY SUPREME COURT JUSTICIES ARE THERE?
55. WHY DID THE PILGRIMS COME TO AMERICA?
56. WHAT IS THE HEAD EXECUTIVE OF A STATE GOVERNMENT CALLED?
57. WHAT IS THE HEAD EXECUTIVE OF A CITY GOVERNMENT CALLED?
58. WHAT HOLIDAY WAS CELEBRATED FOR THE FIRST TIME BY THE AMERICAN COLONISTS?
59. WHO WAS THE MAIN WRITER OF THE DECLARATION OF INDEPENDENCE?
60. WHEN WAS THE DECLARATION OF INDEPENDENCE ADOPTED?
61. WHAT IS THE BASIC BELIEF OF THE DECLARATION OF INDEPENDENCE?
62. WHAT IS THE NATIONAL ANTHEM OF THE UNITED STATES?
63. WHO WROTE THE STAR-SPANGLED BANNER?
64. WHERE DOES FREEDOM OF SPEECH COME FROM?
65. WHAT IS THE MINIMUM VOTING AGE IN THE UNITED STATES?
66. WHO SIGNS BILLS INTO LAW?
67. WHAT IS THE HIGHEST COURT IN THE UNITED STATES?
68. WHO WAS THE PRESIDENT DURING THE CIVIL WAR?
69. WHAT DID THE EMANCIPATION PROCLAMATION DO?
70. WHAT SPECIAL GROUP ADVISES THE PRESIDENT?
71. WHICH PRESIDENT IS CALLED THE "FATHER OF OUR COUNTRY"?
72. WHAT IMMIGRATION AND NATURALIZATION SERVICE FORM IS USED TO APPLY TO BECOME A NATURALIZED CITIZEN?
73. WHO HELPED THE PILGRIMS IN AMERICA?
74. WHAT IS THE NAME OF THE SHIP THAT BROUGHT THE PILGRIMS TO AMERICA?
75. WHAT WERE THE 13 ORIGINAL STATES OF THE UNITED STATES CALLED?
76. NAME 3 RIGHTS OR FREEDOMS GUARANTEED BY THE BILL OF RIGHTS?
77. WHO HAS THE POWER TO DECLARE WAR?
78. WHAT KIND OF GOVERNMENT DOES THE UNITED STATES HAVE?
79. WHICH PRESIDENT FREED THE SLAVES?
80. IN WHAT YEAR WAS THE CONSTITUTION WRITTEN?
81. WHAT ARE THE FIRST 10 AMENDMENTS TO THE CONSTITUTION CALLED?
82. NAME ONE PURPOSE OF THE UNITED NATIONS.
83. WHERE DOES CONGRESS MEET?
84. WHOSE RIGHTS ARE GUARANTEED BY THE CONSTITUTION AND THE BILL OF RIGHTS?
85. WHAT IS THE INTRODUCTION TO THE CONSTITUTION CALLED?
86. NAME ONE BENEFIT OF BEING A CITIZEN OF THE UNITED STATES.
87. WHAT IS THE MOST IMPORTANT RIGHT GRANTED TO U.S. CITIZENS?
88. WHAT IS THE UNITED STATES CAPITOL?
89. WHAT IS THE WHITE HOUSE?
90. WHERE IS THE WHITE HOUSE LOCATED?
91. WHAT IS THE NAME OF THE PRESIDENT'S OFFICIAL HOME?
92. NAME ONE RIGHT GUARANTEED BY THE FIRST AMENDMENT.
93. WHO IS THE COMMANDER IN CHIEF OF THE U.S. MILITARY?
94. WHICH PRESIDENT WAS THE FIRST COMMANDER IN CHIEF OF THE U.S. MILITARY?
95. IN WHAT MONTH DO WE VOTE FOR THE PRESIDENT?
96. IN WHAT MONTH IS THE NEW PRESIDENT INAUGURATED?
97. HOW MANY TIMES MAY A SENATOR BE RE-ELECTED?
98. HOW MANY TIMES MAY A CONGRESSMAN BE RE-ELECTED?
99. WHAT ARE THE 2 MAJOR POLITICAL PARTIES IN THE U.S. TODAY?
100. HOW MANY STATES ARE THERE IN THE UNITED STATES?

ANSWER SHEET

1. RED, WHITE, AND BLUE
2. 50
3. WHITE
4. ONE FOR EACH STATE IN THE UNION
5. 13
6. RED AND WHITE
7. THEY REPRESENT THE ORIGINAL 13 STATES
8. 50
9. INDEPENDENCE DAY
10. JULY 4TH
11. ENGLAND
12. ENGLAND
13. GEORGE WASHINGTON
14. BILL CLINTON
15. AL GORE
16. THE ELECTORAL COLLEGE
17. VICE PRESIDENT
18. FOUR YEARS
19. THE SUPREME LAW OF THE LAND
20. YES
21. AMENDMENTS
22. 26
23. 3
24. LEGISLATIVE, EXECUTIVE, AND JUDICIARY
25. CONGRESS
26. CONGRESS
27. THE SENATE AND THE HOUSE OF REPRESENTATIVES
28. TO MAKE LAWS
29. THE PEOPLE
30. 100
31. **(INSERT LOCAL INFORMATION)**
32. 6 YEARS
33. 435
34. 2 YEARS
35. THE PRESIDENT, CABINET, AND DEPARTMENTS UNDER THE CABINET MEMBERS
36. THE SUPREME COURT
37. TO INTERPRET LAWS
38. THE CONSTITUTION
39. THE FIRST 10 AMENDMENTS OF THE CONSTITUTION
40. **(INSERT LOCAL INFORMATION)**
41. **(INSERT LOCAL INFORMATION)**
42. SPEAKER OF THE HOUSE OF REPRESENTATIVES
43. WILLIAM REHNQUIST
44. CONNECTICUT, NEW HAMPSHIRE, NEW YORK, NEW JERSEY, MASSACHUSETTS, PENNSYLVANIA, DELAWARE, VIRGINIA, NORTH CAROLINA, SOUTH CAROLINA, GEORGIA, RHODE ISLAND, AND MARYLAND
45. PATRICK HENRY
46. GERMANY, ITALY, AND JAPAN
47. HAWAII AND ALASKA
48. 2
49. A CIVIL RIGHTS LEADER
50. **(INSERT LOCAL INFORMATION)**
51. MUST BE A NATURAL BORN CITIZEN OF THE UNITED STATES;
MUST BE AT LEAST 35 YEARS OLD BY THE TIME HE/SHE WILL SERVE;
MUST HAVE LIVED IN THE UNITED STATES FOR AT LEAST 14 YEARS
52. TWO (2) FROM EACH STATE
53. APPOINTED BY THE PRESIDENT
54. NINE (9)
55. FOR RELIGIOUS FREEDOM
56. GOVERNOR
57. MAYOR

58. THANKSGIVING
59. THOMAS JEFFERSON
60. JULY 4, 1776
61. THAT ALL MEN ARE CREATED EQUAL
62. THE STAR-SPANGLED BANNER
63. FRANCIS SCOTT KEY
64. THE BILL OF RIGHTS
65. EIGHTEEN (18)
66. THE PRESIDENT
67. THE SUPREME COURT
68. ABRAHAM LINCOLN
69. FREED MANY SLAVES
70. THE CABINET
71. GEORGE WASHINGTON
72. FORM N-400, "APPLICATION TO FILE PETITION FOR NATURALIZATION"
73. THE AMERICAN INDIANS (NATIVE AMERICANS)
74. THE MAYFLOWER
75. COLONIES
76. (A) THE RIGHT OF FREEDOM OF SPEECH, PRESS, RELIGION, PEACEABLE ASSEMBLY AND REQUESTING CHANGE OF GOVERNMENT.
    (B) THE RIGHT TO BEAR ARMS (THE RIGHT TO HAVE WEAPONS OR OWN A GUN, THOUGH SUBJECT TO CERTAIN REGULATIONS).
    (C) THE GOVERNMENT MAY NOT QUARTER, OR HOUSE, SOLDIERS IN THE PEOPLE'S HOMES DURING PEACETIME WITHOUT THE PEOPLE'S CONSENT.
    (D) THE GOVERNMENT MAY NOT SEARCH OR TAKE A PERSON'S PROPERTY WITHOUT A WARRANT.
    (E) A PERSON MAY NOT BE TRIED TWICE FOR THE SAME CRIME AND DOES NOT HAVE TO TESTIFY AGAINST HIM/HERSELF.
    (F) A PERSON CHARGED WITH A CRIME STILL HAS SOME RIGHTS, SUCH AS THE RIGHT TO A TRIAL AND TO HAVE A LAWYER.
    (G) THE RIGHT TO TRIAL BY JURY IN MOST CASES.
    (H) PROTECTS PEOPLE AGAINST EXCESSIVE OR UNREASONABLE FINES OR CRUEL AND UNUSUAL PUNISHMENT.
    (I) THE PEOPLE HAVE RIGHTS OTHER THAN THOSE MENTIONED IN THE CONSTITUTION.
    (J) ANY POWER NOT GIVEN TO THE FEDERAL GOVERNMENT BY THE CONSTITUTION IS A POWER OF EITHER THE STATE OR THE PEOPLE.
77. THE CONGRESS
78. REPUBLICAN
79. ABRAHAM LINCOLN
80. 1787
81. THE BILL OF RIGHTS
82. FOR COUNTRIES TO DISCUSS AND TRY TO RESOLVE WORLD PROBLEMS; TO PROVIDE ECONOMIC AID TO MANY COUNTRIES.
83. IN THE CAPITOL IN WASHINGTON, D.C.
84. EVERYONE (CITIZENS AND NON-CITIZENS LIVING IN THE U.S.)
85. THE PREAMBLE
86. OBTAIN FEDERAL GOVERNMENT JOBS; TRAVEL WITH A U.S. PASSPORT; PETITION FOR CLOSE RELATIVES TO COME TO THE U.S. TO LIVE
87. THE RIGHT TO VOTE
88. THE PLACE WHERE CONGRESS MEETS
89. THE PRESIDENT'S OFFICIAL HOME
90. WASHINGTON, D.C. (1600 PENNSYLVANIA AVENUE, N.W.)
91. THE WHITE HOUSE
92. FREEDOM OF: SPEECH, PRESS, RELIGION, PEACEABLE ASSEMBLY, AND, REQUESTING CHANGE OF THE GOVERNMENT
93. THE PRESIDENT
94. GEORGE WASHINGTON
95. NOVEMBER
96. JANUARY
97. THERE IS NO LIMIT
98. THERE IS NO LIMIT
99. DEMOCRATIC AND REPUBLICAN
100. FIFTY (50)

*U.S. Government Printing Office: 1997 - 579-725

U.S. Department of Justice
Immigration and Naturalization Service

OMB #1115-0061
Immigrant Petition for Alien Worker

START HERE - Please Type or Print

FOR INS USE ONLY

Part 1. Information about the person or organization filing this petition.

If an individual is filing, use the top Name line. Organizations should use the second line.

Family Name | Given Name | Middle Initial

Company or Organization

Address - Attn:

Street Number and Name | Room #

City | State or Province

Country | ZIP/Postal Code

IRS Tax # | Social Security #

Part 2. Petition Type.

This petition is being filed for: (check one)

a. ☐ An alien of extraordinary ability
b. ☐ An outstanding professor or researcher
c. ☐ A multinational executive or manager
d. ☐ A member of the professions holding an advanced degree or an alien of exceptional ability
e. ☐ A skilled worker (requiring at least two years of specialized training or experience) or professional
f. ☐ An employee of a U.S. business operating in Hong Kong
g. ☐ Any other worker (requiring less than two years training or experience)

Part 3. Information about the person you are filing for.

Family Name | Given Name | Middle Initial

Address - C/O

Street # and Name | Apt. #

City | State or Province

Country | Zip or Postal Code

Date of Birth (month/day/year) | Country of Birth

Social Security # (if any) | A # (if any)

If in the U.S.: Date of Arrival (month/day/year) | I-94#

Current Nonimmigrant Status | Expires on (month/day/year)

Part 4. Processing Information.

Below give the U.S. Consulate you want notified if this petition is approved and if any requested adjustment of status cannot be granted.

U.S Consulate: City | Country

Form I-140 (Rev. 12-2-91)

Continued on back.

FOR INS USE ONLY

Returned | Receipt

Resubmitted

Reloc Sent

Reloc Rec'd

☐ Petitioner Interviewed
☐ Beneficiary Interviewed

Classification
☐ 203(b)(1)(A) Alien Of Extraordinary Ability
☐ 203(b)(1)(B) Outstanding Professor or Researcher
☐ 203(b)(1)(C) Multi-national executive or manager
☐ 203(b)(2) Member of professions w/adv. degree or of exceptional ability
☐ 203(b)(3) (A) (i) Skilled worker
☐ 203(b)(3) (A) (ii) Professional
☐ 203(b)(3) (A) (iii) Other worker
☐ Sec. 124 IMMACT-Employee of U.S. business in Hong Kong

Priority Date | Consulate

Remarks

Action Block

To Be Completed by *Attorney or Representative*, if any
☐ Fill in box if G-28 is attached to represent the petitioner

VOLAG#

ATTY State License #

Part 4. Processing Information. *(continued)*

If you gave a U. S. address in Part 3, print the person's foreign address below. If his/her native alphabet does not use Roman letters, print his/her name and foreign address in the native alphabet.

Name | Address

Are you filing any other petitions or applications with this one? ☐ No ☐ yes attach an explanation
Is the person you are filing for in exclusion or deportation proceedings? ☐ No ☐ yes attach an explanation
Has an immigrant visa petition ever been filed by or in behalf of this person? ☐ No ☐ yes attach an explanation

Part 5. Additional Information about the employer.

Type of petitioner (check one) ☐ Self ☐ Individual U.S. Citizen ☐ Company or organization
☐ Permanent Resident ☐ Other explain ______

If a company, give the following:
Type of business

Date Established	Current # of employees	Gross Annual Income	Net Annual Income

If an individual, give the following:
Occupation | Annual Income

Part 6. Basic Information about the proposed employment.

Job Title | Nontechnical description of job

Address where the person will work if different from address in Part 1.

Is this a full-time position? ☐ yes ☐ No (hours per week ______) Wages per week

Is this a permanent position?: ☐ yes ☐ No | Is this a new position? ☐ yes ☐ No

Part 7. Information on spouse and all children of the person you are filing for.

Provide an attachment listing the family members of the person you are filing for. Be sure to include their full name, relationship, date and country of birth, and present address.

Part 8. Signature. *Read the information on penalties in the instructions before completing this section.*

I certify under penalty of perjury under the laws of the United States of America that this petition, and the evidence submitted with it, is all true and correct. I authorize the release of any information from my records which the Immigration and Naturalization Service needs to determine eligibility for the benefit I am seeking.

Signature Date

Please Note: *If you do not completely fill out this form, or fail to submit required documents listed in the instructions, you cannot be found eligible for the requested document and this application may to be denied.*

Part 9. Signature of person preparing form if other than above. *(Sign below)*

I declare that I prepared this application at the request of the above person and it is based on all information of which I have knowledge.

Signature Print Your Name Date

Firm Name and Address

*U.S. GPO:1992-312-328/51143

Form I-140 (Rev. 12-2-91)

U.S. Department of Justice
Immigration and Naturalization Service

OMB No. 1115-0061
Immigrant Petition for Alien Worker

Purpose Of This Form.
This form is used to petition for an immigrant based on employment.

Who May File.
Any person may file this petition in behalf of an alien who:

- has extraordinary ability in the sciences, arts, education, business, or athletics, demonstrated by sustained national or international acclaim, whose achievements have been recognized in the field; or
- is claiming exceptional ability in the sciences, arts, or business, and is seeking an exemption of the requirement of a job offer in the national interest.

A U.S. employer may file this petition who wishes to employ:

- an outstanding professor or researcher, with at least 3 years of experience in teaching or research in the academic area, who is recognized internationally as outstanding,
    - in a tenured or tenure-track position at a university or institution of higher education to teach in the academic area,
    - in a comparable position at a university or institution of higher education to conduct research in the area, or
    - in a comparable position to conduct research for a private employer who employs at least 3 persons in full-time research activities and has achieved documented accomplishments in an academic field;
- an alien who, in the 3 years preceding the filing of this petition, has been employed for at least 1 year by a firm or corporation or other legal entity and who seeks to enter the U.S. to continue to render services to the same employer or to a subsidiary or affiliate in a capacity that is managerial or executive;
- a member of the professions holding an advanced degree or an alien with exceptional ability in the sciences, arts, or business who will substantially benefit the national economy, cultural or educational interests, or welfare of the U.S.;
- a skilled worker (requiring at least 2 years of specialized training or experience in the skill)- to perform labor for which qualified workers are not available in the U.S.;
- a member of the professions with a baccalaureate degree; or
- an unskilled worker to perform labor for which qualified workers are not available in the U.S.

General Filing Instructions.
Please answer all questions by typing or clearly printing in black ink. Indicate that an item is not applicable with "N/A". If an answer to a question is "none," write "none". If you need extra space to answer any item, attach a sheet of paper with your name and your A#, if any, and indicate the number of the item to which the answer refers. You must file your petition with the required Initial Evidence. Your petition must be properly signed and filed with the correct fee.

Initial Evidence.
If you are filing for an alien of extraordinary ability in the sciences, arts, education, business, or athletics, you must file your petition with:

- evidence of a one-time achievement (i.e., a major, internationally-recognized award), or
- at least three of the following:
    - receipt of lesser nationally or internationally recognized prizes or awards for excellence in the field of endeavor,
    - membership in associations in the field which require outstanding achievements as judged by recognized national or international experts,
    - published material about the alien in professional or major trade publications or other major media,
    - participation on a panel or individually as a judge of the work of others in the field or an allied field,
    - original scientific, scholarly, artistic, athletic, or business-related contributions of major significance in the field,
    - authorship of scholarly articles in the field, in professional or major trade publications or other major media,
    - display of the alien's work at artistic exhibitions or showcases,
    - evidence that the alien has performed in a leading or critical role for organizations or establishments that have a distinguished reputation,
    - evidence that the alien has commanded a high salary or other high remuneration for services, or
    - evidence of commercial successes in the performing arts, as shown by box office receipts or record, casette, compact disk, or video sales.
- If the above standards do not readily apply to the alien's occupation, you may submit comparable evidence to establish the alien's eligibility.

A U.S. employer filing for an outstanding professor or researcher must file the petition with:

- evidence of at least 2 of the following:
    - receipt of major prizes or awards for outstanding achievement in the academic field,
    - membership in associations in the academic field, which require outstanding achievements of their members,
    - published material in professional publications written by others about the alien's work in the academic field,
    - participation on a panel, or individually, as the judge of the work of others in the same or an allied academic field,
    - original scientific or scholarly research contributions to the academic field, or
    - authorship of scholarly books or articles, in scholarly journals with international circulation, in the academic field;
- evidence the beneficiary has at least 3 years of experience in teaching and/or research in the academic field; and
- if you are a university or other institution of higher education, a letter indicating that you intend to employ the beneficiary in a tenured or tenure-track position as a teacher or in a permanent position as a researcher in the academic field, or
- if you are a private employer, a letter indicating that you intend to employ the beneficiary in a permanent research position in the academic field, and evidence that you employ at least 3 full-time researchers and have achieved documented accomplishments in the field.

A U.S. employer filing for a multinational executive or manager must file the petition with a statement which demonstrates that:

- if the alien is outside the U.S., he/she has been employed outside the U.S. for at least 1 year in the past 3 years in a managerial or executive capacity by a firm or corporation or other legal entity, or by its affiliate or subsidiary; or
- if the alien is already in the U.S. working for the same employer, or a subsidiary or affiliate of the firm or corporation or other legal entity, by which the alien was employed abroad, he/she was employed by the entity abroad in a managerial or executive capacity for at least one year in the 3 years preceding his/her entry as a nonimmigrant;
    - the prospective employer in the U.S. is the same employer or a subsidiary or affiliate of the firm or corporation or other legal entity by which the alien was employed abroad;
    - the prospective U.S. employer has been doing business for at least one year; and
    - the alien is to be employed in the U.S. in a managerial or executive capacity and describing the duties to be performed.

A U.S. employer filing for a member of the professions with an advanced degree or a person with exceptional ability in the sciences, arts, or business must file the petition with:

- a labor certification (see GENERAL EVIDENCE) and either:
- an official academic record showing that the alien has a U.S. advanced degree or an equivalent foreign degree, or an official academic record showing that the alien has a U.S. baccalaureate degree or an equivalent foreign degree and letters from current or former employers showing that the alien has at least 5 years of progressive post-baccalaureate experience in the specialty; or
- at least 3 of the following:
    - an official academic record showing that the alien has a degree, diploma, certificate, or similar award from an institution of learning relating to the area of exceptional ability;
    - letters from current or former employers showing that the alien has at least 10 years of full-time experience in the occupation for which he/she is being sought;
    - a license to practice the profession or certification for a particular profession or occupation;
    - evidence that the alien has commanded a salary, or other remuneration for services, which demonstrates exceptional ability;
    - evidence of membership in professional associations; or
    - evidence of recognition for achievements and significant contributions to the industry or field by peers, governmental entities, or professional or business organizations.
- If the above standards do not readily apply to the alien's occupation, you may submit comparable evidence to establish the alien's eligibility.

A U.S. employer filing for a skilled worker must file the petition with:

- a labor certification (see GENERAL EVIDENCE); and requirement is 2 years of training or experience).
- evidence that the alien meets the educational, training, or experience and any other requirements of the labor certification (the minimum requirement is 2 years of training or experience).

A U.S. employer filing for a professional must file the petition with:

- a labor certification (see GENERAL EVIDENCE);
- evidence that the alien holds a U.S. baccalaureate degree or equivalent foreign degree; and
- evidence that a baccalaureate degree is required for entry into the occupation.

A U.S. employer filing for its employee in Hong Kong must file its petition with a statement that demonstrates that:

- the company is owned and organized in the United States
- the employee is a resident of Hong Kong;
- the company, or its subsidiary or affiliate, is employing the person in Hong Kong, and has been employing him or her there for the past 12 months, or the company, or its subsidiary or affiliate, is employing him or her outside of Hong Kong during a temporary absence (i.e., of limited duration) and he or she had been employed in Hong Kong for 12 consecutive months prior to such absence(s), and that such employment is, and for that period has been, as an officer or supervisor, or in a capacity that is executive, managerial or involves specialized knowledge;
- the company employs at least 100 employees in the U.S. and at least 50 employees outside the U.S. and has a gross annual income of at least $50,000,000; and
- the company intends to employ the person in the United States as an officer or supervisor, or in a capacity that is executive, managerial or involves specialized knowledge, with salary and benefits comparable to others with similar responsibilities and experience within the company. A specific job description is required for immediate immigration; a commitment to a qualifying job is required for deterred immigration.

A U.S. employer filing for an unskilled worker must file the petition with:

- a labor certification (see GENERAL EVIDENCE); and
- evidence that the beneficiary meets any education, training, or experience requirements required in the labor certification.

General Evidence.

Labor certification. Petitions for certain classifications must be filed with a certification from the Department of Labor or with documentation to establish that the alien qualifies for one of the shortage occupations in the Department of Labor's Labor Market Information Pilot Program or for an occupation in Group I or II of the Department of Labor's Schedule A. A certification establishes that there are not sufficient workers who are able, willing, qualified, and available at the time and place where the alien is to be employed and that employment of the alien if qualified, will not adversely affect the wages and working conditions of similarly employed U.S. workers. Application for certification is made on Form ETA-750 and is filed at the local office of the State Employment Service. If the alien is in a shortage occupation, or for a Schedule A/Group I or II occupation, you may file a fully completed, uncertified Form ETA-750 in duplicate with your petition for determination by INS that the alien belongs to the shortage occupation.

Translations. Any foreign language document must be accompanied by a full English translation which the translator has certified as complete and correct, and by the translator's certification that he or she is competent to translate from the foreign language into English.

Copies. If these instructions state that a copy of a document may be filed with this petition, and you choose to send us the original, we may keep that original for our records.

Where To File.

File this petition at the INS Service Center with jurisdiction over the place where the alien will be employed.

If the employment will be in Alabama, Connecticut, Delaware, District of Columbia, Florida, Georgia, Maine, Maryland, Massachusetts, New Hampshire, New Jersey, New York, North Carolina, Pennsylvania, Puerto Rico, Rhode Island, South Carolina, Vermont, the Virgin Islands, Virginia, or West Virginia, mail your petition to: USINS Eastern Service Center, 75 Lower Welden Street, St. Albans, VT 05479-0001.

If the employment will be in Arizona, California, Guam, Hawaii, or Nevada, mail your petition to: USINS Western Service Center, P.O. Box 30040, Laguna Niguel, CA 92607-0040.

If the employment will be elsewhere in the U.S., mail your petition to: USINS Northern Service Center, 100 Centennial Mall North, Room, B-26, Lincoln, NE 68508.

Fee.

The fee for this petition is $70.00. The fee must be submitted in the exact amount. It cannot be refunded. DO NOT MAIL CASH. All checks and money orders must be drawn on a bank or other institution located in the United States and must be payable in United States currency. The check or money order should be made payable to the Immigration and Naturalization Service, except that:

- If you live in Guam, and are filing this application in Guam, make your check or money order payable to the "Treasurer, Guam."
- If you live in the Virgin Islands, and are filing this application in the Virgin Islands, make your check or money order payable to the "Commissioner of Finance of the Virgin Islands."

Checks are accepted subject to collection. An uncollected check will render the application and any document issued invalid. A charge of $5.00 will be imposed if a check in payment of a fee is not honored by the bank on which it is drawn.

Processing Information.

Acceptance. Any petition that is not signed or is not accompanied by the correct fee will be rejected with a notice that it is deficient. You may correct the deficiency and resubmit the petition. However, a petition is not considered properly filed until accepted by the Service. A priority date will not be assigned until the petition is properly filed.

Initial processing. Once the petition has been accepted, it will be checked for completeness, including submission of the required initial evidence. If you do not completely fill out the form, or file it without required initial evidence, you will not establish a basis for eligibility, and we may deny your petition.

Requests for more information or interview. We may request more information or evidence or we may request that you appear at an INS office for an interview. We may also request that you submit the originals of any copy. We will return these originals when they are no longer required.

Decision. If you have established eligibility for the benefit requested, your petition will be approved. If you have not established eligibility, your petition will be denied. You will be notified in writing of the decision on your petition.

Meaning of petition approval.

Approval of a petition means you have established that the person you are filing for is eligible for the requested classification. This is the first step towards permanent residence. However, this does not in itself grant permanent residence or employment authorization. You will be given information about the requirements for the person to receive an immigrant visa, or to adjust status, after your petition is approved.

Penalties.

If you knowingly and willfully falsify or conceal a material fact or submit a false document with this request, we will deny the benefit you are filing for, and may deny any other immigration benefit. In addition, you will face severe penalties provided by law, and may be subject to criminal prosecution.

Privacy Act Notice.

We ask for the information on this form, and associated evidence, to determine if you have established eligibility for the immigration benefit you are filing for. Our legal right to ask for this information is in 8 USC 11854. We may provide this information to other government agencies. Failure to provide this information, and any requested evidence, may delay a final decision or result in denial of your request.

Paperwork Reduction Act Notice.

We try to create forms and instructions that are accurate, can be easily understood, and which impose the least possible burden on you to provide us with information. Often this is difficult because some immigration laws are very complex. The estimated average time to complete and file this application is as follows: (1) 20 minutes to learn about the law and form; (2) 15 minutes to complete the form; and (3) 45 minutes to assemble and file the petition; for a total estimated average of 1 hour and 20 minutes per petition. If you have comments regarding the accuracy of this estimate, or suggestions for making this form simpler, you can write to both the Immigration and Naturalization Service, 425 I Street, N.W., Room 5304, Washington, D.C. 20536; and the Office of Management and Budget, Paperwork Reduction Project, OMB No. 1115-0061, Washington, D.C. 20503.

APPENDIX 5-2
Form I-134, Affidavit of Support

OMB No. 1115-0062

U. S. Department of Justice
Immigration and Naturalization Service

Affidavit of Support

(ANSWER ALL ITEMS: FILL IN WITH TYPEWRITER OR PRINT IN BLOCK LETTERS IN INK.)

I, ______________________ (Name), *residing at* ______________________ (Street and Number)

______________________ (City) (State) (ZIP Code if in U.S.) (Country)

BEING DULY SWORN DEPOSE AND SAY:

1. I was born on ____________ (Date) at ____________ (City) ____________ (Country)

   If you are ***not*** a native born United States citizen, answer the following as appropriate:

   a. If a United States citizen through naturalization, give certificate of naturalization number ____________

   b. If a United States citizen through parent(s) or marriage, give citizenship certificate number ____________

   c. If United States citizenship was derived by some other method, attach a statement of explanation.

   d. If a lawfully admitted permanent resident of the United States, give "A" number ____________

2. That I am ________ years of age and have resided in the United States since (date) ____________
3. That this affidavit is executed in behalf of the following person:

Name			Sex	Age
Citizen of—(Country)	Marital Status	Relationship to Deponent		
Presently resides at—(Street and Number)	(City)	(State)	(Country)	

Name of spouse and children accompanying or following to join person:

Spouse	Sex	Age	Child	Sex	Age
Child	Sex	Age	Child	Sex	Age
Child	Sex	Age	Child	Sex	Age

4. That this affidavit is made by me for the purpose of assuring the United States Government that the person(s) named in item 3 will not become a public charge in the United States.

5. That I am willing and able to receive, maintain and support the person(s) named in item 3. That I am ready and willing to deposit a bond, if necessary, to guarantee that such person(s) will not become a public charge during his or her stay in the United States, or to guarantee that the above named will maintain his or her nonimmigrant status if admitted temporarily and will depart prior to the expiration of his or her authorized stay in the United States.

6. That I understand this affidavit will be binding upon me for a period of three (3) years after entry of the person(s) named in item 3 and that the information and documentation provided by me may be made available to the Secretary of Health and Human Services and the Secretary of Agriculture, who may make it available to a public assistance agency.

7. That I am employed as, or engaged in the business of ____________ (Type of Business) with ____________ (Name of concern)

   at ____________ (Street and Number) (City) (State) (Zip Code)

   I derive an annual income of *(if self-employed, I have attached a copy of my last income tax return or report of commercial rating concern which I certify to be true and correct to the best of my knowledge and belief. See instruction for nature of evidence of net worth to be submitted.)* $____________

   I have on deposit in savings banks in the United States $____________

   I have other personal property, the reasonable value of which is $____________

I have stocks and bonds with the following market value, as indicated on the attached list which I certify to be true and correct to the best of my knowledge and belief. $ ______
I have life insurance in the sum of $ ______
With a cash surrender value of $ ______
I own real estate valued at $ ______
With mortgages or other encumbrances thereon amounting to $ ______

Which is located at ______
(Street and Number) (City) (State) (Zip Code)

8. That the following persons are dependent upon me for support: *(Place an "X" in the appropriate column to indicate whether the person named is **wholly or partially** dependent upon you for support.)*

Name of Person	Wholly Dependent	Partially Dependent	Age	Relationship to Me

9. That I have previously submitted affidavit(s) of support for the following person(s). If none, state ***"None"***

Name Date submitted

______

______

10. That I have submitted visa petition(s) to the Immigration and Naturalization Service on behalf of the following person(s). If none, state none.

Name Relationship Date submitted

______

______

11. ***(Complete this block only if the person named in item 3 will be in the United States temporarily.)***
That I ☐ do intend ☐ do not intend, to make specific contributions to the support of the person named in item 3. *(If you check "do intend", indicate the exact nature and duration of the contributions. For example, if you intend to furnish room and board, state for how long and, if money, state the amount in United States dollars and state whether it is to be given in a lump sum, weekly, or monthly, or for how long.)*

______

______

______

OATH OR AFFIRMATION OF DEPONENT

I acknowledge at that I have read Part III of the Instructions, Sponsor and Alien Liability, and am aware of my responsibilities as an immigrant sponsor under the Social Security Act, as amended, and the Food Stamp Act, as amended.

I swear (affirm) that I know the contents of this affidavit signed by me and the statements are true and correct.

Signature of deponent ______

Subscribed and sworn to (affirmed) before me this ______ ***day of*** ______, 19______

at ______ ***My commission expires on*** ______

Signature of Officer Administering Oath ______ ***Title*** ______

If affidavit prepared by other than deponent, please complete the following: I declare that this document was prepared by me at the request of the deponent and is based on all information of which I have knowledge.

______

(Signature) ***(Address)*** ***(Date)***

(Please tear off this sheet before submitting Affidavit)

U. S. Department of Justice
Immigration and Naturalization Service

Affidavit of Support

INSTRUCTIONS

I. EXECUTION OF AFFIDAVIT. A separate affidavit must be submitted for each person. You must sign the affidavit in your full, true and correct name and affirm or make it under oath. If you are **in the United States** the affidavit may be sworn or affirmed before an immigration officer without the payment of fee, or before a notary public or other officer authorized to administer oaths for general purposes, in which case the official seal or certificate of authority to administer oaths must be affixed. If you are **outside the United States** the affidavit must be sworn to or affirmed before a United States consular or immigration officer.

II. SUPPORTING EVIDENCE. The deponent must submit in duplicate evidence of income and resources, as appropriate:

A. Statement from an officer of the bank or other financial institution in which you have deposits giving the following details regarding your account:
1. Date account opened.
2. Total amount deposited for the past year.
3. Present balance.

B. Statement of your employer on business stationery, showing:
1. Date and nature of employment.
2. Salary paid.
3. Whether position is temporary or permanent.

C. If self-employed:
1. Copy of last income tax return filed or,
2. Report of commercial rating concern.

D. List containing serial numbers and denominations of bonds and name of record owner(s).

III. SPONSOR AND ALIEN LIABILITY. Effective October 1, 1980, amendments to section 1614(f) of the Social Security Act and Part A of Title XVI of the Social Security Act establish certain requirements for determining the eligibility of aliens who apply for the first time for Supplemental Security Income (SSI) benefits. Effective October 1, 1981, amendments to section 415 of the Social Security Act establish similar requirements for determining the eligibility of aliens who apply for the first time for Aid to Families with Dependent Children (AFDC) benefits. Effective December 22, 1981, amendments to the Food Stamp Act of 1977 affect the eligibility of alien participation in the Food Stamp Program. These amendments require that the income and resources of any person who, as the sponsor of an alien's entry into the United States, executes an affidavit of support or similar agreement on behalf of the alien, and the income and resources of the sponsor's spouse (*if living with the sponsor*) shall be deemed to be the income and resources of the alien under formulas for determining eligibility for SSI, AFDC, and Food Stamp benefits during the three years following the alien's entry into the United States.

An alien applying for SSI must make available to the Social Security Administration documentation concerning his or her income and resources and those of the sponsor including information which was provided in support of the application for an immigrant visa or adjustment of status. An alien applying for AFDC or Food Stamps must make similar information available to the State public assistance agency. The Secretary of Health and Human Services and the Secretary of Agriculture are authorized to obtain copies of any such documentation submitted to INS or the Department of State and to release such documentation to a State public assistance agency.

Sections 1621(e) and 415(d) of the Social Security Act and subsection 5(i) of the Food Stamp Act also provide that an alien and his or her sponsor shall be jointly and severably liable to repay any SSI, AFDC, or Food Stamp benefits which are incorrectly paid because of misinformation provided by a sponsor or because of a sponsor's failure to provide information. Incorrect payments which are not repaid will be withheld from any subsequent payments for which the alien or sponsor are otherwise eligible under the Social Security Act or Food Stamp Act, except that the sponsor was without fault or where good cause existed.

These provisions do not apply to the SSI, AFDC or Food Stamp eligibility of aliens admitted as refugees, granted political asylum by the Attorney General, or Cuban/Haitian entrants as defined in section 501(e) of P.L. 96-422 and of dependent children of the sponsor or sponsor's spouse. They also do not apply to the SSI or Food Stamp eligibility of an alien who becomes blind or disabled after admission into the United States for permanent residency.

IV. AUTHORITY/USE/PENALTIES. Authority for the collection of the information requested on this form is contained in 8 U.S.C. 1182(a)(15), 1184(a), and 1258. The information will be used principally by the Service, or by any consular officer to whom it may be furnished, to support an alien's application for benefits under the Immigration and Nationality Act and specifically the assertion that he or she has adequate means of financial support and will not become a public charge. Submission of the information is voluntary. It may also, as a matter of routine use, be disclosed to other federal, state, local and foreign law enforcement and regulatory agencies, including the Department of Health and Human Services, the Department of Agriculture, the Department of State, the Department of Defense and any component thereof (if the deponent has served or is serving in the armed forces of the United States), the Central Intelligence Agency, and individuals and organizations during the course of any investigation to elicit further information required to carry out Service functions. Failure to provide the information may result in the denial of the alien's application for a visa, or his or her exclusion from the United States.

Form I-134 (Rev. 12-1-84) Y

U.S. Department of Justice
Immigration and Naturalization Service

OMB No. 1115-0053
Application to Register Permanent Residence or Adjust Status

Purpose of this Form.
This form is for a person who is in the United States to apply to adjust to permanent resident status or register for permanent residence while in the U.S. It may also be used by certain Cuban nationals to request a change in the date their permanent residence began.

Who May File.
Based on an immigrant petition. You may apply to adjust your status if:

- an immigrant visa number is immediately available to you based on an approved immigrant petition; or
- you are filing this application with a complete relative, special immigrant juvenile, or special immigrant military petition which if, approved, would make an immigrant visa number immediately available to you.

Based on being the spouse or child of another adjustment applicant or of a person granted permanent residence . You may apply to adjust status if you are the spouse or child of another adjustment applicant, or of a lawful permanent resident, if the relationship existed when that person was admitted as a permanent resident in an immigrant category which allows derivative status for spouses and children.
Based on admission as the fiance(e) of a U.S. citizen and subsequent marriage to that citizen. You may apply to adjust status if you were admitted to the U.S. as the K-1 fiance(e) of a U.S. citizen and married that citizen within 90 days of your entry. If you were admitted as the K-2 child of such a fiance(e), you may apply based on your parent's adjustment application.
Based on asylum status. You may apply to adjust status if you have been granted asylum in the U.S. and are eligible for asylum adjustment. [Note: In most cases you become eligible after being physically present in the U.S. for one year after the grant of asylum if you still qualify as a refugee or as the spouse or child of refugee.]
Based on Cuban citizenship or nationality. You may apply to adjust status if:

- you are a native or citizen of Cuba, were admitted or paroled into the U.S. after January 1, 1959, and thereafter have been physically present in the U.S. for at least one year; or
- you are the spouse or unmarried child of a Cuban described above, and you were admitted or paroled after January 1, 1959, and thereafter have been physically present in the U.S. for at least one year.

Based on continuous residence since before January 1, 1972. You may apply for permanent residence if you have continuously resided in the U.S. since before January 1, 1972.
Other basis of eligibility. If you are not included in the above categories, but believe you may be eligible for adjustment or creation of record of permanent residence, contact your local INS office.
Applying to change the date your permanent residence began. If you were granted permanent residence in the U.S. prior to November 6, 1966, and are a native or citizen of Cuba, his or her spouse or unmarried minor child, you may ask to change the date your lawful permanent residence began to your date of arrival in the U.S. or May 2, 1964, whichever is later.

Persons Who Are Ineligible.
Unless you are applying for creation of record based on continuous residence since before 1/1/72, or adjustment of status under a category in which special rules apply (such as asylum adjustment, Cuban adjustment, special immigrant juvenile adjustment, or special immigrant military personnel adjustment), **you are not eligible for adjustment of status if <u>any</u> of the following apply to you:**

- you entered the U.S. in transit without a visa;
- you entered the U.S. as a nonimmigrant crewman;
- you were not admitted or paroled following inspection by an immigration officer;
- your authorized stay expired before you filed this application, you were employed in the U.S. , prior to filing this application, without INS authorization, or you otherwise failed to maintain your nonimmigrant status, other than through no fault of your own or for technical reasons; unless you are applying because you are an immediate relative of a U.S. citizen (parent, spouse, widow, widower, or unmarried child under 21 years old), a K-1 fiance(e) or K-2 fiance(e) dependent who married the U.S. petitioner within 90 days of admission, or an "H" or "I" special immigrant (foreign medical graduates, international organization employees or their derivative family members);
- you are or were a J-1 or J-2 exchange visitor, are subject to the two-year foreign residence requirement, and have not complied with or been granted a waiver of the requirement;
- you have A, E or G nonimmigrant status, or have an occupation which would allow you to have this status, unless you complete Form I-508 (I-508F for French nationals) to waive diplomatic rights, privileges and immunities, and if you are an A or G nonimmigrant, unless you submit a completed Form I-566;
- you were admitted to Guam as a visitor under the Guam visa waiver program;
- you were admitted to the U.S. as a visitor under the Visa Waiver Pilot Program, unless you are applying because you are an immediate relative of a U.S. citizen (parent, spouse, widow, widower, or unmarried child under 21 years old);
- you are already a conditional permanent resident;
- you were admitted as a K-1 fiance(e) but did not marry the U.S. citizen who filed the petition for you, or were admitted as the K-2 child of a fiance(e) and your parent did not marry the U.S. citizen who filed the petition.

General Filing Instructions.
Please answer all questions by typing or clearly printing in black ink. Indicate that an item is not applicable with **"N/A"**. If the answer is **"none"**, write **"none"**. If you need extra space to answer any item, attach a sheet of paper with your name and your alien registration number (A#), if any, and indicate the number of the item to which the answer refers. You must file your application with the required **Initial Evidence**. Your application must be properly signed and filed with the correct fee. If you are under 14 years of age, your parent or guardian may sign your application.

Translations. Any foreign language document must be accompanied by a full English translation which the translator has certified as complete and correct, and by the translator's certification that he or she is competent to translate from the foreign language into English.

Copies. If these instructions state that a copy of a document may be filed with this application, and you choose to send us the original, we may keep the original for our records.

Initial Evidence.
You must file your application with following evidence:

- **Birth certificate.** Submit a copy of your birth certificate or other record of your birth.
- **Photos.** Submit two (2) identical natural color photographs of yourself, taken within 30 days of this application [Photos must have a white background, be unmounted, printed on thin paper, and be glossy and unretouched. They must show a three-quarter frontal profile showing the right side of your face, with your right ear visible and with your head bare. You may wear a headdress if required by a religious order of which you are a member. The photos must be no larger than 2 X 2 inches, with the distance from the top of the head to just below the chin about 1 and 1/4 inches. Lightly print your A# (or your name if you have no A#) on the back of each photo, using a pencil.].
- **Fingerprints.** Submit a complete set of fingerprints on Form FD-258 if you are between the ages of 14 and 75 [Do not bend, fold, or crease the fingerprint chart. You should complete the information on the top of the chart and write your A# (if any) in the space marked "Your no. OCA" or "Miscellaneous no. MNU". You should not sign the chart until you have been fingerprinted, or are told to sign by the person who takes your fingerprints. The person who takes your fingerprints must also sign the chart and write his/her title and the date you are fingerprinted in the space provided on the chart. You may be fingerprinted by police, sheriff, or INS officials or other reputable person or organization. You should call the police, sheriff, organization or INS office before you go there, since some offices do not take fingerprints or may take fingerprints only at certain times.].

- **Medical Examination.** Submit a medical examination report on the form you have obtained from INS [Not required if you are applying for creation of record based on continuous residence since before 1/1/72, or if you are a K-1 fiance(e) or K-2 dependent of a fiance(e) who had a medical examination within the past year as required for the nonimmigrant fiance(e) visa.].
- **Form G-325A,** Biographic Information Sheet. You must submit a completed G-325A if you are between 14 and 79 years of age.
- **Evidence of status.** Submit a copy of your Form I-94, Nonimmigrant Arrival/Departure Record, showing your admission to the U.S. and current status, or other evidence of your status.
- **Employment letter/Affidavit of Support.** Submit a letter showing you are employed in a job that is not temporary, an affidavit of support from a responsible person in the U.S., or other evidence that shows that you are not likely to become a public charge [Not required if you are applying for creation of record based on continuous residence since before 1/1/72, asylum adjustment, or a Cuban or a spouse or unmarried child of a Cuban who was admitted after 1/1/59].
- **Evidence of eligibility.**
  - **Based on an immigrant petition.** Attach a copy of the approval notice for an immigrant petition which makes a visa number immediately available to you, or submit a complete relative, special immigrant juvenile, or special immigrant military petition which, if approved, will make a visa number immediately available to you.
  - **Based on admission as the K-1 fiance(e) of a U.S. citizen and subsequent marriage to that citizen.** Attach a copy of the fiance(e) petition approval notice and a copy of your marriage certificate.
  - **Based on asylum status.** Attach a copy of the letter or Form I-94 which shows the date you were granted asylum.
  - **Based on continuous residence in the U.S. since before 1/1/72.** Attach copies of evidence that shows continuous residence since before 1/1/72.
  - **Based on Cuban citizenship or nationality.** Attach evidence of your citizenship or nationality, such as a copy of your passport, birth certificate or travel document.
  - **Based on you being the spouse or child of another adjustment applicant or person granted permanent residence based on issuance of an immigrant visa.** File your application with the application of that other applicant, or with evidence it is pending with the Service or has been approved, or evidence your spouse or parent has been granted permanent residence based on an immigrant visa and:
    - If you are applying as the spouse of that person, also attach a copy of your marriage certificate and copies of documents showing the legal termination of all other marriages by you and your spouse; or
    - If you are applying as the child of that person, also attach a copy of your birth certificate, and, if the other person is not your natural mother, copies of evidence, (such as a marriage certificate and documents showing the legal termination of all other marriages, and an adoption decree), to demonstrate that you qualify as his or her child.
  - **Other basis for eligibility.** Attach copies of documents proving that you are eligible for the classification.

Where To File.
File this application at the local INS office having jurisdiction over your place of residence.

Fee. The fee for this application is **$130**, except that it is **$100** if you are less than 14 years old. The fee must be submitted in the exact amount. It cannot be refunded. **DO NOT MAIL CASH.** All checks and money orders must be drawn on a bank or other institution located in the United States and must be payable in United States currency. The check or money order should be made payable to the Immigration and Naturalization Service, except that:

- If you live in Guam, and are filing this application in Guam, make your check or money order payable to the "Treasurer, Guam."
- If you live in the Virgin Islands, and are filing this application in the Virgin Islands, make your check or money order payable to the "Commissioner of Finance of the Virgin Islands."

Checks are accepted subject to collection. An uncollected check will render the application and any document issued invalid. A charge of $5.00 will be imposed if a check in payment of a fee is not honored by the bank on which it is drawn.

Processing Information.
Acceptance. Any application that is not signed, or is not accompanied by the correct fee, will be rejected with a notice that the application is deficient. You may correct the deficiency and resubmit the application. An application is not considered properly filed until accepted by the Service.

Initial processing. Once an application has been accepted, it will be checked for completeness, including submission of the required initial evidence. If you do not completely fill out the form, or file it without required initial evidence, you will not establish a basis for eligibility, and we may deny your application.

Requests for more information. We may request more information or evidence. We may also request that you submit the originals of any copy. We will return these originals when they are no longer required.

Interview. After you file your application you will be notified to appear at an INS office to answer questions about the application. You will be required to answer these questions under oath or affirmation. You must bring your Arrival-Departure Record (Form I-94) and any passport to the interview.

Decision. You will be notified in writing of the decision on your application.

Travel Outside the U.S. If you plan to leave the U.S. to go to any other country, including Canada or Mexico, before a decision is made on your application, contact the INS office processing your application before you leave. In many cases, leaving the U.S. without advance written permission will result in automatic termination of your application. Also, you may experience difficulty upon returning to the U.S. if you do not have written permission to reenter.

Penalties.
If you knowingly and willfully falsify or conceal a material fact or submit a false document with this request, we will deny the benefit you are filing for, and may deny any other immigration benefit. In addition, you will face severe penalties provided by law, and may be subject to criminal prosecution.

Privacy Act Notice.
We ask for the information on this form, and associated evidence, to determine if you have established eligibility for the immigration benefit you are filing for. Our legal right to ask for this information is in 8 USC 1255 and 1259. We may provide this information to other government agencies. Failure to provide this information, and any requested evidence, may delay a final decision or result in denial of your request.

Paperwork Reduction Act Notice.
We try to create forms and instructions that are accurate, can be easily understood, and which impose the least possible burden on you to provide us with information. Often this is difficult because some immigration laws are very complex. The estimated average time to complete and file this application is computed as follows: (1) **20** minutes to learn about the law and form; (2) **25** minutes to complete the form; and (3) **270** minutes to assemble and file the application, including the required interview and travel time; for a total estimated average of **5** hours and **15** minutes per application. If you have comments regarding the accuracy of this estimate, or suggestions for making this form simpler, you can write to both the Immigration and Naturalization Service, 425 I Street, N.W., Room 5304, Washington, D.C. 20536; and the Office of Management and Budget, Paperwork Reduction Project, OMB No. 1115-0053, Washington, D.C. 20503.

U.S. Department of Justice
Immigration and Naturalization Service

OMB No. 1115-0053

Application to Register Permanent Residence or Adjust Status

START HERE - Please Type or Print

Part 1. Information about you.

Family Name	Given Name	Middle Initial
Address - C/O		
Street Number and Name		Apt. #
City		
State	Zip Code	
Date of Birth (month/day/year)	Country of Birth	
Social Security #	A # (if any)	
Date of Last Arrival (month/day/year)	I-94 #	
Current INS Status	Expires on (month/day/year)	

Part 2. Application Type. *(check one)*

I am applying for adjustment to permanent resident status because:

a. ☐ an immigrant petition giving me an immediately available immigrant visa number has been approved (attach a copy of the approval notice), or a relative, special immigrant juvenile, or special immigrant military visa petition filed with this application will give me an immediately available visa number if approved.

b. ☐ My spouse or parent applied for adjustment of status or was granted lawful permanent residence in an immigrant visa category which allows derivative status for spouses and children.

c. ☐ I entered as a K-1 fiance(e) of a U.S. citizen whom I married within 90 days of entry, or I am the K-2 child of such a fiance(e) (attach a copy of the fiance(e) petition approval notice and the marriage certificate).

d. ☐ I was granted asylum or derivative asylum status as the spouse or child of a person granted asylum and am eligible for adjustment.

e. ☐ I am a native or citizen of Cuba admitted or paroled into the U.S. after January 1, 1959, and thereafter have been physically present in the U.S. for at least 1 year.

f. ☐ I am the husband, wife, or minor unmarried child of a Cuban described in (e) and am residing with that person, and was admitted or paroled into the U.S. after January 1, 1959, and thereafter have been physically present in the U.S. for at least 1 year.

g. ☐ I have continuously resided in the U.S. since before January 1, 1972.

h. ☐ Other-explain____________________________

I am already a permanent resident and am applying to have the date I was granted permanent residence adjusted to the date I originally arrived in the U.S. as a nonimmigrant or parolee, or as of May 2, 1964, whichever is later, and: *(Check one)*

i. ☐ I am a native or citizen of Cuba and meet the description in (e), above.

j. ☐ I am the husband, wife or minor unmarried child of a Cuban, and meet the description in (f), above.

FOR INS USE ONLY

Returned	Receipt
Resubmitted	
Reloc Sent	
Reloc Rec'd	
☐ Applicant Interviewed	

Section of Law
- ☐ Sec. 209(b), INA
- ☐ Sec. 13, Act of 9/11/57
- ☐ Sec. 245, INA
- ☐ Sec. 249, INA
- ☐ Sec. 1 Act of 11/2/66
- ☐ Sec. 2 Act of 11/2/66
- ☐ Other____________

Country Chargeable

Eligibility Under Sec. 245
- ☐ Approved Visa Petition
- ☐ Dependent of Principal Alien
- ☐ Special Immigrant
- ☐ Other____________

Preference

Action Block

To Be Completed by *Attorney or Representative*, if any

☐ Fill in box if G-28 is attached to represent the applicant

VOLAG#

ATTY State License #

Form I-485 (09-09-92)N

Continued on back.

Part 3. Processing Information.

A. City/Town/Village of birth	Current occupation
Your mother's first name	Your father's first name

Give your name exactly how it appears on your Arrival /Departure Record (Form I-94)

Place of last entry into the U.S. (City/State)	In what status did you last enter? *(Visitor, Student, exchange alien, crewman, temporary worker, without inspection, etc.)*
Were you inspected by a U.S. Immigration Officer? ☐ Yes ☐ No	
Nonimmigrant Visa Number	Consulate where Visa was issued
Date Visa was issued (month/day/year) / Sex: ☐ Male ☐ Female	Marital Status: ☐ Married ☐ Single ☐ Divorced ☐ Widowed

Have you ever before applied for permanent resident status in the U.S? ☐ No ☐ Yes (give date and place of filing and final disposition):

B. List your present husband/wife, all of your sons and daughters (if you have none, write "none". If additional space is needed, use separate paper).

Family Name	Given Name	Middle Initial	Date of Birth (month/day/year)
Country of birth	Relationship	A #	Applying with you? ☐ Yes ☐ No
Family Name	Given Name	Middle Initial	Date of Birth (month/day/year)
Country of birth	Relationship	A #	Applying with you? ☐ Yes ☐ No
Family Name	Given Name	Middle Initial	Date of Birth (month/day/year)
Country of birth	Relationship	A #	Applying with you? ☐ Yes ☐ No
Family Name	Given Name	Middle Initial	Date of Birth (month/day/year)
Country of birth	Relationship	A #	Applying with you? ☐ Yes ☐ No
Family Name	Given Name	Middle Initial	Date of Birth (month/day/year)
Country of birth	Relationship	A #	Applying with you? ☐ Yes ☐ No

C. List your present and past membership in or affiliation with every political organization, association, fund, foundation, party, club, society, or similar group in the United States or in any other place since your 16th birthday. Include any foreign military service in this part. If none, write "none". Include the name of organization, location, dates of membership from and to, and the nature of the organization. If additional space is needed, use separate paper.

Part 3. Processing Information. *(Continued)*

Please answer the following questions. (If your answer is **"Yes"** on any one of these questions, explain on a separate piece of paper. Answering **"Yes"** does not necessarily mean that you are not entitled to register for permanent residence or adjust status).

1. Have you ever, in or outside the U. S.:
   a. knowingly committed any crime of moral turpitude or a drug-related offense for which you have not been arrested?
   b. been arrested, cited, charged, indicted, fined, or imprisoned for breaking or violating any law or ordinance, excluding traffic violations?
   c. been the beneficiary of a pardon, amnesty, rehabilitation decree, other act of clemency or similar action?
   d. exercised diplomatic immunity to avoid prosecution for a criminal offense in the U. S.? ☐ Yes ☐ No

2. Have you received public assistance in the U.S. from any source, including the U.S. government or any state, county, city, or municipality (other than emergency medical treatment), or are you likely to receive public assistance in the future? ☐ Yes ☐ No

3. Have you ever:
   a. within the past 10 years been a prostitute or procured anyone for prostitution, or intend to engage in such activities in the future?
   b. engaged in any unlawful commercialized vice, including, but not limited to, illegal gambling?
   c. knowingly encouraged, induced, assisted, abetted or aided any alien to try to enter the U.S. illegally?
   d. illicitly trafficked in any controlled substance, or knowingly assisted, abetted or colluded in the illicit trafficking of any controlled substance? ☐ Yes ☐ No

4. Have you ever engaged in, conspired to engage in, or do you intend to engage in, or have you ever solicited membership or funds for, or have you through any means ever assisted or provided any type of material support to, any person or organization that has ever engaged or conspired to engage, in sabotage, kidnapping, political assassination, hijacking, or any other form of terrorist activity? ☐ Yes ☐ No

5. Do you intend to engage in the U.S. in:
   a. espionage?
   b. any activity a purpose of which is opposition to, or the control or overthrow of, the Government of the United States, by force, violence or other unlawful means?
   c. any activity to violate or evade any law prohibiting the export from the United States of goods, technology or sensitive information? ☐ Yes ☐ No

6. Have you ever been a member of, or in any way affiliated with, the Communist Party or any other totalitarian party? ☐ Yes ☐ No

7. Did you, during the period March 23, 1933 to May 8, 1945, in association with either the Nazi Government of Germany or any organization or government associated or allied with the Nazi Government of Germany, ever order, incite, assist or otherwise participate in the persecution of any person because of race, religion, national origin or political opinion? ☐ Yes ☐ No

8. Have you ever engaged in genocide, or otherwise ordered, incited, assisted or otherwise participated in the killing of any person because of race, religion, nationality, ethnic origin, or political opinion? ☐ Yes ☐ No

9. Have you ever been deported from the U.S., or removed from the U.S. at government expense, excluded within the past year, or are you now in exclusion or deportation proceedings? ☐ Yes ☐ No

10. Are you under a final order of civil penalty for violating section 274C of the Immigration Act for use of fraudulent documents, or have you, by fraud or willful misrepresentation of a material fact, ever sought to procure, or procured, a visa, other documentation, entry into the U.S., or any other immigration benefit? ☐ Yes ☐ No

11. Have you ever left the U.S. to avoid being drafted into the U.S. Armed Forces? ☐ Yes ☐ No

12. Have you ever been a J nonimmigrant exchange visitor who was subject to the 2 year foreign residence requirement and not yet complied with that requirement or obtained a waiver? ☐ Yes ☐ No

13. Are you now withholding custody of a U.S. Citizen child outside the U.S. from a person granted custody of the child? ☐ Yes ☐ No

14. Do you plan to practice polygamy in the U.S.? ☐ Yes ☐ No

Form I-485 (Rev. 09-09-92)N ***Continued on back***

Part 4. Signature. *(Read the information on penalties in the instructions before completing this section. You must file this application while in the United States.)*

I certify under penalty of perjury under the laws of the United States of America that this application, and the evidence submitted with it, is all true and correct. I authorize the release of any information from my records which the Immigration and Naturalization Service needs to determine eligibility for the benefit I am seeking.

Signature	Print Your Name	Date	Daytime Phone Number

Please Note: *If you do not completely fill out this form, or fail to submit required documents listed in the instructions, you may not be found eligible for the requested document and this application may be denied.*

Part 5. Signature of person preparing form if other than above. *(Sign Below)*

I declare that I prepared this application at the request of the above person and it is based on all information of which I have knowledge.

Signature	Print Your Name	Date	Day time Phone Number

Firm Name
and Address

Form I-485 (Rev. 09-09-92) N

*U.S. Government Printing Office: 1996 — 405-024/440

Form I-817, Application for Voluntary Departure under the Family Unity Program

U.S. Department of Justice
Immigration and Naturalization Service

OMB No. 1115-0166
Application for Voluntary Departure under the Family Unity Program

Purpose.

This form is used to apply for Voluntary Departure under the Family Unity Program based on being the spouse or child of a "legalized alien." A legalized alien is a temporary or permanent resident adjusted under sections 210, or 245A of the Immigration and Nationality Act, or a permanent resident adjusted under Section 202 of the Immigration Reform and Control Act of 1986 (Cuban/Haitian Adjustment).

Who May File.

Each person must file a separate application. You may file this application if you entered the United States before May 5, 1988, and have resided in the United States since that date, and since May 5, 1988 you have been, and remain, either:

- the spouse of a legalized alien; or
- the unmarried child under the age of 21 of a legalized alien, except that you are ineligible if you are an adopted child and the adoption took place after you became 16 years old, or you were not in the legal custody and living with the adoptive parent(s) for at least two years on May 5, 1988. You are also ineligible if you are a stepchild and the marriage that created this relationship took place after you became 18 years old.

General Filing Instructions.

Please answer all questions by typing or clearly printing in black ink. Indicate that an item is not applicable with "N/A." If an answer to a question is "none," write "none." If you need extra space to answer any item, attach a sheet of paper with your name and your A#, if any, and indicate the number of the item to which the answer refers. You must file your application with the required Initial Evidence. Your application must be properly signed and filed with the correct fee.

Initial Evidence.

Evidence you entered the United States before May 5, 1988. File your application with copies of evidence demonstrating the date of your entry, such as:

- your passport;
- your Form I-94, Nonimmigrant Arrival-Departure Record;
- Copies of residency documents, specified below.

Evidence you have resided in the U.S. since May 5, 1988. File your application with copies of at least 3 of the following:

- Employment records, such as pay stubs, W-2 Forms, certification of the filing of Federal income tax returns, state verification of the filing of state income tax returns, letters from employer(s) or, if you are self employed, letters from banks and other firms with whom you have done business. In all of the above, your name and the name of the employer or other interested organization must appear on the form or letter, as well as relevant dates. Letters from employers must be in affidavit form, and must be signed and attested to by the employer under penalty of perjury. Such letters must include:
  - your address(es) at the time of employment;
  - the exact period(s) of employment, including the dates of any layoffs and:
  - your duties with the company.

  If these records are unavailable, the employer's affidavit stating that your employment records are unavailable and why they are unavailable may be submitted. This affidavit shall be signed and attested to by the employer under penalty of perjury.
- Rent receipts, utility bills (gas, electric, phone, etc.), receipts, or letters from companies showing the dates during which you received service.
- School records (letters, report cards, etc.) from the schools you or your children have attended in the United States, which show the name of the school and periods of school attendance.
- Hospital or medical records showing treatment or hospitalization of you or your children, which show the name of the medical facility or physician and the date(s) of the treatment or hospitalization.
- Attestations by churches, unions, or other organizations to your residence by letter which:
  - identify you by name;
  - are signed by an official (whose title is shown);
  - show inclusive dates of membership;
  - state the address where you resided during membership period;
  - include the seal of the organization impressed on the letter or the letterhead of the organization, if the organization has letterhead stationery;
  - establish how the author knows you; and
  - establish the origin of the information being attested to.
- Any other relevant documents, such as money order receipts for money sent in or out of the country; passport entries; birth certificates of children born in the United States; bank books with dated transactions; correspondence between you and another person or organization; Social Security card; Selective Service card, automobile license receipts, title, vehicle registration; deeds, mortgages, contracts to which you have been a party; tax receipts; insurance policies, receipts, or letters.

Evidence you are the spouse or unmarried child of a legalized alien. You must file your application with a copy of the document issued by the Service to your spouse or parent granting legalized status (examples are: Form I-688, Temporary Resident Card, Form I-94 reflecting temporary proof of lawful permanent residence, or Form I-551, Alien Registration Receipt Card). You must also file your application with the following:

- **If you are the legalized alien's spouse,** file your application with:
  - a copy of your marriage certificate; and
  - if either you or your spouse were married before, file copies of documents to show that any prior marriage was legally ended.
- **If you are the legalized alien's unmarried child and are under 21 years of age,** file your application with a copy of your birth certificate showing your parent(s) names and:
  - if you are the legitimate child of your legalized alien father or stepparent, file a copy of the certificate of marriage of your parents and copies of proof of the legal termination of their prior marriages;
  - if you are the legitimated child of your legalized alien father, file copies of evidence of the legitimation, which must have occurred prior to your eighteenth birthday, and copies of proof of the legal termination of your parent's prior marriages if legitimation resulted from your natural parents' marriage to each other;
  - if you are a child born out-of-wedlock of a legalized alien who purports to be your father, file copies of evidence to show that your father is your natural father and that a bona fide parent-child relationship exists or did exist while you are or were unmarried and under twenty-one (21) years of age. Such a relationship exists or has existed where your father shows, or has shown, an active concern for your support, instruction, and general welfare. Evidence to show that your father is your natural parent may include, but is not limited to the following: a copy of your birth certificate or religious document relating to your birth or baptism; copies of local civil records; affidavits from knowledgeable witnesses, and/or; copies of evidence of your financial support by your putative father.
  - if you are the child of a legalized alien adoptive parent, file a certified copy of your adoption decree showing that you were adopted while under the age of 16 years, a copy of the legal custody decree if your custody was obtained before adoption, and a statement showing the dates and places you and your adoptive parent have lived together.

Fingerprint Cards. If you are age 14 or older, you must file this application with 2 completed and signed Fingerprint Cards, Form FD-258.

Photos. You must submit 2 identical natural color photographs of yourself taken within 30 days of this application. The photos must have a white background, be unmounted, printed on thin paper, and be glossy and unretouched. They should show a three-quarter frontal profile showing the right side of your face, with your right ear visible and with your head bare (unless you are wearing a headdress as required by a religious order of which you are a member).

The photos should be no larger than 2 X 2 inches, with the distance from the top of the head to just below the chin about 1 and 1/4 inches. Lightly print your A# on the back of each photo with a pencil.

General Evidence.

Change of name. If either you or the legalized alien are using a name other than that shown on the relevant documents, you must file your application with copies of the legal documents that made the change, such as a marriage certificate, adoption decree or court order.

Secondary Evidence. All of the documents listed in "INITIAL EVIDENCE" should be issued by the civil registrar, vital statistics office, or other civil authority. If such documents are unavailable, you must file your petition with original evidence from those authorities to establish that all primary evidence is unavailable, and must also submit secondary evidence to establish the facts in question. Submit as many types of secondary evidence as possible to verify the claimed relationship. Listed below are some types of secondary evidence. Any evidence submitted must contain enough information (birth dates, parents' names, etc.) to establish the event you are trying to prove.

- Baptismal certificate. A certificate under the seal of the church where the baptism occurred within two months after birth showing date and place of the child's birth, date of baptism, and the names of the child's parents.
- School record. A letter from the school authorities having jurisdiction over school attended (preferably the first school), showing the date of admission to the school, child's date of birth or age at that time, place of birth, and the names and places of birth of parents, if shown in the school records.
- Census record. State or federal census record showing the name(s) and place(s) of birth, and date(s) of birth or age(s) of the person(s) listed.

If all forms of primary and secondary evidence are unavailable, you must file your petition with original evidence to establish such unavailability, and also submit at least 2 affidavits sworn to, or affirmed, by persons who were living at the time, and have direct personal knowledge of the event you are trying to prove (date and place of birth, marriage, death, etc.). These persons may be relatives and need not be citizens of the United States. Each affidavit should give the person's full name and address, date and place of birth, and any relationship to you. Each affidavit must also fully describe the circumstances or event in question, and fully explain how how he or she acquired knowledge of the event.

Translations. Any foreign language document must be accompanied by a full English translation which the translator has certified as complete and correct, and by the translator's certification that he or she is competent to translate from the foreign language into English.

Copies. If these instructions state that a copy of a document may be filed with this application, and you choose to send us the original, we may keep that original for our records.

Where To File.

If you live in Connecticut, Delaware, District of Columbia, Maine, Maryland, Massachusetts, New Hampshire, New Jersey, New York, Pennsylvania, Puerto Rico, Rhode Island, Vermont, the Virgin Islands, Virginia, or West Virginia, mail your application to: USINS Eastern Service Center, 75 Lower Welden Street, St. Albans, VT 05479-0001.

If you live in Alabama, Arkansas, Florida, Georgia, Kentucky, Louisiana, Mississippi, New Mexico, North Carolina, Oklahoma, South Carolina, Tennessee, or Texas, mail your application to: USINS Southern Service Center, P.O. Box 152122, Dept. A, Irving, TX 75015-2122.

If you live in Arizona, California, Guam, Hawaii, or Nevada, mail your application to: USINS Western Service Center, P.O. Box 30040, Laguna Niguel, CA 92607-0040.

If you live elsewhere in the U.S., mail your application to: USINS Northern Service Center, 100 Centennial Mall North, Room, B-26, Lincoln, NE 68508.

Fee.

The fee for this application is $75.00. The fee must be submitted in the exact amount. It cannot be refunded. DO NOT MAIL CASH.

All checks and money orders must be drawn on a bank or other institution located in the United States and must be payable in United States currency. The check or money order should be made payable to the Immigration and Naturalization Service, except that:

- If you live in Guam, and are filing this application in Guam, make your check or money order payable to the "Treasurer, Guam."
- If you live in the Virgin Islands, and are filing this application in the Virgin Islands, make your check or money order payable to the "Commissioner of Finance of the Virgin Islands."

Checks are accepted subject to collection. An uncollected check will render the application and any document issued invalid. A charge of $5.00 will be imposed if a check in payment of a fee is not honored by the bank on which it is drawn.

Processing Information.

Rejection. Any application that is not signed or is not accompanied by the correct fee will be rejected with a notice that it is deficient. You may correct the deficiency and resubmit the application. However, an application is not considered properly filed until accepted by the Service. If you do not completely fill out the form, or file it without required initial evidence, you will not establish a basis for eligibility, and we may deny your application.

Initial processing. Once the application has been accepted, it will be checked for completeness, including submission of the required initial evidence.

Requests for more information or interview. We may request more information or evidence or we may request that you appear at an INS office for an interview. We may also request that you submit the originals of any copy. We will return these originals when they are no longer required.

Decision. You will be notified in writing of the decision on your application. If your application is approved, you will be issued evidence of your Voluntary Departure Status.

If your application is denied, your case will be referred to the INS office that has jurisdiction over your place of residence, for consideration of whether to issue an Order to Show Cause as to why you should not be deported from the United States. Your case will not be referred for at least 60 days after the date the denial of this application to allow you to file another I-817 application if you feel that the denial can be overcome.

Penalties.

If you knowingly and willfully falsify or conceal a material fact or submit a false document with this request, we will deny the benefit you are filing for, and may deny any other immigration benefit. In addition, you will face severe penalties provided by law, and may be subject to criminal prosecution.

Privacy Act Notice.

We ask for the information on this form, and associated evidence, to determine if you have established eligibility for the immigration benefit you are filing for. Our legal right to ask for this information is in 8 USC 1154. We may provide this information to other government agencies. Failure to provide this information, and any requested evidence, may delay a final decision or result in denial of your application.

Paperwork Reduction Act Notice.

We try to create forms and instructions that are accurate, can be easily understood, and which impose the least possible burden on you to provide us with information. Often this is difficult because some immigration laws are very complex. The estimated average time to complete and file this application is as follows: (1) 25 minutes to learn about the law and form; (2) 1 hour to complete the form; and (3) 1 hour and 10 minutes to assemble and file the petition; for a total estimated average of 2 hours and 35 minutes per petition. If you have comments regarding the accuracy of this estimate, or suggestions for making this form simpler, you can write to both the Immigration and Naturalization Service, 425 I Street, N.W., Room 5304, Washington, D.C. 20536; and the Office of Management and Budget, Paperwork Reduction Project, OMB No. 1115-0166, Washington, D.C. 20503.

U.S. Department of Justice
Immigration and Naturalization Service

OMB No. 1115-0166
Application for Voluntary Departure Under the Family Unity Program

START HERE - Please Type or Print

PART 1. Information about you, the applicant for Family Unity Benefits

Family Name	Given Name	Middle Initial

Address C/O

Street		Apt. #
City	State	Zip Code

Date of Birth (month/day/year)	Country of Birth
Social Security # (If any)	A# (If any)
Date of Arrival month/day/year	I-94# (If any)
Current Immigration Status	Expires on (month/day/year)

Part 2. Type of Application.

1. Relationship to a legalized alien (check one):
   - a. ☐ I am the spouse of a legalized alien and have been married to him or her since at least May 5, 1988.
   - b. ☐ I am the unmarried child of a legalized alien and this relationship was established before May 5, 1988.
2. I am applying for (check one):
   - a. ☐ Initial voluntary departure under the Family Unity Program.
   - b. ☐ An extension of voluntary departure granted under the Family Unity Program.

Part 3. Information about the legalized alien you are related to.

Family Name	Given Name	Middle Initial

Address - C/O

Street Number and Name		Apt. #
City	State	Zip Code

Date of Birth (month/day/year)	Country of Birth
Social Security #	A#

Part 4. Processing Information.

A. If separate applications for Family Unity benefits are also being submitted for other relatives, give names of each and list relationship. ______________________

B. Have you ever applied for Family Unity benefits before? ☐ Yes ☐ No

C. If "Yes", give name under which you applied, place and date of filing, #A assigned, and result.

____

____

Form I-817 (Rev. 09/10/91)N *Continued on back.*

FOR INS USE ONLY

	Receipt
Returned	
Resubmitted	
Reloc Sent	
Reloc Rec'd	

Remarks

Action Block

To Be Completed by Attorney or Representative, if any
☐ Fill in box if G-28 is attached to represent the applicant

VOLAG#

ATTY State License #

Part 4. Processing Information *(con't).*

D. Have you ever been in exclusion or deportation proceedings? ☐ No ☐ Yes. If yes, explain on a separate sheet, including where and when the proceedings took place.

E. Address where you resided in the United States on May 5, 1988

Street	Apt. #	City	State	Zip Code

F. Answer the following. If your answer is yes to any question, explain in detail on a separate sheet.

1. Have you ever, in or outside the U. S.:
   a. knowingly committed a crime for which you have not been arrested? ☐ Yes ☐ No
   b. been arrested, cited, charged, indicted, fined, or imprisoned for breaking or violating any law or ordinance, excluding traffic violations? ☐ Yes ☐ No
   c. been the beneficiary of a pardon, amnesty, rehabilitation decree, other act of clemency or similar action? ☐ Yes ☐ No
2. Have you been convicted of any felony or 3 or more misdemeanors committed in the United States? ☐ Yes ☐ No
3. Have you ever exercised diplomatic immunity to avoid prosecution for a criminal offense in the U. S.? ☐ Yes ☐ No
4. Have you received public assistance from any source, including the U.S. government or any state, county, city, or municipality; or are you likely to request public assistance in the future? ☐ Yes ☐ No
5. Do you have, or have you ever had, a mental or physical disorder which does or may pose a threat to yourself or others? ☐ Yes ☐ No
6. Have you ever:
   a. practiced polygamy or plan to practice polygamy? ☐ Yes ☐ No
   b. within the past 10 years been a prostitute or procured anyone for prostitution, or intend to engage in such activities? ☐ Yes ☐ No
   c. engaged in any unlawful commercialized vice, including, but not limited to, gambling? ☐ Yes ☐ No
   d. knowingly encouraged, induced, assisted, abetted or aided, any alien to try to enter the U.S. illegally? ☐ Yes ☐ No
   e. illicitly trafficked in any controlled substance, or knowingly assisted, abetted or colluded in the illicit trafficking of any controlled substance? ☐ Yes ☐ No
7. Have you ever engaged in, conspired to engage in, or intend to engage in, or ever solicited membership or funds for, or through any means ever assisted or provided any type of material support to, any person or organization that has ever engaged or conspired to engage, in:
   a. sabotage, espionage, hijacking, or any other form of terrorist activity? ☐ Yes ☐ No
   b. any activity a purpose of which is opposition to, or the control of overthrow of, the Government of the United States, by force, violence or other unlawful means? ☐ Yes ☐ No
   c. any activity to violate or evade any law prohibiting the export from the United States of goods, technology or sensitive information? ☐ Yes ☐ No
8. Have you ever been, a member of, or in any way affiliated with, the Communist Party or any other totalitarian party? ☐ Yes ☐ No
9. Did you, during the period March 23, 1933 to May 8, 1945, in association with either the Nazi Government of Germany or any organization or government associated or allied with the Nazi Government of Germany, ever order, incite, assist or otherwise participate in the persecution of any person because of race, religion, national origin or political opinion? ☐ Yes ☐ No
10. Have you ever engaged in genocide, or otherwise ordered, incited, assisted or otherwise participated in the killing of any person because of race, religion, national origin or political opinion? ☐ Yes ☐ No
11. Have you ever been excluded from the U.S. within the past year, ever been deported from the U.S., or ever been removed from the U.S. at government expense, or are you now in exclusion or deportation proceedings? ☐ Yes ☐ No
12. Are you under a final order of civil penalty for violating section 274C of the Immigration Act for use of fraudulent documents, or have you, by fraud or willful misrepresentation of a material fact, ever sought to procure, or procured, a visa, other documentation, entry into the U.S., or any other immigration benefit? ☐ Yes ☐ No
13. Have you ever left the U.S. to avoid being drafted into the U.S. Armed Forces? ☐ Yes ☐ No

Form I-817 (Rev 09-10-91)N Continued on back

Part 4. Processing Information *(con't).*

14. Have you ever been a J nonimmigrant exchange visitor who was subject to the 2 year foreign residence requirement and not yet complied with that requirement? ☐ Yes ☐ No

15. Are you now withholding custody of a child outside the U.S. from a person granted custody of the child? ☐ Yes ☐ No

Part 5. Complete only if legalized alien is your spouse.

Section 1. *Additional Information about you, the applicant.*

Home Phone ( ) | Work Phone ( )

List all other names used (i.e. maiden name, aliases)

Sex: ☐ Male ☐ Female | Number of Prior Marriages: ______

Section 2. *Additional Information about your legalized alien spouse.*

Home Phone of Legalized Alien ( ) | Work Phone of Legalized Alien ( )

List all other names used (i.e. maiden name, aliases)

Sex: ☐ Male ☐ Female | Number of Prior Marriages: ______

Section 3. *Information about your marriage.*

We were married on: *(date)* / /

We were married in *(City, U.S. State or Country)*

Type of Ceremony: ☐ Religious ☐ Civil ☐ None

We are: ☐ Now living together ☐ Not living together

We are or intend to: *(Check one)*

- ☐ Live together in a home or apartment
- ☐ Live together with my family
- ☐ Live together with my spouse's family
- ☐ Live together with non-relatives
- ☐ Live separately from each other

We have the following Joint Financial Assets or Contracts: *(Check one)*

- ☐ Checking and/or Savings account
- ☐ Lease for apartment we occupy
- ☐ Mortgage for home we occupy
- ☐ Credit cards
- ☐ Consumer Loans

List three people (such as relatives, friends neighbors, co-workers, or employers) who know of your relationship:

1.	Name	Relationship	How long known
	Address		Phone number
2.	Name	Relationship	How long known
	Address		Phone number
3.	Name	Relationship	How long known
	Address		Phone number

Form I-817 (Rev. 09-10-91)N

Continued on back

Part 6. Complete only if you are the child of a legalized alien.

Sex: ☐ Male ☐ Female | Are you married? ☐ Yes ☐ No

My legalized alien parent is my: *(check one)*

☐ biological mother

☐ biological father who was married to my mother when I was born

☐ biological father who was not married to my mother when I was born

☐ adoptive parent:

1. Did the adoption occur before your 16th birthday? ☐ Yes ☐ No
2. Did your parent have custody of you for at least 2-years after the adoption? ☐ Yes ☐ No
3. Did you live with your parent for at least 2 years after the adoption? ☐ Yes ☐ No

☐ stepparent based on marriage to my parent which occurred before my 18th birthday.

☐ parent based on circumstances not described above *(explain in detail on separate paper).*

'art 7. Signature. *(Read the information on penalties in the instructions before completing this part. You must file this application while in the United States.)*

certify under penalty of perjury under the laws of the United States of America that this application, and the evidence submitted with it, is all true and orrect. I authorize the release of any information from my records which the Immigration and Naturalization Service needs to determine eligibility for e benefit I am seeking

'ignature *Print Your Name* *Date*

ddress

'art 8. Signature of person preparing form if other than above. *(Sign Below)*

declare that I prepared this application at the request of the above person and it is based on all information of which I have knowledge.

ignature *Print Your Name* *Date* *Day time Phone Number*

irm Name
nd Address

Form I-817 (Rev. 09/10/91)N

APPENDIX 7-2
Form I-246, Application for Stay of Deportation

U.S. Department of Justice
Immigration and Naturalization Service

Application for Stay of Deportation

OMB No. 1115-0055
Expires 4/86

Fee Stamp

SUBMIT IN DUPLICATE

Read instructions on reverse before filling out application

File No.

Date

1. Name (Family Name in Capital letters) (First Name) (Middle Name)

2. Present Address (Apt. No.) (Number and Street) (Town or City) (State) (Zip Code)

3. Country of Citizenship

4. Date to which passport is valid (Attach passport)

5. Country to which deportation has been ordered

6. Date to which stay of deportation is requested

7. Reasons for requesting stay of deportation:

8. I certify that all the statements I have made in this application are true and correct to the best of my knowledge and belief.

(Signature of Applicant) (Dated at) (Date)

9. SIGNATURE OF PERSON PREPARING FORM, IF OTHER THAN APPLICANT

I declare that this document was prepared by me at the request of the applicant and is based on all information of which I have any knowledge.

(Signature) (Address) (Date)

APPLICANT: DO NOT WRITE BELOW THIS LINE

Stay ☐ Denied ☐ Granted Until (Date) at (Place Where Granted)

By (Signature) (Title) (Date)

Form I-246 (Rev. 1-15-86) Y

RECEIVED	TRANS. IN	RET'D-TRANS. OUT	COMPLETED

INSTRUCTIONS

1. A fee of seventy dollars ($70) must be paid for filing this application. It cannot be refunded regardless of the action taken on the application. DO NOT MAIL CASH. ALL FEES MUST BE SUBMITTED IN THE EXACT AMOUNT. Payment by check or money order must be drawn on a bank or other institution located in the United States and be payable in United States currency. If applicant resides in Guam, check or money order must be payable to the "Treasurer, Guam." If applicant resides in the Virgin Islands, check or money order must be payable to the "Commissioner of Finance of the Virgin Islands." All other applicants must make the check or money order payable to the "Immigration and Naturalization Service." When check is drawn on account of a person other than the applicant, the name of the applicant must be entered on the face of the check. If application is submitted from outside the United States, remittance may be made by bank international money order or foreign draft drawn on a financial institution in the United States and payable to the Immigration and Naturalization Service in United States currency. Personal checks are accepted subject to collectibility. An uncollectible check will render the application and any document issued pursuant thereto invalid. A charge of $5.00 will be imposed if a check in payment of a fee is not honored by the bank on which it is drawn.

2. Submit a passport valid for at least 60 days beyond the expiration of requested stay with this application, or state why this is not possible.

3. Additional evidence in support of application may be attached.

4. Neither the filing of this application nor the failure to receive a notice of decision thereon shall relieve or excuse the applicant from presenting himself or herself for deportation at the time and place designated for deportation.

5. No appeal can be made from a denial of this application for a stay of deportation.

6. PENALTIES––Severe penalties are provided by law for knowingly falsifying or concealing a material fact or using any false document in the submission of this application.

U. S. Government Printing Office 1995 387-154/22704

Form I-590, Registration for Classification as Refugee

U.S. Department of Justice
Immigration and Naturalization Service

OMB No. 1115-0057
Registration for Classification as Refugee

Type or print the following information. *(Read instructions on reverse)* A File No.: ____________

1. Name: *(First)* *(Middle)* *(Last)*

2. Present address:

3. Date of birth: *(month/day/year)* | Place of birth *(city or town)* | *(Province)* | *(Country)* | Present nationality:

4. Country from which I fled or was displaced: | On or about *(month/day/year)*:

5. Reasons *(State in detail)*: ____________

6. My present immigration status in ____________ is: ____________
(country in which residing)

Evidence of my immigration status is:
(Describe)

7. Name of spouse: | 8. Present address of spouse *(if different)*: | 9. Nationality of spouse:

10. My spouse ☐ will ☐ will not accompany me to the United States.

11. Name of child (ren)	Date of birth	Place of birth	Present address *(if different)*

Place a mark (x) in front of name of each child who will accompany you to the United States.

12. Schooling or education

Name and location of school	Type	Dates attended	Title of degree or diploma

13. Military service

Country	Branch and organization	Dates	Serial No.	Rank attained

Form I-590 (Rev. 11-13-92)Y

Page - 2

14. Political, professional or social organizations of which I am now or have been a member or with which I am now or have been affiliated since my 16th birthday (If you have never been a member of any organization, state "None.")

15. I ☐ have ☐ have not been charged with a violation of law. (If you have ever been charged with a violation of law, give date, place and nature of each charge and the final result.)

16. I ☐ have ☐ have not been in the United States. (If you have ever been in the United States, show the dates of entry and departure and the purpose of your entry (visitor, permanent resident, student, seaman, etc.).

File or Alien Registration Number:

17. I have the following close relatives in the United States:

Name	Relationship	Present address

18. I am being sponsored by (Name and address of United States sponsor):

Date: Signature of registrant:

DO NOT WRITE BELOW THIS LINE

I, ______________________, do swear (affirm) that I know the contents of this registration subscribed by me including the attached documents, that the same are true to the best of my knowledge, and that corrections numbered ( ) to ( ) were made by me or at my request, and that this registration was signed by me with my full, true name:

(Complete and true signature of registrant)

Subscribed and sworn to before me by the above-named registrant at ______________________ on ______________
(month/day/year)

(Signature and title of officer)

INTERVIEW DATE AT Immigration Officer	APPROVED DATE Officer in Charge	

INSTRUCTIONS

This form should be executed, signed and submitted to the Officer in Charge of the nearest overseas office of the United States Immigration and Naturalization Service. When your name has been reached as a registrant you will be furnished additional instructions.

Registration - A separate Registration Form must be executed by each registrant and submitted in one copy. A Registration Form in behalf of a child under 14 years of age shall be executed by the parent of guardian.

Public reporting burden for this collection of information is estimated to average 35 minutes per response. If you have comments regarding the accuracy of this estimate or suggestions for simplifying this form, you can write to both the U.S. Department of Justice, Immigration and Naturalization Service Policy Directives and Instructions Branch (HQPDIB), Washington, D.C. 20536 and to the Office of Management and Budget, Paperwork Reduction Project: OMB No. 1115-0057, Washington, D.C. 20503.

Form I-589, Application for Asylum and for Withholding of Removal

U.S. Department of Justice
Immigration and Naturalization Service

OMB No. 1115-0086

Application for Asylum and for Withholding of Removal

Start Here - Please Type or Print. USE BLACK INK. SEE THE SEPARATE INSTRUCTION PAMPHLET FOR INFORMATION ABOUT ELIGIBILITY AND HOW TO COMPLETE AND FILE THIS APPLICATION.

PART A. INFORMATION ABOUT YOU.

1. Alien Registration Number(s), if any (A#'s)	2. Social Security Number	
3. Complete Last Name	4. First Name	5. Middle Name
6. What Other Names Have You Used? *(Include maiden name and aliases.)*		
7. Residence in the U.S. C/O		Telephone Number
Street Number and Name		Apt. No.
City	State	ZIP Code
8. Mailing Address in the U.S. if Other than Above C/O		Telephone Number
Street Number and Name		Apt. No.
City	State	ZIP Code
9. Sex Male Female	10. Marital Status: ☐ Single ☐ Married ☐ Divorced ☐ Widowed	
11. Date of Birth *(Mo/Day/Yr)*	12. City and Country of Birth	
13. Present Nationality *(Citizenship)*	14. Nationality at Birth	
15. Race, Ethnic or Tribal Group	16. Religion	

17. *Check each box that applies.*

I am not now in removal, deportation or exclusion proceedings.

I was previously in removal, deportation or exclusion proceedings.

I am now in removal, deportation or exclusion proceedings.

I have never been in removal, deportation or exclusion proceedings.

18. *Complete 18a through 18g.*

a. When did you last leave your country? *(Mo/Day/Yr)*	d. What was your status when you last entered the U.S.? *(What type of visa did you have, if any)?*
b. When did you last enter the U.S.? *(Mo/Day/Yr)*	e. What is your I-94 Number?
c. Where did you last enter the U.S.?	f. What is the expiration date of your authorized stay, if any?

g. Have you previsously entered the U.S.? No Yes. If YES, list place, date, and your status for each entry. *(Attach additional sheets as needed.)*

Date ____________ Place ____________________ Status ____________

Date ____________ Place ____________________ Status ____________

Date ____________ Place ____________________ Status ____________

FOR INS USE ONLY

Returned	Receipt
Resubmitted	
Reloc Sent	
Reloc Rec'd	
Action: Interview Date:	

Asylum:
Granted
Denied
Referred
Recommended Approval Date ____________

Date A.O. final decision or referral issued ____________

Total number of persons granted asylum ____________

For EOIR Use Only

To Be Completed by Attorney or Representative, if any

Check if G-28/EOIR-28 is attached showing you represent the applicant.

INS VOLAG or PIN #

ATTY State License # ____________

OMB No. 1115-0086

Information About You - Continued.

19. What is your native language?	20. Are you fluent in English? Yes No	21. What other languages do you speak fluently?

22. Have you ever applied to the United States Government or to any other Government(s) for refugee status, asylum, withholding of deportation, or withholding of removal?
   - ☐ No.
   - ☐ I was included in a pending application of my parent(s). However, I am now 21 years old or married so I am filing my own application.
   - ☐ I was included in my spouse's application, but now I wish to file my own application.
   - ☐ Yes. (In what country and what was the decision? Also specify the date of the decision.) *Country* ______________________ *Date* __________

   Decision ______________________

23. What country issued your last passport or travel document?	24. Passport # Travel Document #	25. Expiration Date

26. Prior address in last country of residence or country in which you fear persecution. *(List Address, City/Town, Province, State, Department, and Country)*

27. Provide the following information about your education, beginning with the most recent.

Name of School	Type of School	Location	Attended From *(Mo/Yr)*	To *(Mo/Yr)*

28. Provide the following information about your residences during the last five years. List your present address first. *(Use additional sheets of paper if necessary.)*

Number and Street	City	Province or State	Country	Dates From *(Mo/Yr)*	To *(Mo/Yr)*

29. Provide the following information about your employment during the last five years. List your present employment first. *(Use additional sheets of paper if necessary.)*

Name and Address of Employer	Your Occupation	Dates From *(Mo/Yr)*	To *(Mo/Yr)*

30. Provide the following information about your parents.

Name	Country and City of Birth	Location

Page 2 (Rev. 05-01-98) N

OMB No. 1115-0086

PART B. INFORMATION ABOUT YOUR SPOUSE AND CHILDREN.

Your Spouse. ☐ I am not married. *(Skip to Part B, Your Children.)*

1. Alien Registration Number (A#)		2. Passport/ID Card, etc.#	
3. Complete Last Name	4. First Name	5. Middle Name	6. Date of Birth *(Mo/Day/Yr)*
7. Date of Marriage *(Mo/Day/Yr)*	8. Place of Marriage	9. City and Country of Birth	
10. Nationality *(Citizenship)*	11. Race, Ethnic or Tribal Group		12. Sex ☐ Male ☐ Female
13. Is this person in the U.S.? ☐ Yes. *(Complete blocks 13 to 24.)* ☐ No. *(Specify Location)*			14. Social Security #
15. Place of Last Entry in the U.S.?	16. Date of Last Entry in the U.S.? *(Mo/Day/Yr)*	17. I-94#	18. Status when Last Admitted *(Visa type, if any)*
19. Expiration of Status *(Mo/Day/Yr)*	20. Is your spouse in removal, deportation or exclusion proceedings? ☐ Yes ☐ No	21. If previously in the U.S., Date of Previous Arrival *(Mo/Day/Yr)*	
22. Place of Previous Arrival		23. Status at Time of Previous Arrival	

24. If in the U.S., is this person to be included in this application? *(Check the appropriate box.)*

- ☐ Yes. *(Attach one (1) photograph of your spouse in the upper right hand corner of Page 3 on the extra copy of the application submitted for this person.)*
- ☐ No, because my spouse is/has:
  - ☐ Filing separately.
  - ☐ Separate application pending.
  - ☐ Other reasons.

All of Your Children, Regardless of Age or Marital Status.
(Use Supplement A Form or attach additional pages and documentation if you have more than two (2) children.)

1. Alien Registration Number (A#)		2. Passport/ID Card, etc.#	
3. Complete Last Name	4. First Name	5. Middle Name	6. Date of Birth *(Mo/Day/Yr)*
7. City and Country of Birth	8. Nationality *(Citizenship)*	9. Race, Ethnic or Tribal Group	10. Sex ☐ Male ☐ Female
11. Is this child in the U.S.? ☐ Yes. *(Complete blocks 12 to 22.)* ☐ No. *(Specify Location)*			12. Social Security #
13. Place of Last Entry in the U.S.?	14. Date of Last Entry in the U.S.? *(Mo/Day/Yr)*	15. I-94#	16. Status when Last Admitted *(Visa type, if any)*
17. Expiration of Status *(Mo/Day/Yr)*	18. Is this child in removal, deportation or exclusion proceedings? ☐ Yes ☐ No	19. If previously in the U.S., Date of Previous Arrival *(Mo/Day/Yr)*	
20. Place of Previous Arrival		21. Status at Time of Previous Arrival	

22. If in the U.S., is this person to be included in this application? *(Check the appropriate box.)*

- ☐ Yes. *(Attach one (1) photograph of your child in the upper right hand corner of Page 3 on the extra copy of the application submitted for this person.)*
- ☐ No, because child is/has:
  - ☐ Filing separately.
  - ☐ Separate application pending.
  - ☐ Over 21 years of age.
  - ☐ Married.
  - ☐ Other reasons.

Page 3 (Rev. 05-01-98) N

OMB No. 1115-0086

Information About Your Spouse and Children - Continued. *(Use Supplement A Form or attach additional sheets of paper to list additional children.)*

All of Your Children, Regardless of Age or Marital Status.

1. Alien Registration Number (A#):		2. Passport/ID Card, etc. #	
3. Complete Last Name	4. First Name	5. Middle Name	6. Date of Birth *(Mo/Day/Yr)*
7. City and Country of Birth	8. Nationality *(Citizenship)*	9. Race, Ethnic or Tribal Group	10. Sex ☐ Male ☐ Female
11. Is this person in the U.S.? ☐ Yes. *(Complete blocks 11 to 22.)* ☐ No. *(Specify Location)*			12. Social Security #
13. Place of Last Entry in the U.S.?	14. Date of Last Entry in the U.S.? *(Mo/Day/Yr)*	15. I-94#	16. Status when Last Admitted *(Visa type, if any)*
17. Expiration of Status *(Mo/Day/Yr)*	18. Is this child in removal, deportation or exclusion proceedings? ☐ Yes ☐ No		19. If previously in the U.S., Date of Previous Arrival *(Mo/Day/Yr)*
20. Place of Previous Arrival			21. Status at Time of Previous Arrival

22. If in the U.S., is this person to be included in this application? *(Check the appropriate box.)*

☐ Yes. *(Attach one (1) photograph of your child in the upper right hand corner of Page 3 on the extra copy of the application submitted for this person.)*
☐ No, because child is/has:
- ☐ Filing separately.
- ☐ Separate application pending.
- ☐ Over 21 years of age.
- ☐ Married.
- ☐ Other reasons.

PART C. INFORMATION ABOUT YOUR CLAIM TO ASYLUM.
(Use Supplement B Form or attach additional sheets of paper as needed to complete your responses to the questions contained in Part C.)

1. Why are you seeking asylum? Explain in detail what the basis is for your claim. *(Attach additional sheets of paper as needed.)*

Page 4 (Rev. 05-01-98) N

OMB No. 1115-0086

Information About Your Claim to Asylum - Continued.

2. Have you or any member of your family ever belonged to or been associated with any organizations or groups in your home country, such as, but not limited to, a political party, student group, labor union, religious organization, military or paramilitary group, civil patrol, guerrilla organization, ethnic group, human rights group, or the press or media?

   No. ☐ Yes. If yes, provide a detailed explanation of your or your relatives' involvement with each group and include the name of each organization or group; the dates of membership or affiliation; the purpose of the organization; your duties or your relatives' duties or responsibilities in the group or organization; and whether you or your relatives are still active in the group(s). *(Attach additional sheets of paper as needed.)*

3. Have you or any member of your family ever been mistreated or threatened by the authorities of your home country or any other country or by a group or groups that are controlled by the government, or that the government of the country is unable or unwilling to control?

   ☐ No. ☐ Yes. If YES, was it because of any of the following reasons? *(Check each of the following boxes that apply.)*

   ☐ Race ☐ Religion ☐ Nationality ☐ Membership in a particular social group ☐ Political Opinion

   On a separate sheet of paper, specify for each instance, what occurred and the circumstances; the relationship to you of the person involved; the date; the exact location; who it was who took such action against you or your family member(s); his/her position in the government or group; the reason why the incident occurred. Attach documents referring to these incidents, if they are available. *(Attach additional sheets of paper as needed.)*

4. Have you or any member of your family ever been accused, charged, arrested, detained, interrogated, convicted and sentenced, or imprisoned in your country or any other country, including the United States?

   ☐ No. ☐ Yes. If YES, for each instance, specify what occurred and the circumstances; dates; location; the duration of the detention or imprisonment; the reason(s) for the detention or conviction; the treatment received during the detention or imprisonment; any formal charges that were lodged against you or your relatives; the reason for release; treatment after release. Attach documents referring to these incidents if they are available. *(Attach additional sheets of paper as needed.)*

OMB No. 1115-0086

Information About Your Claim to Asylum - Continued.

5. Do you fear being subjected to torture (severe physical or mental pain or suffering, including rape or other sexual abuse) in your home country or any other country if you return?

☐ No. ☐ Yes. If YES, explain why. *(Attach additional sheets of paper as needed.)*

6. What do you think would happen to you if you returned to the country from which you claim you would be subjected to persecution? Explain in detail and provide information or documentation to support your statement, if available. *(Attach additional sheets of paper as needed.)*

7. Describe in detail your trip to the United States from your home country. After leaving the country from which you are claiming asylum, did you or your spouse or child(ren), who are now in the United States, travel through or reside in any other country before entering the United States?

☐ No. ☐ Yes. If YES, for each person, identify each country and indicate the length of stay; the person's status while there; the reasons for leaving; whether the person is entitled to return for residence purposes; and if the person applied for refugee status or for asylum while there; or why he or she did not do so. *(Attach additional sheets of paper as needed.)*

Page 6 (Rev. 05-01-98) N

OMB No. 1115-0086

PART D. ADDITIONAL INFORMATION ABOUT YOUR APPLICATION FOR ASYLUM.

(Use Supplement B Form or attach additional sheets of paper as needed to complete your responses to the questions contained in Part D.)

1. Do you, your spouse, or your child(ren) now hold, or have you ever held, permanent residence, other permanent status, or citizenship, in any country other than the one from which you are now claiming asylum?

☐ No. ☐ Yes. If YES, explain. *(Attach additional sheets of paper as needed).*

2. Have you, your spouse, your child(ren), your parents ever filed for, been processed for, or been granted or denied refugee status or asylum by the United States Government?

☐ No. ☐ Yes. If YES, explain the decision and what happened to any status you received as a result of that decision. If you have been denied asylum by an Immigration Judge or the Board of Immigration Appeals, please describe any change in country conditions or your own circumstances since the date of the denial that may affect your eligibility for asylum. *(Attach additional sheets of paper as needed.)*

3. Have you, your spouse, your child(ren), or your parents ever filed for, been processed for, or been granted or denied refugee status or asylum by any other country?

☐ No. ☐ Yes. If YES, explain the decision and what happened to any status you received as a result of that decision. *(Attach additional sheets of paper as needed.)*

4. Have you, your spouse, or child(ren) ever caused harm or suffering to any person because of his or her race, religion, nationality, membership in a particular social group or belief in a particular political opinion, or ever ordered, assisted, or otherwise participated in such acts?

☐ No. ☐ Yes. If YES, describe, in detail, each such incident and your own or your spouse's or child(ren)'s involvement. *(Attach additional sheets of paper as needed.)*

5. After you left your country of claimed persecution for the reasons you have described, did you return to that country?

☐ No. ☐ Yes. If YES, describe, in detail, the circumstances of your visit, for example, the date(s) of the trip(s), the purpose(s) of the trip(s), and the length of time you remained in that country for the visit(s). *(Attach additional sheets of paper as needed.)*

6. Are you filing the application more than one year after your last arrival in the United States?

☐ No. ☐ Yes. If YES, explain why you did not file within the first year after you arrived. You should be prepared to explain at your interview or hearing why you did not file your asylum application within the first year after you arrived. For guidance in answering this question see Part 1: Filing Instructions, Section V. "Completing the Form," Part D. *(Attach additional sheets of paper as needed.)*

OMB No. 1115-0086

PART E. SIGNATURE.

After reading the information on penalties in the instructions, complete and sign below. If someone helped you prepare this application, he or she must complete Part F.

I certify, under penalty of perjury under the laws of the United States of America, that this application and the evidence submitted with it is all true and correct. Title 18, United States Code, Section 1546, provides in part: "Whoever knowingly makes under oath, or as permitted under penalty of perjury under Section 1746 of Title 28, United States Code, knowingly subscribes as true, any false statement with respect to a material fact in any application, affidavit, or other document required by the immigration laws or regulations prescribed thereunder, or knowingly presents any such application, affidavit, or other document containing any such false statement or which fails to contain any reasonable basis in law or fact -- shall be fined in accordance with this title or imprisoned not more than five years, or both". I authorize the release of any information from my record which the Immigration and Naturalization Service needs to determine eligibility for the benefit I am seeking.

Staple your photograph here.

WARNING: **Applicants who are in the United States illegally are subject to removal if their asylum or withholding claims are not granted by an asylum officer or an Immigration Judge. Any information provided in completing this application may be used as a basis for the institution of, or as evidence in, removal proceedings even if the application is later withdrawn. Applicants determined to have knowingly made a frivolous application for asylum will be permanently ineligible for any benefits under the Immigration and Nationality Act. See INA 208(d)(6) and 8 CFR 208.18.**

Signature of Applicant *(The person named in Part A)*

[______________________________] ____________________

Sign your name so it all appears within the brackets. Date *(Mo/Day/Yr)*

Print Name	Write your name in your native alphabet

Did your spouse, parent or child(ren) assist you in completing this application? No Yes *(If YES, list their name(s) and relationship.)*

(Name) ______ *(Relationship)* ______ *(Name)* ______ *(Relationship)* ______

Did someone other than you or your spouse, parent or child(ren) prepare this application? No Yes *(Complete Part F)*

Asylum applicants may be represented by counsel. Have you been provided with a list of persons who may be available to assist you, at little or no cost, with your asylum claim? No Yes

PART F. SIGNATURE OF PERSON PREPARING FORM IF OTHER THAN ABOVE. *Sign below.*

I declare that I have prepared this application at the request of the person named in Part E, that the responses provided are based on all information of which I have knowledge, or which was provided to me by the applicant and that the completed application was read to the applicant in his or her native language for verification before he or she signed the application in my presence. I am aware that the knowing placement of false information on the Form I-589 may also subject me to civil penalties under 8 U.S.C. Section 1324(c).

Signature of Preparer	Print Name	Date *(Mo/Day/Yr)*
Daytime Telephone Number ( )	Address of Preparer: Street Number and Name	

Apt. No.	City	State	ZIP Code

PART G. TO BE COMPLETED AT INTERVIEW.

You will be asked to complete this Part when you appear before an asylum officer of the Immigration and Naturalization Service (INS), or an Immigration Judge of the Executive Office for Immigration Review (EOIR) for examination.

I swear (affirm) that I know the contents of this application that I am signing, including the attached documents and supplements, that they are all true or not all true to the best of my knowledge and that corrections numbered ______ to ______ were made by me or at my request.

Signed and sworn to before me by the above-name applicant on:

Signature of Applicant Date *(Mo/Day/Yr)*

Write your Name in your Native Alphabet Signature of Asylum Officer or Immigration Judge

Page 8 (Rev. 05-01-98) N

OMB No. 1115-0086
SUPPLEMENT A FORM I-589

A# *(If available)*	Date
Applicant's Name	Applicant's Signature

ALL OF YOUR CHILDREN, REGARDLESS OF AGE OR MARITAL STATUS.
(Attach additional pages and documentation if you have more than two (2) children.)

1. Alien Registration Number (A#):		2. Passport/ID Card, etc.#	
3. Complete Last Name	4. First Name	5. Middle Name	6. Date of Birth *(Mo/Day/Yr)*
7. City and Country of Birth	8. Nationality *(Citizenship)*	9. Race, Ethnic or Tribal Group	10. Sex ☐ Male ☐ Female

11. Is this child in the U.S.? ☐ Yes. *(Complete blocks 12 to 22.)* ☐ No. *(Specify Location)*			12. Social Security #
13. Place of Last Entry in the U.S.?	14. Date of Last Entry in the U.S.? *(Mo/Day/Yr)*	15. I-94#	16. Status when Last Admitted *(Visa type, if any)*
17. Expiration of Status *(Mo/Day/Yr)*	18. Is this child in removal, deportation or exclusion proceedings? ☐ Yes ☐ No		19. If previously in the U.S., Date of Previous Arrival *(Mo/Day/Yr)*
20. Place of Previous Arrival			21. Status at Time of Previous Arrival

22. If in the U.S., is this person to be included in this application? *(Check the appropriate box.)*

- ☐ Yes. *(Attach one (1) photograph of your child in the upper right hand corner of Page 3 on the extra copy of the application submitted for this person.)*
- ☐ No, because child is/has:
  - ☐ Filing separately.
  - ☐ Separate application pending.
  - ☐ Over 21 years of age.
  - ☐ Married.
  - ☐ Other reasons.

1. Alien Registration Number (A#):		2. Passport/ID Card, etc.#	
3. Complete Last Name	4. First Name	5. Middle Name	6. Date of Birth *(Mo/Day/Yr)*
7. City and Country of Birth	8. Nationality *(Citizenship)*	9. Race, Ethnic or Tribal Group	10. Sex ☐ Male ☐ Female

11. Is this child in the U.S.? ☐ Yes. *(Complete blocks 12 to 22.)* ☐ No. *(Specify Location)*			12. Social Security #
13. Place of Last Entry in the U.S.?	14. Date of Last Entry in the U.S.? *(Mo/Day/Yr)*	15. I-94#	16. Status when Last Admitted *(Visa type, if any)*
17. Expiration of Status *(Mo/Day/Yr)*	18. Is this child in removal, deportation or exclusion proceedings? ☐ Yes ☐ No		19. If previously in the U.S., Date of Previous Arrival *(Mo/Day/Yr)*
20. Place of Previous Arrival			21. Status at Time of Previous Arrival

22. If in the U.S., is this person to be included in this application? *(Check the appropriate box.)*

- ☐ Yes. *(Attach one (1) photograph of your child in the upper right hand corner of Page 3 on the extra copy of the application submitted for this person.)*
- ☐ No, because child is/has:
  - ☐ Filing separately.
  - ☐ Separate application pending.
  - ☐ Over 21 years of age.
  - ☐ Married.
  - ☐ Other reasons.

OMB No. 1115-0086
SUPPLEMENT B FORM I-589

ADDITIONAL INFORMATION ABOUT YOUR CLAIM TO ASYLUM.

A# *(If available)*	Date
Applicant's Name	Applicant's Signature

Use attached blank response sheet to supplement any information requested. Please copy and complete as needed.

PART ___

QUESTION ___

Page 10 (Rev. 05-01-98) N

OMB No. 1115-0086
SUPPLEMENT B FORM I-589

ADDITIONAL INFORMATION ABOUT YOUR CLAIM TO ASYLUM.

A# *(If available)*	Date
Applicant's Name	Applicant's Signature

Use attached blank response sheet to supplement any information requested. Please copy and complete as needed.

PART ___

QUESTION ___

APPENDIX 8-3
Form FD-258, Fingerprint Chart

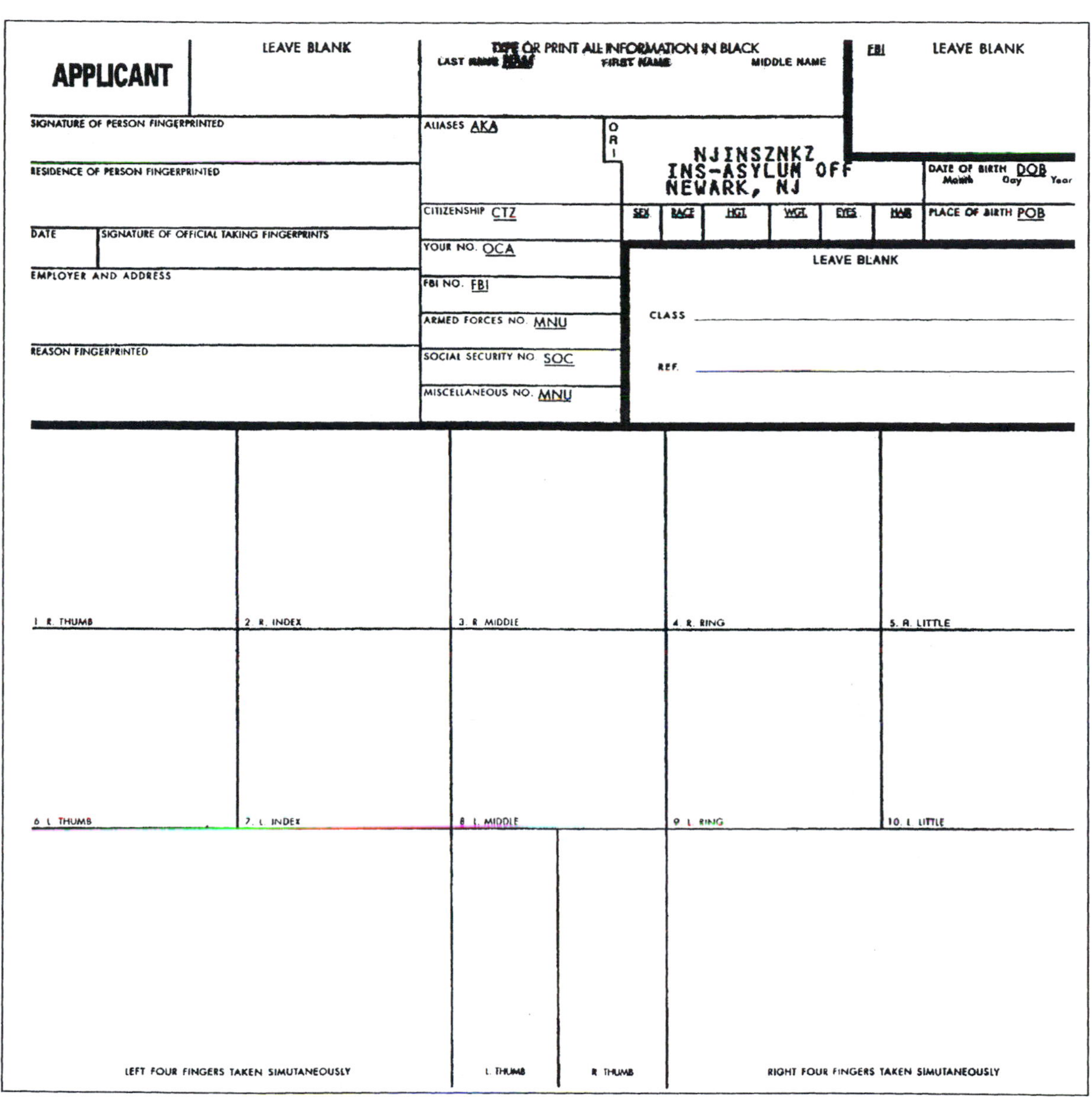

APPLICANT

LEAVE BLANK

TYPE OR PRINT ALL INFORMATION IN BLACK

LAST NAME NAM FIRST NAME MIDDLE NAME

FBI LEAVE BLANK

SIGNATURE OF PERSON FINGERPRINTED

ALIASES AKA

ORI NJINSZNKZ INS-ASYLUM OFF NEWARK, NJ

RESIDENCE OF PERSON FINGERPRINTED

DATE OF BIRTH DOB Month Day Year

CITIZENSHIP CTZ

SEX RACE HGT. WGT. EYES HAIR

PLACE OF BIRTH POB

DATE

SIGNATURE OF OFFICIAL TAKING FINGERPRINTS

YOUR NO. OCA

LEAVE BLANK

EMPLOYER AND ADDRESS

FBI NO. FBI

CLASS

ARMED FORCES NO. MNU

REASON FINGERPRINTED

SOCIAL SECURITY NO. SOC

REF.

MISCELLANEOUS NO. MNU

1. R. THUMB	2. R. INDEX	3. R. MIDDLE	4. R. RING	5. R. LITTLE
6. L. THUMB	7. L. INDEX	8. L. MIDDLE	9. L. RING	10. L. LITTLE

LEFT FOUR FINGERS TAKEN SIMUTANEOUSLY

L. THUMB

R. THUMB

RIGHT FOUR FINGERS TAKEN SIMUTANEOUSLY

FEDERAL BUREAU OF INVESTIGATION
UNITED STATES DEPARTMENT OF JUSTICE
WASHINGTON, D.C. 20537

APPLICANT

1. LOOP

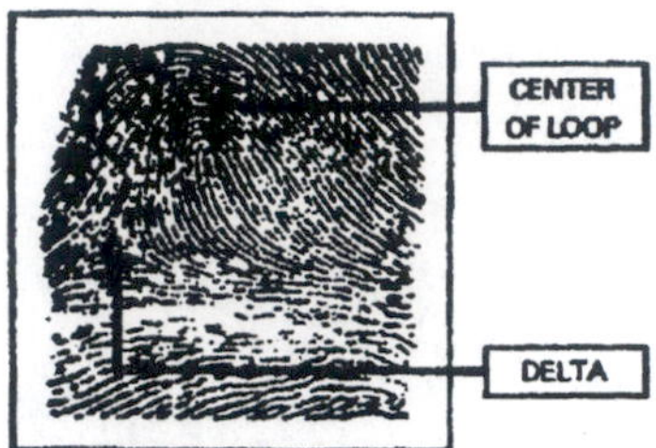

THE LINES BETWEEN CENTER OF LOOP AND DELTA MUST SHOW

2. WHORL

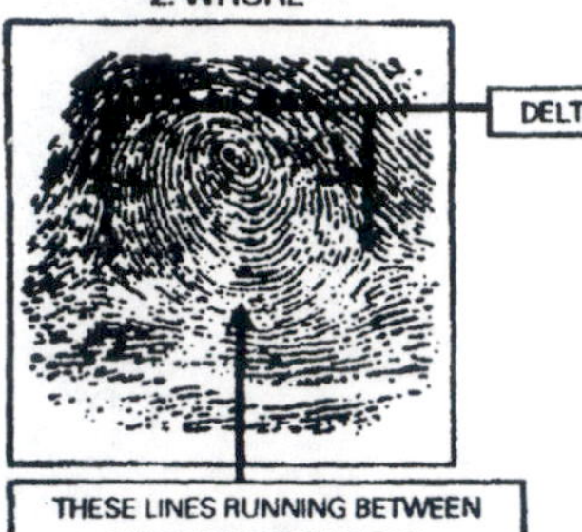

THESE LINES RUNNING BETWEEN DELTAS MUST BE CLEAR

3. ARCH

ARCHES HAVE NO DELTAS

FD-258 (REV. 12-29-82)

TO OBTAIN CLASSIFIABLE FINGERPRINTS:

1. USE BLACK PRINTER'S INK.
2. DISTRIBUTE INK EVENLY ON INKING SLAB.
3. WASH AND DRY FINGERS THOROUGHLY.
4. ROLL FINGERS FROM NAIL TO NAIL, AND AVOID ALLOWING FINGERS TO SLIP.
5. BE SURE IMPRESSIONS ARE RECORDED IN CORRECT ORDER.
6. IF AN AMPUTATION OR DEFORMITY MAKES IT IMPOSSIBLE TO PRINT A FINGER, MAKE A NOTATION TO THAT EFFECT IN THE INDIVIDUAL FINGER BLOCK.
7. IF SOME PHYSICAL CONDITION MAKES IT IMPOSSIBLE TO OBTAIN PERFECT IMPRESSIONS, SUBMIT THE BEST THAT CAN BE OBTAINED WITH A MEMO STAPLED TO THE CARD EXPLAINING THE CIRCUMSTANCES.
8. EXAMINE THE COMPLETED PRINTS TO SEE IF THEY CAN BE CLASSIFIED, BEARING IN MIND THAT MOST FINGERPRINTS FALL INTO THE PATTERNS SHOWN ON THIS CARD (OTHER PATTERNS OCCUR INFREQUENTLY AND ARE NOT SHOWN HERE).

THIS CARD FOR USE BY:

1. LAW ENFORCEMENT AGENCIES IN FINGERPRINTING APPLICANTS FOR LAW ENFORCEMENT POSITIONS.*
2. OFFICIALS OF STATE AND LOCAL GOVERNMENTS FOR PURPOSES OF EMLOYMENT, LICENSING, AND PERMITS, AS AUTHORIZED BY STATE STATUTES AND APPROVED BY THE ATTORNEY GENERAL OF THE UNITED STATES. LOCAL AND COUNTY ORDINANCES, UNLESS SPECIFICALLY BASED ON APPLICABLE STATE STATUTES DO NOT SATISFY THIS REQUIREMENT.*
3. U.S. GOVERNMENT AGENCIES AND OTHER ENTITIES REQUIRED BY FEDERAL LAW.**
4. OFFICIALS OF FEDERALLY CHARTERED OR INSURED BANKING INSTITUTIONS TO PROMOTE OR MAINTAIN THE SECURITY OF THOSE INSTITUTIONS.

LEAVE THIS SPACE BLANK

INSTRUCTIONS:

*1. PRINTS MUST FIRST BE CHECKED THROUGH THE APPROPRIATE STATE IDENTIFICATION BUREAU, AND ONLY THOSE FINGERPRINTS FOR WHICH NO DISQUALIFYING RECORD HAS BEEN FOUND LOCALLY SHOULD BE SUBMITTED FOR FBI SEARCH.

2. PRIVACY ACT OF 1974 (P.L. 93-579) REQUIRES THAT FEDERAL, STATE, OR LOCAL AGENCIES INFORM INDIVIDUALS WHOSE SOCIAL SECURITY NUMBER IS REQUESTED WHETHER SUCH DISCLOSURE IS MANDATORY OR VOLUNTARY, BASIS OF AUTHORITY FOR SUCH SOLICITATION, AND USES WHICH WILL BE MADE OF IT.

**3. IDENTITY OF PRIVATE CONTRACTORS SHOULD BE SHOWN IN SPACE "EMPLOYER AND ADDRESS". THE CONTRIBUTOR IS THE NAME OF THE AGENCY SUBMITTING THE FINGERPRINT CARD TO THE FBI.

4. FBI NUMBER, IF KNOWN, SHOULD ALWAYS BE FURNISHED IN THE APPROPRIATE SPACE.

MISCELLANEOUS NO. RECORD: OTHER ARMED FORCES NO., PASSPORT NO (PP), ALIEN REGISTRATION NO. (AR), PORT SECURITY CARD NO. (PS), SELECTIVE SERVICE NO. (SS), VETERANS' ADMINISTRATION CLAIM NO. (VA).

☆U.S. GPO: 1996—405-015/20049

Form I-821, Application for Temporary Protected Status

U.S. Department of Justice
Immigration and Naturalization Service

OMB # 1115-0170
Application for Temporary Protected Status

START HERE - Please Type or Print

FOR INS USE ONLY

Remarks
Action Stamp
Fee Stamp
Case ID#:
A#:

Part 1. Type of Application *(check one)*

1. ________ This is my first application to register for Temporary Protected Status.
2. ________ This is my application for annual registration/re-registration. I have previously been granted Temporary Protected Status. I have maintained and continue to maintain the conditions of eligibility for Temporary Protected Status.

Part 2. Information about You

Family Name	First	Middle Initial

U.S. Mailing Address - Care of

Street Number and Name	Apt. #
Town/City	County
State	ZIP Code
Place of Birth (Town or City)	(State/Country)
Country of Residence	Country of Citizenship
Date of Birth *(month/day/year)*	Sex ☐ Male ☐ Female
Marital Status ☐ Single ☐ Married ☐ Divorced ☐ Widowed	Other Names Used *(including maiden name)*
Date of entry into the U.S.	Place of entry into the U.S.

Manner of Arrival *(Visitor, student, stowaway, without inspection, etc.)*

Arrival/Departure Record (I-94) Number	Date authorized stay expired/or will expire, as shown on form I-94 or I-95

Your current immigration Status

In Status *(state nonimmigrant classification e.g. F-1, etc.)*

Out of Status *(state nonimmigrant violation e.g. overstay student etc.; EWI)*

Alien Registration Number *(If any)*	Social Security Number

Are you now or have you ever been under immigration proceedings?

☐ Yes ☐ No Where________________ When______________

☐ Exclusion ☐ Deportation ☐ Rescission ☐ Judicial Proceedings

Part 3. Information about Your spouse and children *(if any)*

Name of Spouse Last	First	Middle Initial
Address (number and street)		Apt #
Town/City	State	
Country	Zip/Postal Code	

To Be Completed by *Attorney or Representative*, if any

☐ Fill in box if G-28 is attached to represent the applicant

VOLAG#

ATTY State License #

Form I-821 (Rev. 5/22/91)N

Continued on back.

Part 3. Information about your spouse and children (con't)

Date of Birth *(month/day/ year)*	Date and Place of Present Marriage
Name of prior husbands/wives	Date(s) Marriage(s) Ended

List the names, ages, and current residence of any children

Name - (Last)	(First)	(Middle Initial)	Date of Birth	Residence

Part 4. Eligibility Standards

1. Fill in the necessary information:

   I am a national of the foreign state of ________________, and I entered the United States on ________________________________, and I have resided in the United States since that time.

2. To be eligible for Temporary Protected Status, you must be admissible as an immigrant to the United States, with certain exceptions. Do any of the following apply to you?

   a. have you been convicted of any felony or 2 or more misdemeanors committed in the United States;

   b. (i) have you ordered, incited, assisted, or otherwise participated in the persecution of any person on account of race, religion, nationality, membership in a particular social group or political opinion;

      (ii) have you been convicted by a final judgment of a particularly serious crime, constituting a danger to the community of the United States (an alien convicted of an aggravated felony is considered to have committed a particularly serious crime);

      (iii) have you committed a serious nonpolitical crime outside of the United States prior to your arrival in the United States; or

      (iv) have you engaged in or are you still engaged in activities that could be reasonable grounds for concluding that you are a danger to the security of the United States;

   c. (i) have you been convicted of, or have you committed acts which constitute the essential elements of a crime (other than a purely political offense) or a violation of or a conspiracy to violate any law relating to a controlled substance as defined in Section 102 of the Controlled Substance Act;

      (ii) have you been convicted of 2 or more offenses (other than purely political offenses) for which the aggregate sentences to confinement actually imposed were 5 years or more;

      (iii) have you trafficked in or do you continue to traffic in any controlled substance or are or have been a knowing assister, abettor, conspirator, or colluder with others in the illicit trafficking of any controlled substance;

      (iv) have you engaged or do you continue to engage solely, principally, or incidentally in any activity related to espionage or sabotage or violate any law involving the export of goods, technology, or sensitive information, any other unlawful activity, or any activity the purpose of which is in opposition, or the control, or overthrow of the government of the United States;

Form I 821 (Rev. 05/22/91)

Continued on next page

Part 4. Eligibility Standards (con't)

(v) have you engaged in or do you continue to engage in terrorist activities;

(vi) have you engaged in or do you continue to engage or plan to engage in activities in the United States that would have potentially serious adverse foreign policy consequences for the United States;

(vii) have you been or do you continue to be a member of the Communist or other totalitarian party, except when membership was involuntary; and

(viii) have you participated in Nazi persecution or genocide.

d. have you been arrested, cited, charged, indicted, fined, or imprisoned for breaking or violating any law or ordinance, excluding traffic violations, or been the beneficiary of a pardon, amnesty, rehabilitation decree, other act of clemency or similar action;

e. have you committed a serious criminal offense in the United States and asserted immunity from prosecution;

f. have you within the past 10 years engaged in prostitution or procurement of prostitution or do you continue to engage in prostitution or procurement of prostitution;

g. have you been or do you intend to be involved in any other commercial vice;

h. have you been excluded and deported from the United States within the past year, or have you been deported or removed from the United States at government expense within the last 5 years (20 years if you have been convicted of an aggravated felony);

i have you ever assisted any other person to enter the United States in violation of the law;

j (i) do you have a communicable disease of public health significance,

(ii) do you have or have you had a physical or mental disorder and behavior (or a history of behavior that is likely to recur) associated with the disorder which has posed or may pose a threat to the property, safety or welfare of yourself or others;

(iii) are you now or have you been a drug abuser or drug addict;

k. have you entered the United States as a stowaway;

l. are you subject to a final order for violation of section 274C (producing and/or using false documentation to unlawfully satisfy a requirement of the Immigration and Nationality Act);

m. do you practice polygamy;

n. were you the guardian of, and did you accompany another alien who was ordered excluded and deported from the United States;

o. have you detained, retained, or withheld the custody of a child, having a lawful claim to United States citizenship, outside the United States from a United States citizen granted custody.

If any of the above statements apply to you, indicate which one(s) by number reference on the line below (for example "2 k") and include a full explanation on a separate piece of paper. If you were ever arrested you should provide the disposition (outcome) of the arrest (for example, "case dismissed") from the appropriate authority.

____

PLEASE NOTE: If you placed any of the following numbered references on the line above you may be eligible for a waiver of the grounds described in the statements: 2e; 2f; 2g; 2h; 2i; 2j; 2k; 2l; 2m; 2n; 2o. Form I-601 or I-724 are the Service forms used to request a waiver. These forms are available at INS offices.

Form I-821 (Rev. 05/22/91) *Continued on back*

Part 5. Your Certification

Your Certification: I certify, under penalty of perjury under the laws of the United States of America, that the foregoing is true and correct. Copies of documents submitted are exact photocopies of unaltered original documents and I understand that I may be required to submit original documents to the INS at a later date. Furthermore, I authorize the release of any information from my records which the Immigration and Naturalization Service needs to determine eligibility for the benefit that I am seeking.

Signature:________________ Date:__________ Telephone No.:______________

Signature of Person Preparing Form if other than above:

I declare that I prepared this document at the request of the person above and that it is based on all information of which I have any knowledge.

Print Name:________________ Signature:________________ Date:__________

Address:________________________________

Part 6. Checklist

___ Have you answered each question?
___ Have you signed the application?

Have you enclosed:

___The filing fee for this application or a written request for a waiver of the filing fee (see instructions, item 12)?

___Supporting evidence to prove identity, nationality, date of entry and residence?

___Other required supporting documents (fingerprint charts, pictures etc.) for each application?

IT IS NOT POSSIBLE TO COVER ALL THE CONDITIONS FOR ELIGIBILITY OR TO GIVE INSTRUCTIONS FOR EVERY SITUATION. IF YOU HAVE CAREFULLY READ ALL THE INSTRUCTIONS AND STILL HAVE QUESTIONS, PLEASE CONTACT YOUR NEAREST INS OFFICE. IT IS RECOMMENDED THAT YOU KEEP A COMPLETE COPY OF THIS APPLICATION FOR YOUR RECORDS.

Form I-821 (Rev. 05/22/91)

Form I-765, Application for Employment Authorization

U. S. Department of Justice
Immigration and Naturalization Service

OMB # 1115-0163
Application for Employment Authorization

Do Not Write In This Block

Remarks	Action Stamp	Fee Stamp
A#		
Applicant is filing under 274a.12 ________		

☐ Application Approved. Employment Authorized / Extended (Circle One) ______________ (Date).
until ______________ (Date).
Subject to the following conditions: ______________
☐ Application Denied.
☐ Failed to establish eligibility under 8 CFR 274a.12 (a) or (c).
☐ Failed to establish economic necessity as required in 8 CFR 274a.12(c) (14), (18) and 8 CFR 214.2(f)

I am applying for: ☐ Permission to accept employment
☐ Replacement (of lost employment authorization document).
☐ Renewal of my permission to accept employment (attach previous employment authorization document).

1. Name (Family Name in CAPS) (First) (Middle)

2. Other Names Used (Include Maiden Name)

3. Address in the United States (Number and Street) (Apt. Number)

(Town or City) (State/Country) (ZIP Code)

4. Country of Citizenship/Nationality

5. Place of Birth (Town or City) (State/Province) (Country)

6. Date of Birth (Month/Day/Year)

7. Sex ☐ Male ☐ Female

8. Marital Status ☐ Married ☐ Single ☐ Widowed ☐ Divorced

9. Social Security Number (Include all Numbers you have ever used)

10. Alien Registration Number (A-Number) or I-94 Number (if any)

11. Have you ever before applied for employment authorization from INS?
☐ Yes (If yes, complete below) ☐ No
Which INS Office? Date(s)

Results (Granted or Denied - attach all documentation)

12. Date of Last Entry into the U.S. (Month/Day/Year)

13. Place of Last Entry into the U.S.

14. Manner of Last Entry (Visitor, Student, etc.)

15. Current Immigration Status (Visitor, Student, etc.)

16. Go to Part 2 of the instructions, Eligibility Categories. In the space below, place the letter and number of the category you selected from the instructions (For example, (a)(8), (c)(17)(iii), etc.).
Eligibility under 8 CFR 274a.12
( ) ( ) ( )

Certification

Your Certification: I certify, under penalty of perjury under the laws of the United States of America, that the foregoing is true and correct. Furthermore, I authorize the release of any information which the Immigration and Naturalization Service needs to determine eligibility for the benefit I am seeking. I have read the Instructions in Part 2 and have identified the appropriate eligibility category in Block 16.

Signature Telephone Number Date

Signature of Person Preparing Form If Other Than Above: I declare that this document was prepared by me at the request of the applicant and is based on all information of which I have any knowledge.

Print Name Address *Signature* Date

Initial Receipt	Resubmitted	Relocated		Completed		
		Rec'd	Sent	Approved	Denied	Returned

GLOSSARY

ABC settlement — Court case that permits rehearing of denials of application for asylum for Salvadorans and Guatemalans because of U.S. discrimination.

Adjustment of status — Changing an alien's classification from one category to another.

Aggravated felony — Grounds for removal.

Alien — A person who is not a citizen of the country in question.

Alien Prescreening Office — Government office that interviews prospective refugees.

Asiatic Barred Zone — 1917 congressional act barring certain Asian immigrants but exempting others.

Asylee — Person granted asylum.

Asylum — Status granted to qualifying refugees who apply for status as asylees either within the U.S. or at its borders.

Asylum officer — Government official who decides on applications for refuge or asylum for persons not subject to removal proceedings.

Board of Immigration Appeals (BIA) — The Department of Justice board created to hear appeals from the immigration court.

Border patrol — Government officials authorized to maintain U.S. borders and to keep out undocumented aliens.

Bureau of Immigration — Forerunner of the INS created to administer the immigration laws.

Cancellation of removal — A form of discretionary relief from removal.

Central Office of Refugees, Asylum, Parole (CORAP) — INS office with jurisdiction over refugees and asylees.

Chinese Exclusion Act of 1882 — Federal statute designed to limit immigration of Chinese nationals.

Citizenship — Owing allegiance to a particular geographic and political unit.

Clear probability (credible fear) — Standard of documenting a likelihood of persecution in the applicant's home country; a more severe standard than well-founded fear.

Commuter alien — Citizen of Canada or Mexico who enters and leaves the United States every day to work.

Conditional status — Basis on which an alien who marries a U.S. citizen and obtains permanent resident status can remain in the U.S. for two years.

Constructive residence — Meeting U.S. residency requirements for naturalization by serving on a U.S. public vessel or a vessel with a U.S. home port.

Coolie labor contract — Contract used to hire Chinese immigrants at low wages.

Culturally unique — Typical of a particular country or ethnic group.

Deferred removal — Discretionary relief from removal granted on humanitarian grounds.

Denaturalization — The process by which a naturalized citizen loses citizenship.

Deportation — The process of removing aliens from the United States (now termed "removal").

Diversity immigrant — Immigrant classification for persons whose country of origin has had few immigrants in the past few years.

Diversity visa — Classification of preference given to persons who come from countries under-represented in the U.S. population.

Dual citizenship — Owing allegiance to two countries at the same time; not recognized by the United States.

Employment creator — Alien given preference if he or she guarantees to invest at least $1 million in a U.S. business and employ at least ten U.S. citizens.

Enemy aliens — Citizens and nationals of countries the United States government has declared to be an enemy of the country.

Estoppel — Form of relief from removal for an alien who has relied on the representations of a government official with respect to immigration matters.

Ex post facto — Latin for "after the fact."

Exchange visitor — A student, scholar, teacher or specialist who has been invited to participate in an exchange program by the U.S. Information Agency.

Exclusion — Process of denying an alien the right to enter the U.S. (now termed "removal").

Exclusion hearing — Administrative hearing to determine an alien's right to enter the United States; now called removal proceeding.

Expatriation — A voluntary act by which a citizen renounces his or her citizenship.

Extended voluntary departure — Special category that permits aliens to remain in the United States after issuance of a removal order because of problems in their homelands.

Extraordinary ability — Being recognized either nationally or internationally as having specialized knowledge or skill.

Green card — Document authorizing an alien to work in the U.S.

Hardship waiver — Waiver granted by the attorney general if removing an alien would result in undue hardship to a U.S. citizen.

Head tax — Fee that immigrants formerly paid when entering the United States.

Illegal Immigration Reform and Immigrant Responsibility Act of 1996 — Most recent federal statute concerning undocumented aliens.

Immigrant — Person from one country who wishes to resettle permanently in another country.

Immigration — The migration of people from their place of citizenship or nationality to a geographic location to which they owe no automatic allegiance.

Immigration Act of 1875 — The first national act restricting the categories of persons permitted to enter the U.S.

Immigration Act of 1990 — Current federal legislation governing immigration.

Immigration Court — Specialty court established to hear immigration matters.

Immigration Marriage Fraud Act — Enacted in 1986 to prevent sham marriages designed to circumvent immigration law.

Immigration and Nationality Act of 1952 (INA) — Federal law governing immigration and naturalization of foreigners to the U.S.

Immigration and Naturalization Service (INS) — Federal agency under the Department of Justice authorized to implement the immigration laws.

Immigration Nursing Relief Act of 1989 — Enacted in 1989 to alleviate shortage of nurses in the U.S.

Immigration officer — Government official under the Department of State whose function is to maintain U.S. borders and make the initial determination on an application for naturalization.

Immigration preference — Under the INA, four categories of persons receive preference over other immigrants.

Immigration Reform and Control Act of 1986 (IRCA) — Federal law designed to deal with the question of undocumented aliens residing in the United States.

Immigration judge — Government official with jurisdiction over refugees and asylees subject to removal proceedings.

Immigration law judge — Administrative law judge presiding over removal hearings.

Insular cases — Refers to Supreme Court determination that persons in the U.S. territories were U.S. nationals, but not U.S. citizens.

Interdiction — Special procedure for Haitians attempting to enter the U.S.

Judicial review — The ability of a court of law to review decisions of an administrative agency.

Jus sanguinis — Citizenship by blood.

Jus soli — Citizenship by place of birth.

Labor condition application — Document to be filed by H-category employers.

Lawful permanent resident — An alien who has entered the U.S. with an immigrant visa.

Legal Immigration and Family Equity Law Act — Statute permitting limited adjustment of status for certain undocumented aliens.

Moral turpitude — Behavior considered reprehensible by society's norms.

Nationality — A political subdivision of citizenship.

Naturalization — The process of becoming a citizen of a country by a voluntary act.

Naturalization officer — Governmental official authorized to handle the naturalization process.

National Origin Formula — One of the early methods of limiting immigration of persons from non-Western Hemisphere countries.

Nationality Act of 1802 — First federal statute dealing with questions of nationality.

Nonimmigrant — Alien who wishes to enter the country for a terminable period of time rather than permanently.

Nonpriority status — Same as "deferred removal."

Normal-flow refugee — A refugee who enters under the normal refugee ceilings.

Numerical limitations — Ceiling on the amount of visas that can be issued to persons who are not the immediate family members of U.S. citizens.

Order to Show Cause — Document served on the alien as part of the removal proceedings prior to the 1996 Act.

Parole — Procedure for allowing aliens limited entry into the United States pending investigation prior to a removal proceeding.

Priority worker — Classification of immigrant in the employment related category who has extraordinary skill and abilities.

Private bill — Legislation intended to affect only the person named in the law.

Quota — Method of limiting the number of aliens who may enter the country each year.

Refugee — Alien seeking entry into the U.S. because he or she is persecuted in his or her homeland because of race, religion, sex, national origin or political beliefs.

Refugee Act of 1980 — Federal statute covering the entry of refugees into the country.

Refugee on special humanitarian grounds — Category of refugee who enters under special circumstances not limited to the typical refugee ceilings.

Registry — Permitted for a limited time under the 1996 Act to permit aliens who had resided in the United States for a long time to adjust their status and remain in the country.

Removal — The process of denying entry to aliens and removing undocumented aliens from the country.

Removal Order — Document requiring an alien to leave the United States.

Removal prior to entry — Term under the 1996 Act for what used to be called exclusion.

Removal proceeding — Term under the 1996 Act for what used to be called exclusion or deportation hearings.

Removal subsequent to entry — Term under the 1996 Act for what used to be called deportation.

Secondary inspection — INS inspection of aliens when they attempt to enter the U.S.

Special immigrant — A religious worker or the former employee of a U.S. government or international organization.

Specialty occupation — Job requiring theoretical and practical application of a highly specialized body of knowledge.

Stay of removal — Discretionary relief permitting an alien to stay in the U.S. pending a reopening of his or her case or while the alien attempts to obtain a status adjustment.

Suspension of removal — Permitting the alien to remain in the U.S. for a period longer than that specified in the removal order.

Temporary protected status — Status granted to aliens in the United States so that they may remain in the U.S. while their homelands are in turmoil.

Treaty investor — Person who, subject to a valid U.S. treaty, plans to invest funds in a U.S. enterprise.

Treaty trader — Person who, subject to a valid U.S. treaty, plans to participate in an enterprise in the United States.

Undocumented aliens — Formerly "illegal aliens." Persons who enter the U.S. without lawful authorization.

Visa — Government grant of entry to the country for aliens.

Visa Waiver Pilot Program — Special provision for persons from 24 specified countries to come to the U.S. without first obtaining a visa.

Voluntary departure — Permitting the alien to leave the country on his or her own volition without the stigma of removal.

Well-founded fear — The statutory standard that must be met with respect to the applicant's worry about being persecuted in his or her homeland.

Withholding of removal — Similar to seeking asylum; must be requested at the commencement of the removal proceedings.

INDEX